TOM MOR

HOLY

WATERS

SEARCHING FOR THE
SACRED IN A GLASS

WATKINS

Sharing Wisdom Since 1893

This edition first published in the UK and USA in 2022 by

Watkins, an imprint of Watkins Media Limited

Unit 11, Shepperton House

89-93 Shepperton Road

London

N1 3DF

enquiries@watkinspublishing.com

1 2 3 4 5 6 7 8 9 10

Typeset by Lapiz

Printed and bound in the United Kingdom

A CIP record for this book is available from the British Library

ISBN: 978-1-78678-656-2 (Paperback)

ISBN: 978-1-78678-657-9 (eBook)

www.watkinspublishing.com

MIX

Paper from
responsible sources

FSC® C013056

CONTENTS

"Questa e la vera acqua santa!"

("This is the real holy water!")

Pope Francis, on being presented with a
bottle of Oban Single Malt Whisky

Before We Begin: Advice on Drinking and Reading at the Same Time

Just before you settle down to absorb this text, may I suggest a quick visit to the local off-licence, bottle shop, supermarket or your favourite online beverage dealer? Because if we are to search for the sacred in a glass, it may be necessary, even advisable, to take our liquid salvation in our own hands. And fill that glass right up.

What we're going to do in this book is go on a journey. I know, I know. That word "journey" has been terribly demeaned by hundreds of TV talent shows, but nevertheless, that's what we're doing: travelling.

We're going to investigate the connections between religion and alcohol: the attempts faith has made to prohibit or moderate its consumption or to harness it to a particular belief's purpose; the uses it has been put to within worship, and the many divine and very human legends and stories associated with it.

We will be moving, sometimes a little unsteadily, across the planet – from Scotland to India, Japan, the USA, Europe, Africa, the Caribbean – and encountering God, gods, goddesses, witches, warlocks, demons and every conceivable drink from cider to mead to Norse spittle. Not all of these libations will be delicious.

It will be interesting. It will be fun. And if you drink as you read, it could even be … spiritually enlightening.

Please do drink and read. Or not, depending on the circumstances you find yourself in with this book. Maybe you're driving and listening to the audio version, in which case the consumption of alcoholic liquids would be both ill-advised and illegal. However, what could be more conducive to literary appreciation or the enjoyable absorption of information than the occasional sip of a suitable libation? Perhaps you're reading and quaffing by a roaring fire or even a gently whirring air conditioner? Something internally warming or cooling, or vice versa, would surely be appropriate.

Each chapter in this book is preceded by a short list of drinks either mentioned in the text or that could, in this author's opinion, highlight, reinforce or simply enhance what is written about. A small measure of each will suffice and there is no requirement to consume all or any of the drinks mentioned. I have, however, tried to make each chapter's "flight" (a technical term borrowed from the esoteric world of malt whisky appreciation) an informative and enjoyable progression of tastes.

I love the stories associated with drinks; they nearly all reflect the places and personalities that brought them into being and the ideologies, the beliefs, the moments in history when they were first made. I've never been so sure about so-called "tasting notes", which tend to vary wildly depending on the taster, their level of sobriety, what they had for breakfast, lunch or dinner and whatever form of prose, poetry or gobbledygook they were last exposed to. I write this as a regular World Whisky Awards judge who has been nosing and tasting whiskies professionally for 40 years.

Better by far to come to your own conclusions about a drink. Give it a chance, even if you don't initially like the taste. Then, at the end of each chapter, you will find my attempt to describe my own reactions to the drams or tipples mentioned at the start – and that will, for the most part, be in the traditional format: colour, nose or smell, palate or mouthfeel and aftertaste or finish. Drink it neat, or in the case of spirits, with enough water to bring the alcohol content down past the point of burning your mouth. Water will release some aroma too, but don't drown it.

Sniff. Don't heat the glass with your palm. I like straight glasses – tumblers – but I appear to be unique in this. Some say you should hold a spirit in your mouth for the number of seconds it is years old, if that figure is available. Let it rest until you taste it thoroughly. Swallow and enjoy the afterlife.

We are dealing in these pages with the links between alcoholic drinks and religion, and occasionally I may make claims for the spiritual insights induced by specific concoctions. Often these sensations or insights will be about memory, history, the people I associate with particular liquids or the places they come from. I will be telling stories. My story. I believe religion is about story. The tales we tell each other that explain the world and how we live in it. How we ought to live. How we'd like to.

There is a fashion in the international spirits industry to portray hustlers and salespeople tasked with flogging their favoured booze as "brand evangelists". "Evangel" is from the Greek *euangelion*, which means "good news". The good news about the best alcoholic drinks – and with certain exceptions, the drinks I have chosen for these holy flights are the best I could find – is that, in moderation, they can illuminate, relax, provide conviviality and seal friendship. And consumption leads, always, to the telling of, and listening to, stories. At least I believe so.

Should you feel that my descriptions of the sensations associated with said drinks are somehow pretentious or fanciful, I apologize. And offer you the following lines as one rather addled professional drinks taster's thoughts on the matter.

The Guided Tasting

There's vanilla, sherry, oak, molasses
But there nearly always is
There's coconut and lemongrass
Or perhaps I didn't wash the glass
Because – and I do have a little guilt –
I had a Malibu and Lilt

To freshen up my nosing skills
A residue may linger still
I'll rinse out this receptacle
And use my strongest spectacles
To read the label – oh, I see
Distilled in 1953
A fine year for this lovely dram
And warehoused, I see, in Amsterdam …
I do apologize, I'm wrong
It was aged in Glasgow all along
Made three years past, in Glen Aldi –
A lovely spot, you will agree.
At any rate, let's have a sniff
Aha! you see! Sea! Seaweed! Salt! We're on a cliff
Breakers down below are breaking
Oceanic shakers of sea salt are shaking
Now, swirl it round your mouth – don't spit
You really need to swallow it
To gain the cosmic realization
The truly marvellous sensation
Of life, and rediscovered youth
It's almost 50 per cent proof
It's like being hit with a fencing mallet
It's removed a layer from my palate
I'm getting … mildew, smoking tyres
A waste disposal plant on fire
My mother's burned raspberry jam
Perhaps my friend Archie's dear old nan
Whose imminent incontinence
Entire rooms could always sense
But really, that is quite enough
This is incandescent stuff
Still, I should warn you to take care
Of Glen Aldi amateurs must beware
I'll give it five stars out of four

As long as I can have some more
A case or two will be just fine
I'll get a decent price online
Now, that's enough from me, I think
It's time to have a proper drink …

The Holy Flights

Nearly all of these drinks are available worldwide at what I consider a reasonable price, though customs regulations may prevent imports into some countries. If you go to my personal blog at thebeatcroft.com you will find a list of online retailers who should be able to supply most, if not all of the drinks mentioned. Some retailers will supply "sample"-size single-drink versions and of course in a good bar you will be able to get the single or double measure you want or need. At thebeatcroft.com you will also find updates with extra essays, and news of the *Holy Waters Live* show, which will include guided tastings, music and readings. Not to mention a possible appearance of "the God Helmet" (see Chapter 3).

The Holy Flights

Introduction
Highland Park Viking Honour 12-Year-Old Single Malt Whisky
Cutty Sark Blended Malt Whisky
Arbikie Haar Vodka

Chapter 1
St Columba Garden Gin
Bushmills Black Bush Irish Whiskey
Ledaig 10-Year-Old Isle of Mull Single Malt Whisky
Graham's 10-Year-Old Tawny Port

Chapter 2
Lindores Abbey New Make Spirit Drink 2021 (63.5 per cent alcohol)
Lindores Abbey Distillery Aqua Vitae (40 per cent alcohol)
Lindores Lowland Single Malt Scotch Whisky MCDXCIV (46 per cent alcohol)

Chapter 3
North Uist Distillery Downpour Scottish Dry Gin
Courvoisier VS Cognac
Châteauneuf-du-Pape 2014 (Marc Perrin for the Co-operative Society, UK)

Chapter 4
Amrut Peated Single Malt Whisky
Cobra Premium Lager
Murree Beer

Chapter 5
Ribena (Blackurrant cordial)
Kool-Aid (Grape drink)
Chateau Musar 2015

Chapter 6
Buckfast Tonic Wine
Dom Pérignon Vintage Champagne 2010
(Cheaper alternative: Freixenet Cordon Negro Cava)
Green Chartreuse
Barr's Irn Bru (1901 edition)

Chapter 7
Murphy's Stout (canned)
Weihenstephaner Hefe Weissbier
Weltenburger Kloster Dunkle Weissbier
Tynt Meadow English Trappist Ale

Chapter 8
Perrier
Highland Spring
Whatever comes out of your tap (faucet)

Chapter 9
Jose Cuervo Especial Gold
Evan Williams Kentucky Straight Bourbon Whiskey
Elijah Craig Kentucky Straight Bourbon Whiskey
Heaven Hill Corn Whiskey 9-Year-Old (That Boutique-y Whisky Company)

Chapter 10
Smith Hayne Dry Still Cider
Burrow Hill Sparkling Perry
Arran 10-Year-Old Single Malt Whisky

Chapter 11
Clairin Communal
Clément VSOP Rhum Agricole
Watson's Trawler Rum

Chapter 12
Ben Nevis 10-Year-Old Single Malt Whisky
Isake Classic Sake
Yoichi Single Malt Whisky

Chapter 13
Lerwick Brewery Blindside Stout
Scapa Skiren Single Malt
Lindisfarne Mead

Chapter 14
Theakston's Old Peculier
Newcastle Brown Ale

WIDE-EYED AND LEGLESS

Holy Flight
– *Highland Park Viking Honour 12-Year-Old Single Malt Whisky*
– *Cutty Sark Blended Malt Whisky*
– *Arbikie Haar Vodka*

Alcohol is a psychoactive substance that also affects the body, and in religion it serves two purposes: it is both a gateway drug and a crucial piece of symbolism. How it works and how it is made feed into the theatrical power of its ritual use, so it's worth delving into both the chemistry and the history.

The alcohol we find in the liquids we commonly consume – wine, beer, gin, absinthe, whisky, whatever – is ethanol, though in most cases this is not pure ethanol (chemical formula $C2H6O$) as the brewing and distilling process throws up a number of different alcohols. Pure ethanol can be produced by petrochemical processes but for the most part it comes from fermentation and subsequent distillations. In other words, it's all about the rot.

According to Professor David Nutt, a man whose job title is longer than most – neuropsychopharmacologist – and who has combined, at various times, the treatment of alcoholics with owning a wine bar, alcohol "has glamour and history, and our art and culture are steeped in it. It's thought to be nearly as old as human society. There's a theory that the roots of agriculture weren't in the search for food but in the cultivation of crops to make alcohol."[1]

---

[1]　Nutt, Professor D, *Drink,* Yellow Kite, London, 2020, p.5

At its most basic, once fruit or grain begins to rot in liquid, the presence of yeast – wild or cultured – will produce ethanol and some other not so palatable organic compounds that need not concern us here, but which, in the form of congeners, are responsible for much suffering in the form of hangovers.

John Barleycorn Must Die

This is where the chemistry leaches into holy symbolism. Let me introduce you to my friend John Barleycorn. Who, as many know, will die.

Aged seven, I arrived in the school system of Ayrshire, Scotland, straight from a private prep school in Glasgow where the concern was to hammer us into polite shape and get us to speak "proper". Miss Kemmet belted us (the tawse, a seasoned leather bludgeon traditional to Scots schools, first met my hands when I was six in punishment for running in the girls' playground). Miss Fountain nurtured our plosives and fricatives in elocution ("p-p-p-p-p-p ... *please* speak clearly"). I was parachuted into a state (public), Protestant primary school dressed in my green (indicative of Catholicism in the west of Scotland) St Ronan's blazer (spat upon) and cap (stolen). And then I was forced to begin memorizing the work of Robert Burns, laureate of Ayrshire and southern Scotland, lover of whisky, women, mice and haggis.

"Tam O' Shanter", first published in 1791, is an enormous poem, and as an adult I can appreciate its humour, pace, poise and power. But as a child, I was all but overwhelmed by its immense length, and terribly impressed that one of my classmates, Evelyn, had memorized all 228 lines of it. It is a poem about drink, domestic strife, witchcraft, religion, hallucination and a horse called Meg. It was "Tam" who helped make John Barleycorn what he is today – a synonym for booze.

Inspiring bold John Barleycorn!
What dangers thou canst make us scorn!
With ale, we fear no evil

With whisky, we'll face the devil!

The term "John Barleycorn" had been used for centuries previously and is the title of a traditional English song going back to Elizabethan times. But Burns, a man whose tippling caused him no end of bother and whose expertise in matters alcohol-related led to his later career as a customs officer, brought John into common usage. Not just through Tam O'Shanter but in his version of the song:

There was three kings into the east,
Three kings both great and high,
And they hae sworn a solemn oath
John Barleycorn must die.

They took a plough and plough'd him down,
Put clods upon his head,
And they hae sworn a solemn oath
John Barleycorn was dead.

But the cheerful Spring came kindly on'
And show'rs began to fall.
John Barleycorn got up again,
And sore surprised them all.

The sultry suns of Summer came,
And he grew thick and strong;
His head well arm'd wi' pointed spears,
That no one should him wrong.

The sober Autumn enter'd mild,
When he grew wan and pale;
His bendin' joints and drooping head
Show'd he began to fail.

His colour sicken'd more and more,
And he faded into age;
And then his enemies began
To show their deadly rage.

They took a weapon, long and sharp,
And cut him by the knee;
They ty'd him fast upon a cart,
Like a rogue for forgerie.

They laid him down upon his back,
And cudgell'd him full sore.
They hung him up before the storm,
And turn'd him o'er and o'er.

They filled up a darksome pit
With water to the brim,
They heav'd in John Barleycorn.
There, let him sink or swim!

They laid him upon the floor,
To work him farther woe;
And still, as signs of life appear'd,
They toss'd him to and fro.

They wasted o'er a scorching flame
The marrow of his bones;
But a miller us'd him worst of all,
For he crush'd him between two stones.

And they hae taen his very hero blood
And drank it round and round;
And still the more and more they drank,
Their joy did more abound.

John Barleycorn was a hero bold,
Of noble enterprise;
For if you do but taste his blood,
'Twill make your courage rise.

'Twill make a man forget his woe;
'Twill heighten all his joy;
'Twill make the widow's heart to sing,
Tho' the tear were in her eye.

Then let us toast John Barleycorn,
Each man a glass in hand;
And may his great posterity
Ne'er fail in old Scotland![2]

What we have here is the process of planting, growing, flourishing, harvesting, threshing, malting and brewing barley. It is the cycle of agriculture, of rural life, of death and rebirth. The poetic character of John is so ancient that he probably goes back into the pagan era of British history, but the cycle of death and rebirth he symbolizes is crucial to many religions, not least, and most obviously perhaps, Christianity. The death and rebirth of the Messiah is, as Jesus himself says in John 12:24, necessary for salvation and just like Johnny B: "Verily, verily, I say unto you, Except a corn of wheat fall into the ground and die, it abideth alone: but if it die, it bringeth forth much fruit."[3]

It was James Frazer in his seminal 1890 book *The Golden Bough*, who popularized the notion that the so-called "dying-and-rising god" was central to religion in the widest sense. Osiris from Egypt, Dionysus and Adonis from Greece, Tammuz from Mesopotamia and of course Christ. However, some scholars since have argued that the idea is not universal. Some gods just, well, die, notably in Viking mythology, where the warfare

2   http://www.robertburns.org.uk/Assets/Poems_Songs/john_barleycorn.htm

3   John 12:24

culture is perhaps a bit blunter: Poor old Baldur – gone, and an inadequate number of tears shed to restore him. A blind brother shoots one mistletoe-tipped arrow and the gods are doomed! Pass me some mead (or, in fact, beer, which was the liquid of sustenance on those long Viking voyages).

Death and rebirth is a central theme in all religions and a psychological trope most famously analysed and mused upon by Carl Gustav Jung. Here he waxes poetic, though not perhaps with the same versifying verve as Burns:

The moon is dead.
Your soul went to the moon, to the preserver of souls.
Thus the soul moved toward death.
I went into the inner death and saw that outer dying is
better than inner death.
And I decided to die outside and to live within.
For that reason I turned away and sought the place of the
inner life.[4]

Jung was a big fan of Osiris, linking Egyptian mythology to Christianity in a way that still infuriates some Evangelical Christians. The explicit linking of Osiris to the rebirth of vegetable crops in agriculture led those who participated in the Osiris festivities to "experience the permanence and continuity of life which outlasts all changes of form". Jung argued that it was through Osiris that the Christian concept of the soul emerged.

In step with Persephone, Ishtar and many other deities, John Barleycorn stalks the Earth, and so the death/rebirth cycle you can see so explicitly rendered on the malting floor of a traditional distillery becomes central to religious thought. The malting of barley for whisk(e)y production is not just one of the most beautiful and indeed spectacular aspects of the whole distillation process, it is also, in its most old-fashioned form, my favourite. Go if you can to Highland Park Distillery in Orkney, Scotland or the

---

4   Jung, C G, *The Red Book*, p.267

Hillrock Distillery at Ancram NY, USA, and take in the (literally) breath-taking business. What happens is this: grains of barley, harvested and dried, are spread out in an even layer on an open space. They are dead. Water is sprayed on the floor – not a lot, just enough to dampen the grain, which is left until each individual grain begins to sprout. This massively increases the sugar content, which is the whole point. For brewing and distilling, germination provides that extra sugar, so you can actually extract the alcohol.

However, you don't want the grain to keep sprouting or else you'd end up with a field of whitish-green indoor stalks. You need to stop the growth process at the optimum point for sugar production. This you do in a small-scale, old-school malting operation by shovelling the sprouted barley into a kiln, where a combination of heat and smoke stops the germination. I was going to say stops it dead, but the really life-restoring magic is yet to happen. It's after the kilning that the malt is brewed with yeast to turn it into beer, and then, if you're going the whole hog, it can be distilled into spirit.

And there you have the water of life. It's like magic, it's elemental and it's a truly wonderful experience to see even a small malting in production. At Highland Park, the one I know best, and indeed one in which I have both shovelled malt and stoked the peat furnace, the smells are overwhelming: the cereal flavours of damp barley; the deep, oily smokiness of burning peat. And later, as you process through the production chain, the pungent reek of the wort as malt and water brew, and the high, zingy alcoholic whiff of new-make spirit as it runs like a miniature waterfall through the spirit safes.

So there is religious symbolism here in the way that alcohol is produced, which is similar in grape-based drinks. Brandy is essentially distilled wine and the death/rebirth cycle in wine production is even more pronounced. First witness for the prosecution (of anyone done for being drunk in charge of a human body): Dionysus, Greek, then Roman god of wine-making, wine, drinking, ecstasy (the condition not the substance), fertility and ritual madness. He is also known as Bacchus. This is where we get the notion of Bacchanalian rites and festivals, though by all accounts these were not the dissolute orgies we sometimes see portrayed in movies or TV series, such as *A Funny Thing Happened on the Way to the Forum*; *I, Claudius*; or *Asterix and Obelix Go to the Colosseum*. Although wine was seen according to the cult of Dionysus as the manifestation of the god himself on Earth, its consumption was a form of worship and a means to enlightenment, not oblivion. The notion of "divine madness" was completely different from being blind, blazing drunk.

Incidentally, the words used for drunkenness are many, each language having dozens of them, especially English. This is a poem from the show I wrote and performed for several years, *The Malt and Barley Revue*, and it contains as many words as I could find in English for the variations of inebriation:

Full of Loudmouth Soup: An A to Z of Drunkenness

Ankled, banjaxed, bladdered bleezin'
Why? Do I really need a reason?
I'm cabbaged clobbered, Chevy Chased
But not a broken vein upon my face
Despite being thoroughly Dot Cottoned
Sobriety almost forgotten
I'm etched – egregiously and completely
That creme de menthe went down so sweetly
So now, I'm fleemered and I'm flecked
So many snifters have been necked
That guttered, sweaty, ganted, howling
I'm wearing shirts made out of towelling
Inebriated, kaed up, jaxied
I've been ill in every single taxi
In every city kiboshed, kaned
Bernhard Langered, legless, debrained
Dhuisg, it is in Gaelic, mottled
(I must recycle all my bottles)
I'm Newcastled, out of my tree

There's really not much wrong with me
On the skite, overly refreshed
I swear I'd still pass my driving "tesht"
For drink improves pronounciation
Adds sparkle to enunciation
Predicting earthquakes, kissing pavements
Quite quoited, rubbered, I've made arrangements
To remain forever snobbled
Sleeping on tarmac or on cobbles
Thora Hirded, trousered, trashed
I've spent great lakes of liquid cash
Unca' fou, marocced, it's easy
Discombobulated, queasy
My wobbly boots are on, I'm wellied
But only very slightly smelly
Xenophoned, Yorkshired as a skunk
Zombied
But not even slightly drunk.

Holy Flight – Tasting Notes

Highland Park Viking Honour 12-Year-Old Single Malt Whisky

In my opinion, one of the best-value whiskies you can buy. Normally available at an entry-level price, I know from frequent visits to the distillery that it is one of the most carefully and thoughtfully produced whiskies on the market. Highland Park is also, as I write, the northernmost distillery in the UK and its location in Kirkwall in the Orkney Islands is a beautiful and historic small town full of fascinating charm. St Magnus Cathedral is my favourite church, its warm red sandstone glowing with welcome. It's a church that does not intimidate but somehow nurtures even the most casual visitor.

There are various bars in Kirkwall selling obscure and often very expensive bottles of the local whiskies (there are two distilleries in Orkney: Highland Park and Scapa) but my favourite is Helgi's Viking-themed pub on the Kirkwall waterfront. Often very busy, if you can get a seat it offers flights of whisky that will take you to Valhalla – the hall of the gods slain in battle – and back again. The food is excellent, too.

The distillery malts some of its own barley using peat from its own moorland banks on Orkney itself. As a visitor experience, it is second to none. This whisky has a mild peatiness that never overwhelms what is a complex and rewarding dram and is balanced by the oaky, winey notes from the used sherry barrels made of wood from distillery-owned forests. They treat the barrels with sherry, too. Heather or clumps of very heathery peat goes into the malting furnace, and you can taste it.

Colour: Red-gold, the shade of Orcadian sunsets or a longboat going up in flames.

Nose: Spicy and controlled, fragrant and fruity with just a hint of smoke.

Palate: Smooth, sweet and with overtones of citrus fruit and that vegetal smoke. Malty.

Finish: Long and warming, with the smoke coming through more strongly, but never dominating. A superb whisky for what is a very moderate price in most markets.

Cutty Sark Blended Malt Whisky

A blend originally made by the London company Berry Brothers and Rudd, named for the tea clipper *Cutty Sark*, once the fastest ship of her time and now a visitor attraction at the Royal Museums in Greenwich.

The ship was built in Dumbarton, Scotland, launched in 1869 and named after Tam's delighted shout in Burns' poem "Tam o'Shanter", as he watches witches, warlocks and demons dance in the old Alloway kirk:

And thought his very een enrich'd;
Even Satan glowr'd and fidg'd fu' fain,
And hotch'd and blew wi' might and main:

Till first ae caper, syne anither,
Tam tint his reason a' thegither,
And roars out, "Weel done, Cutty-sark!"
And in an instant all was dark:
And scarcely had he Maggie rallied,
When out the hellish legion sallied.

A "cutty sark" was a short nightdress. The ship, as portrayed on the label of every bottle of Cutty Sark whisky, was painted by Swedish artist Carl Georg August Wallin. The whisky itself does not really match up to the wild and uproarious events experienced by Tam, but it is deceptively smooth enough to seduce the careless drinker into a state where he or she may find themselves seeing things they perhaps had not anticipated … holy or unholy.

Colour: Buttery-yellow, a summer field of barley in a warm wind.

Nose: Fairly light and mildly caressing. The pungency comes with sweet floral notes and just a bit of graininess, with touches of citrus.

Palate: Barley to the fore with orange peel and a hint of vanilla pods.

Finish: Malty with a lengthy afterglow.

Arbikie Haar Wheat Vodka

Arbikie Estate is a family-owned working farm on the east coast of Angus in Scotland. They plant, sow, tend and harvest the fields and the drinks made on site use those crops. So, this is wheat vodka (there's also one made from potatoes), the true product of the land itself. It really is a product of the whole process from field to bottle.

The soil is red from the local sandstone, and the effect of the sea – the farm faces Lunan Bay – is obvious. The distillery was made from an old barn, and the family make everything from rye whiskey to gin here. Arbikie Haar Vodka is named after the rolling and chilly coastal fog that frequently envelops the distillery.

This is vodka in an old-school Russian sense, only very Scottish. And if you're going to drink alcohol, this is as pure an expression of it, both in its clarity and purity and its journey from crop to glass, as you will find.

Colour: Crystal clear, as it should be.

Nose: Wild honey, croissants, a bakery in early morning as the bread is just coming out of the oven.

Palate: You can taste the sea and the land. There's a graininess coming from the wheat, the spicy bursts of alcohol and a custardy undercurrent, too.

Finish: Warming, but clean and not too aggressive.

CHAPTER I

BURIED ALIVE BY A WARRIOR MONK

Ireland, Scotland (Iona, Mull, Ayrshire)
Gin, whiskey, whisky and port

Holy Flight
– *St Columba Garden Gin*
– *Bushmills Black Bush Irish Whiskey*
– *Ledaig 10-Year-Old Isle of Mull Single Malt Whisky*
– *Graham's 10-Year-Old Tawny Port*

St Columba, Colum, Columcille in Gaelic, Irish warrior monk of royal descent, miracle worker, bringer of Christianity to Scotland, whence his followers spread the word throughout the whole of Britain and eventually beyond to most of mainland Europe.

Picture him if you can, though descriptions after more than 1,500 years are understandably vague. Charismatic, a natural leader, physically strong, imposing. A prince by birth and temperament, rough monk's robes or not. Haunted, perhaps by his past, but full of determination, passion and strength. Given the hygiene limitations of the time, probably a bit smelly. His (male) followers were fond of shaving the front of their heads, presumably in imitation of St Columba's male pattern receding hairline, and letting their hair grow long at the back, thus pioneering what we now call a "skullet", a variation on the infamous Michael Bolton/Billy Ray Cyrus/ Mel Gibson mullet.

St Columba came to Scotland in about AD 563 with a dozen companions, bent on penance for his sins. A senior religious and political figure and also an abbot, he had royally messed things up back home, sparking off a series of tribal conflicts and many deaths due to a dispute over the copying of a Gospel manuscript. So he and his followers came first to Dunaverty on the Kintyre peninsula aboard a curragh, a leather and basketweave boat. However, they could still see the coast of Ireland from there, so Columba decreed they would land elsewhere and eventually they arrived on the island of Iona.

And with them they brought whisky. Or, coming as they did from Ireland, maybe we should say they brought whiskey with an "e". I will explain the origins of that particular spelling discrepancy in due course (see page 26).

To be completely honest, we don't know if Columba had a flask or two of firewater with him on that curragh, though one sincerely hopes he and his boys did. The North Channel can be a cold, rough and unforgiving stretch of water. But there is little doubt that whisky and the expertise needed to make it arrived in Scotland courtesy of Columba and his band of brothers.

As the Columban missionaries spread their gospel of salvation, the knowledge of distillation went with them. Ideas and the ability to produce alcoholic spirits moved hand in hand, glass to lip. Holy water and the water of life intermingled. And eventually, as folk began to move across the Atlantic to the Americas, often forced to leave their native lands on religious grounds, stills and the ability to use them went, too. When God moves, or gods move a people, the spirits that people produce also move.

Columba was a charismatic figure. Building his abbey on Iona, he supposedly discovered that its foundations would only be secure if a living person was buried beneath them. Was there a volunteer? One of his original twelve disciples, Oran, also once an abbot in Ireland, came forward and was duly interred. His face was left uncovered until he began proclaiming that in fact there was no such place as heaven or hell, and Columba decided to quite literally shut him up. Permanently.

Columba's encounters with kings and other creatures, notably the Loch Ness Monster (Columba won that skirmish), have been dealt with in many books over the past 500 years. He worked many miracles, converted kings and chieftains. His spirit, fuelled perhaps by the spirits whose distillation techniques he brought to Scotland, haunts the world today. But for now, come with me back to Ireland, back across the North Channel near to a spot from where on a clear day you can see the Scottish coast. Indeed, there was a time when strict presbyterians of a particular denominational bent would row on a Sunday morning over to Scotland to worship. Following in Columba's oar-sweeps.

By the Rill of St Colum

Forty years of motorcycling, and I'd never fallen off once. Now here I was, in the deceptively sloping car park of Bushmills Distillery in Northern Ireland, lying underneath a Triumph Street Triple R – 675cc of rampant, hooligan motorcycle – which had just toppled with a sickening crunch onto my legs and torso.

I was on a pilgrimage. A journey of the spirit. Having already blended a whisky using the products of distilleries at the extreme points of the compass in Scotland, I was now engaged in collecting whisky from distilleries in each of the United Kingdom's four component countries – Scotland, Ireland, England and Wales. By motorcycle. I'm sure there was a sensible reason for this. Whisky production in Wales and England was still rare, and I think myself and my travelling companions wished to contrast, compare and celebrate. Or just go for a long road trip involving bikes and ferries. At any rate, it seemed like a good idea at the time. Until that moment in the Bushmills car park.

There was no pain at first. Briefly, there had been horror, a sense of awful inevitability as, while swinging my leg over the heavily laden bike to get off, I caught my foot on the tailpack, fell to the ground and watched the Grey Beast teeter on its dodgy kickstand and then descend toward my aged body.

Worse, there were witnesses. As I lay on the ground waiting for the inevitable agony and revelations of damage to both myself and the motorbike (brand new and borrowed, amid much dubiety about its insurance status, from the Triumph factory), I saw the horrified expression on the face of Gordon Donoghue, manager of Bushmills and a keen motorcyclist himself. Manoeuvring my bike close to his immaculate Triumph Bonneville had provoked my awkward and ultimately failed attempt to dismount. The dishonourable idea that it was all Gordon's fault flashed through my mind. I could see in his eyes he thought so, too. Or rather, that it was all the fault of Bushmills Whiskey, its manager, then-owners Pernod Ricard, and possibly the Protestant God who inhabits this part of Northern Ireland. The same God who makes the populace paint the paving stones red, white and blue; spreads Him- (or Her-) self among the dozens of competing churches of a Sabbath morning; and turns a blind presbyterian eye to the fact that Jameson's, that good Catholic whiskey made in Cork in the Republic of Ireland, was for years tankered north and bottled at Bushmills. By some Protestants. Although of course many Bushmills staff were Catholics, not that this is widely advertised. It's still common in parts of the USA for drinkers to affirm their Roman Catholic Irish heritage, or indeed Republicanism, by ordering Jameson's. And many remember Detective Jimmy McNulty in the TV series *The Wire* having a famous interchange with a bartender: Could he have a Jameson's? Well, no, they didn't have any. Would a Bushmills be all right? That, replied McNulty in high dudgeon, was Protestant whiskey.

Gordon had already told me that during the "Troubles", there had never been an attack by either Republican or Loyalist forces on the distillery. Some things are too important for politics.

But back to the car park, and me lying with a motorbike on my leg. In the milliseconds the whole incident took to play out,

I could see Gordon's brain turning over various considerations. After the array of Bushmills new-make spirit and finished whiskeys I had inhaled, but not drunk, that morning, had I addled my motorcycling body and brain, despite a rigid adherence to the sniff-spit-don't-swallow rule? Would there have to be a full Health and Safety inquiry into the incident? Would I sue for bad car park camber?

The answer to all of the above was, of course, no. And miraculously, I was completely uninjured, being able to withdraw my leather-clad leg without even an abrasion. The bike, though, that was another story. Three months after Triumph silently took it back, a letter arrived detailing the £1,500-worth of repairs that had been necessary. Did I wish to make a contribution to the cost?

I did not. But I was unhurt. It was a miracle.

The Real Holy Water

Miracles happen at Bushmills, as you might expect when the water of St Columb's rill is being transformed into *uisge beatha*, the water of life. It's thought that whiskey has been made on this site since the 13th century. Long, long after Columcille had become St Columba and departed for the Inner Hebrides of Scotland.

Alcohol and Christianity have always walked hand in hand. And even today, at the very top of the Roman Catholic Church, there is evidently the taste for a dram. At the Vatican in 2019, Pope Francis was presented with a bottle of Oban single malt whisky by a group of Scottish student priests. He was, it's fair to say, delighted, and he was caught on video holding the bottle up to the light and telling the young men, "*Questa e la vera acqua santa!*" "This is the *real* holy water!"

Ripples of unease spread across Roman Catholicism. Though it was recognized that the Holy Father had his tongue firmly in his cheek, he had form with whisky. The previous year, a gift of whisky from Scottish priest Father Jim Walls had provoked a reference to holy water, and the same year Father Jim Sichko had presented him with a bottle of 23-year-old Pappy Van Winkle Bourbon. "This," said Pope Francis knowledgeably, "is really good bourbon." What he thinks of Bushmills – or Jameson's – is not recorded.

And that would be Irish whiskey, not whisky. The additional "e" applies in most of the USA and all of Ireland, but not in Canada. It depends where the majority of settlers originally came from.

With or without an "e", the pronunciation is identical, and the name comes from Gaelic (pronounced "Gaylic", if we're talking in Irish), or Gaelic (pronounced "Gallic", if we happen to be in Scotland). Scots Gaelic developed from the Irish version of the language, and it seems certain that the magical recipe for whisky came from there too. *Uisge beatha*, in Scots Gaelic, *Uisce beatha* in Irish. Water of Life. How do you say that? How much have you had to drink? Ooshkiva! Ooooshhhkivaaah … Oosh … Ooshhka … Oooshki … Whisky.

Or, if you prefer, whiskey. Or whisky.

If you're thinking that this water-of-life stuff sounds awfully similar to the Latin aqua vitae, as in Aquavit, or eau de vie, as in Cognac, Armagnac or Calvados, then you're absolutely right. But in almost every culture and country, distilled alcohol has been seen as a life-affirming, life-giving liquid. Magical. An elixir, in fact. Of course, in large quantities, it will kill you, but its origin was as a medicine. And to go back to Gaelic (Scots), that's why it's best to moderate your intake by asking for "*te bheag*" (chay-vaik). A wee one. You can have several wee ones. Lots of wee ones. Sufficient wee ones to sink the proverbial Titanic. But stick to just a few wee ones and you'll be all right. Probably.

Alcohol, then. Distilled spirit. Did the Irish monks discover how to produce it? Some find it impossible to believe that alcohol could first have been distilled anywhere else. But no, Celts did not pioneer the hard stuff. Distilled alcohol for drinking is a Middle Eastern discovery. Beer and wine go back to the beginnings of agriculture. Traces of a beery drink made around 13,000 years ago have been found in Israel, and a fermented concoction of rice, honey and fruit is thought to have been made in China somewhere between 7000 and 6600 BC.

Distillation is what the Columbans brought from Ireland to Scotland – so-called "pure" distillation; there's been a form of it on the Indian subcontinent since AD 500. Ethanol – C_2H_5OH – boils at 78.4°C (173.12°F), which is lower than water. That means it comes wafting off heated, fermented liquid before watery steam does. All you have to do is condense it on something cool, and bingo: there you have it – life!

Forget all that mystical Celtic twilight nonsense about some heathery crofter accidentally boiling up beer and licking shockingly strong ethanol off the top of his curiously shaped early Superlager can. It was all happening way to the east. The basics of the technology would have been picked up by Irish monks, known for their travels in the Middle East, and brought back home. Meanwhile, Arab and Persian chemists, at the absolute cutting edge of science in their day, perfected the technology, developing processes and equipment that would be recognized and admired today, even within the hallowed precincts of Heriot-Watt University's Brewing and Distilling of Mind-Altering Liquids Department. By the AD 800s, the legend that was Persian alchemist Abu Musa Jabir ibn Hayyan was perfecting what we would recognize today as the alembic still. It's unlikely that his activities would be welcomed today in what his homeland has become – the Islamic Republic of Iran.

The word "alcohol" itself comes from the Middle East. The term appears in English in the 16th century, entering the language via French from medical Latin, ultimately from either the Arabic *al-k'ohl* or *al-ghawl*. *Kuhl* (kohl) is a powder used as an antiseptic and eyeliner then and now, and *al* is the Arabic for "the". So alcohol might take its name from eye shadow, though not because it caused a natural equivalent to occur in those who've been up all night sampling the stuff. One explanation is that *k'ohl* was seen as the essence of Indian Devilwood, the plant it was extracted from, and it became a generic term for the essential spirit of something. Better than "Max Factor", anyway. Alternatively, the word *k'ohl* may come from *kahala*, which means to colour or stain.

Type *al-kuhl, al k'ohl or a variant into* an internet search engine, however, and a stranger and more chilling story will come pouring out of your device. You will be informed, sometimes by what appear to be authorities on the subject, that *al-kohl* is Arabic for "body-eating spirit". In fact, this is *al-ghawl*. The two terms are often confused. The argument, often but not always associated with extreme fundamentalist Christianity, then usually hops to the practice of alchemy, in which apparently alcohol is used to extract the soul of an entity. If a human being consumes alcohol, the liquid in effect extracts the very essence of the soul, allowing the body to be more susceptible to neighbouring entities, most of which are of low frequencies. Demon possession, in other words. Evil spirits. *Al-ghawl* is supposedly where the English word "ghoul" comes from.

The English-language and fundamentalist Christian arguments that boozing means imbibing demons has a lot to do with a remarkable man called Dr Walter Johnson, one of the proponents of hydropathy or water treatment. He practised around Great Malvern in England (home of the internationally famous mineral water) and was Florence Nightingale's favourite doctor. He is quoted in *The Temperance Dictionary* as believing that:

> "When the spirit (alcohol) was first discovered and had proved its infuriating power, the oriental fancy connected it with the belief in ghouls – spirits believed to assume human forms, and to feed upon the dead. Hence would come the designation *al-ghoul*, the ghoul, afterwards changed by western mispronunciation into alcohol."[1]

---

[1]   Burns, Rev Dawson, *The Temperance Dictionary*, J Caudwell, London, 1861. Volume One on Google Books.

The author of the dictionary, Rev Dawson Burns, was a staunch teetotaller and very much a product of the 19th-century temperance movement, which sought to ban the consumption of all forms of what Scottish comedian Norman Maclean called "the old mood-altering". Burns, however, is lofty in his dismissal of Johnson: "The theory is ingenious, but the supposed fact on which it is based is without historical support, and contrary to historical probability."[2] Certainly, the Oxford English Dictionary goes for the *al-k'ohl* etymology and English texts going back to the 17th century affirm this.

Ghoul or Kohl, alcohol, an apparently magical substance, made its way from the Middle East to Ireland, and it did so because of religion. Faith was the focus and impetus of all learning in Ireland, and the monasteries sent their monks out in search of knowledge and converts. As well, of course, as Islam itself being a colonizing force. The Iberian Peninsula was under Islamic control from 711, but by that time it is arguable that distillation was already established far to the north, the skills and secrets travelling with holy men. The spirit moves. Time passes. Especially when there's drink involved.

In the Irish *Annals of Clonmacnoise*, the death of a chieftain is recorded in 1405. He perished at Christmas after "taking a surfeit of aqua vitae". As for Scotland, we have to leap forward 89 years, to 1494, for the famous entry in the Exchequer Rolls of James IV where "Eight bolls of malt" were sent "to Friar John Cor, by order of the king, to make aquavitae" – the first written record of whisky-making in Scotland. Cor's home was Lindores Abbey in Fife, and this was, interestingly, not an offshoot of an Irish monastic order but of the Tironensians, originally Benedictines from Tiron in France, who were extremely powerful in Scotland, with abbeys not just in Fife but at Kilwinning, Kelso and Arbroath. This raises the interesting question: while distilling methodology was almost certainly already in Scotland by 1405 thanks to Columba, was it French expertise that perfected it? Sacre Bleu!

---

[2]   Ibid.

As I began writing this book, the new distillery at Lindores bottled and released its first single malt whisky. I will tell the story more fully in the next chapter, but it's worth saying here that the distillery has dubbed itself "the spiritual home of whisky". I suggest that some folk on Iona may disagree. Although there is no proof that whisky was made on the island, Maxwell Macleod, son of Lord George Macleod, who masterminded the rebuilding of Iona Abbey last century, told me of stories that the monks would race cats around the cloisters while under the influence of distilled spirits. It seems an odd enough tale to be believable.

By the mid-18th century, alcohol was solidly, indeed soberly, defined in English as the "intoxicating ingredient in strong liquor". What was to become a worldwide industry worth billions began to establish itself. The world's favourite mood-altering substance gradually became more and more industrialized. Its effects became for many an escape from the grim realities of urban poverty. Cheap gin and bad booze were obvious methods of personal oblivion and social control, and the source of huge health problems in fast-developing societies. That demon, drink.

Now we are sold ethanol in a million different forms, branded to appeal to all age groups, tastes and cultures, producers inciting us to celebrate, to indulge but never, on any billboard or TV advert, to over-indulge. It's a commodity, a drug, an illusion and for many, sadly, a dependency.

But alcohol, pure, impure and diluted, is more than indulgence, more than drunkenness. It is of great symbolic importance in various faiths. It plays roles in magic and is an object of constant scientific investigation. It provides conviviality and solitary insight. It can be transformational and, yes, destructive. To those who say all forms of alcohol are the same, in that they produce the same effects … well, yes. You're right. And you're also wrong. The difference between a ferocious but deceptively smooth George T Stagg 2009 small-batch Kentucky straight bourbon, bottled at 70.7 per cent alcohol and a stunningly sophisticated Glen Rothes 1994 should be obvious to any taster. As should that between a Bacardi Breezer and an Aftershock, a Buckfast Tonic wine and a frozen Stolichnaya.

Speaking of George T Stagg and Kentucky Bourbon, I will be discussing the uneasy but often enthusiastic relationship between alcohol and the USA in due course, but it's worth pointing out that the connection between religious missionary activity and alcohol is at the root of Kentucky Bourbon production, thanks to the activities of renegade Baptist preacher Rev Elijah Craig (note the Scottish surname), who was allegedly the first to age whiskey in charred oak barrels. And, of course, there's William Laird distilling applejack in New Jersey after he arrived from the Scottish Highlands in 1698. They came, they went to church, they made the water of life.

So many tastes, so many sources, so much spiritual comfort in a glass! But these days many call themselves connoisseurs, and the enlivening qualities of an alcoholic drink – the sheer ability to alter someone's mood – is disguised by intense discussion and description of aroma, taste, manufacturing process and that lovely French word *terroir* – meaning the land, the soil – even the cultural context a drink comes from. We can so easily get lost in our attempts to categorize and describe.

Then there is The Truth According to Hamish Henderson. Henderson was (he died in 2002) an intellectual, lecturer, folksong collector, hero of the Resistance against Hitler, pacifist, soldier (he personally accepted the surrender of Italy from Marshall Graziani) and poet, seen by many as Scotland's greatest since Robert Burns. In many ways he personifies Scotland: difficult, controversial, inspirational, charming, and that old Scots word *thrawn*, meaning intransigent. He was great company, a cheerful invader of personal space. Once, a friend of his who was involved in the whisky industry decided it would be a good idea to obtain the great man's verdict on a few rare single malts, for possible marketing purposes. After all, wouldn't the famous poet capture the grandeur and greatness of these fine spirits with words of deathless beauty, aesthetic insight and intellectual rigour?

The tasting began with due ceremony. The correct glasses, the small jug of water, the holy libations themselves. Henderson sniffed and sipped, a beatific expression on his face. Time passed. At length the poet was asked to describe the experience of drinking an excessively expensive, hugely aged dram. What, he was asked, was it like? There was a long pause. And then Henderson smiled, shook his head, and held out his glass for a refill.

"I'll tell you what it was like," he said. "It was like … whisky."

This book is about "discerning the spirits", as the Bible instructs on many occasions, perhaps most notably in 1 John 4, verse one: "Beloved, believe not every spirit, but try the spirits whether they are of God: because many false prophets are gone out into the world." The associations of alcohol with the Divine are many, and we shall seek those connections, finding them in some perhaps unexpected places. But it's in humanity's agricultural interactions with the planet that alcohol has its origins – as does, some would argue, religion.

Put together clean water, carefully grown crops, yeast and fire, and you can produce real magic. If you have the knowledge. If you have the faith. It is a matter of the spirit. For alcohol and belief have always walked hand in hand.

Germ-Free Communion and the Lost Evangelist

My first encounters with alcohol were intrinsically religious. First there was a communion or "the morning meeting", and then there was witnessing drunks.

"The silver", said my dad, "reacts with the alcohol and actually kills germs. So despite the fact that everyone is drinking from a common cup, infection cannot spread."

I believed him. But then, the wonder and mystery of the Sunday morning communion service at Bethany Gospel Hall was overwhelming for a ten-year-old. How could you not believe? There was the glint and glitter of the two big silver communion cups, a bottle of Old Tawny fortified wine in each. I knew it was Old Tawny as my pal Stewart and I had raided the Gospel Hall bins one bored summer weekday and found the brown bottles lurking at the bottom. Empty, or we'd have had a swallow. What I have never been able to establish is whether this was "proper" Old Tawny port, or a cheap fortified wine masquerading as such. I have drunk all sorts of fortified wines in my post-Brethren years, including a Madeira at least some of which was originally made in the 18th century and a port that cost £55 for a small glass in the Ubiquitous Chip restaurant in Glasgow (Scottish Television were paying). Communion on an Ayrshire Sabbath was no place for connoisseurship. It was strong. It was heady. It was Old Tawny and it was the blood of Christ.

A loaf of unsliced bread sat on a silver platter between the communion chalices, draped with a starched linen napkin. And the smell was the first thing that hit you when you entered the building. The warm, domestic embrace of the bread; the pungent, heady reek of the wine. All I wanted to do was eat and drink. At that age I was always hungry. And thirsty.

"Plymouth" (that seaport so crucial in the history of the USA) or "Christian" Brethren services were – in theory if not entirely in practice – open to anyone (anyone male, that is); to contribute a prayer, a hymn, a sermon or to launch communion by "giving thanks for the bread and wine". There was always a failsafe fallback of senior elders who would keep things moving along if there was a lull, sometimes nudged by wives anxious about the Sunday roast sitting in the oven at home. But once the bread started moving from hand to hand, fingers tearing a piece out for consumption, the bakery aromas would send me almost into convulsions of starvation.

The wine, as the massive cup moved along the pews, could make you slightly drunk just by inhaling its aroma. There was great amusement in watching certain elderly members of the congregation swilling back a couple of massive swallows, their cheeks flushing rosy pink in holy ecstasy.

You didn't get to partake of communion in the Brethren unless you'd been baptised (full immersion, minimum age 16), and then you had to confess your belief in front of "the meeting", or its representatives on Earth, "the oversight" – a selection of male elders. Eventually, amid a welter of adolescent doubt and desperation to belong, I was submerged and welcomed into the fellowship, and I got to taste Old Tawny myself.

"This is my body broken for you … This is my blood …" The wine, beefed up with brandy or some distillate or other, burned my throat. It was acrid and sweet at the same time, sour and sugary and thick, like treacle. As motes of dust danced in the sunlight streaming through the windows, I felt my head swimming with pride. I belonged. I was part of this. The wine was a symbol of Christ's blood, poured out at Calvary for our eternal redemption, but it was also a mysterious seal on my faith. And if you sneaked a second sip, it made you feel … good.

I remember the first time I saw a drunk, on the streets of Bellshill in Central Lanarkshire. An elderly man, falling over, stumbling and singing. He cannoned off another man, known to him, who refused to drink from the bottle of Eldorado or Lanliq he was bearing, the electric soups as they were known. Or it may have been Old Tawny.

"Have a drink, Billy! Have a drink with me!" His sober companion shook his head.

"No, Gerry, that's fine. But I'm just glad to see you so happy."

I was walking with my dad, through the winter's darkness, the ashiness of a 1960s Lanarkshire night, and he was holding my hand. We passed the pair and went on toward the Gospel Hall there, which sat between a steelworks and a pig farm: the aromas of industry and excrement.

"Happiness," Dad said, shaking his head. "Happiness. Wine that maketh glad the heart of man." And even as a child I knew that Gerry's happiness wasn't something to aspire to. I looked back as Billy gently lowered his acquaintance to the ground, placed the bottle in his lap and walked on.

After you'd been absorbed into the Assembly, as the church was called, you had a duty to spread the word, and this was where things became scary. Because that meant door-to-door visiting of strangers, the handing out of leaflets outside pubs at closing time and the conducting of open-air Gospel meetings on street corners, again just at the time when the happily or unhappily inebriated were making their disinhibited way home. Pubs closed at ten in those far-off days in Scotland. There was a lot of liver-loading in the fifteen minutes' drinking-up time; street-corner preachers needed nerves of steel and the holy patter of Billy Connolly to cope with hecklers.

And there was sometimes a physical threat. Fortunately, among the converted in the essentially working-class Brethren were usually one or two robust ex-shipyard workers or miners who could defuse the situation with their advanced social skills or the firm grasping of a bicep. Muscular Christianity.

I preached sometimes. I sang soberly into the maelstrom of a Glasgow Friday night in Buchanan Street, was propositioned, scolded, offered sips from brown-bagged bottles. There were fights, glassings, cops on horses. Ministers who later fled the country in tabloid disgrace.

And later, I would be the one staggering along the street, as half-remembered believers shouted salvation through bad PA systems. After I'd taken disbelieving communion for the final time, in a church that used Ribena (a popular British blackcurrant cordial), diluted and in individual glasses. No risk of infection. No chance of getting a taste for it.

Not like me.

Dad, Scotland and the Whole Wide Western World

Today I am remembering my father, who, as I write this, died aged 90 a few short weeks ago. One of our last conversations was about alcohol.

"When we get through this," he said, during his last struggles with illness and fatigue, "when I'm feeling better, I'm going to buy a really nice bottle of Nuits St Georges and we'll have a drink together."

Through the years, Dad had grown to take a much more

liberal attitude toward alcohol than during his earlier Gospel Hall days and had become something of a wine connoisseur. He even, again in his final week, told me how much he appreciated the bottle of Berry Brothers and Rudd Sherry Cask Matured Blended Malt Scotch Whisky I'd bought him for Christmas.

But now, right now, I'm remembering him and his faith – the faith that reared and still marks me – with a glass of as near to Old Tawny as I can find: Graham's 10-Year-Old Tawny Port. And as I open the bottle, the release of that heavy smell takes me back first to Bethany Hall in Troon and then unleashes all kinds of other memories: Sunday School, witnessing drunks, holidays in camper vans, including one to near Southend in Kintyre, to Dunaverty. Where Columba first landed. And then moved on. Taking his stories with him. Stories of faith and distillation, which would eventually spread throughout the western world.

Holy Flight – Tasting Notes

St Columba Garden Gin

There are many so-called "craft" gins, and most, like St Columba, are made with neutral alcohol (usually, but not always, neutral grain spirit), which is then added to a mixture of neutral alcohol and water that has been re-distilled, incorporating various botanicals and herbs to flavour the finished product as required.

I'm sorry to take away from the mystique surrounding these drinks, but I regard a lot of "craft" gins with suspicion. Remember that most people will drink gin in a cocktail, often with tonic, and that most specialist cocktail bartenders favour the famous old standbys – Bombay Sapphire, Gordon's, Beefeater and Tanqueray, with those upmarket upstarts Sipsmith and Hendricks bringing up the rear. Other bars will use whatever they're paid to.

However, some small hotels and pubs have their own gins made up to reflect where they are and the atmosphere of the location. That's what's happened here. The St Columba Hotel,

Bar and Larder on Iona is set in an almost impossibly atmospheric position, right next door to the Abbey, and the herbs and botanicals used in their gin are from their own Iona garden. So, when you drink this (preferably neat), you are drinking in the spirit of Iona in a very real sense. Also, no matter where in the world you drink it, it will take you in the space of a sip right back to that beautiful and historic island. Oh, and I'm drinking it without tonic or water. Or ice.

At the moment, this gin is only available on Iona, from the hotel itself. As a substitute, you may wish to try the much more easily obtained Whitetail Gin from the nearby island of Mull. The name was inspired by the white-tailed sea eagles that nest close to the distillery – the first new distillery on the island in 220 years. It uses a selection of local flavourings such as pine needles, heather and sea-kelp from shores of Loch Scridain.

Colour: Clear as the Atlantic rain.

Nose: Sharp and cleansing, with ozone and the crisp and wintry marine zing of juniper, mint and fresh seaweed.

Palate: Slight oiliness doesn't detract from the bracing freshness. Citrus notes, all bitter lemon and with vegetal elements – sage, juniper of course, and grassiness. With the sea always there in the background.

Finish: Coolness and poise turns to a long, warm embrace.

Bushmills Black Bush Irish Whiskey

There are several expressions – varieties – of Bushmills you can buy, ranging from the absurdly expensive, very old bottlings that tend to end up in the hands of collectors and are destined never to be drunk, to the classic Bushmills original, a light Irish blend. Red Bush (nothing to do with the tea) is four years old and aged in once-used American oak Bourbon barrels. Black Bush is in my opinion the most characterful of the bunch – 80 per cent single malt whiskey (from a pot still, using malted barley) and aged not just in the American oak barrels, which lend a lighter finish to the spirit, but in Oloroso sherry casks, too.

Colour: Deep amber; gold verging on burned orange.

Nose: A sweet apple and grape scent followed by hints of caramel and toffee, with a ginger snap nuttiness.

Palate: Vanilla pods and cinnamon balls with an embracing oakiness and orange peel wedding cake; a well-worn leather armchair, recently cleaned.

Finish: Plum pudding with home-made sponge cake or English digestive biscuits. Also stewed "builder's" tea with sugar.

Ledaig 10-Year-Old Isle of Mull Single Malt Whisky

I could have chosen the St Columba Hotel's single malt whisky, but on Mull (you have to go through Mull to catch the ferry to Iona) the spectacularly colourful village of Tobermory houses a distillery that invites visitation. And if not in person, then in spirit.

It produces two different styles of whisky. Tobermory itself, which is unpeated, and Ledaig, which has the phenolic tang of the fuel known in Ireland as turf, and which, when barley is malted using its smoke, lends that distinctive pungency to mostly island whiskies. It's pronounced "lech-aik", by the way, which was one of the distillery's previous names. It's a smoky, fruity and very reasonably priced bottling at 10 years old.

Colour: Ripe, golden wheat.

Nose: The smokiness you might expect is gentle and controlled, but the sea is ever-present in that ozone whiff. A little pine forest and some fruit-and-nut chocolate, too.

Palate: Just a touch of pepper and smoky peat, but this is not a brutal attack, face-down-in-a-bog, as you might expect from some of the Islay malts such as Lagavulin or Laphroaig. But fear not, we will get to Islay in due course. Medium-bodied with a bit of burned oak and a wedding-cake fruitiness. A good alcohol level of 46.3 per cent.

Finish: Spicy and slightly smoky, fading not too quickly.

Graham's 10-Year-Old Tawny Port

You can pay astonishing amounts of money for tawny port, and I've chosen this particular bottling as it's reasonably priced and

I think reflects what I would have drunk at communion back at Bethany Hall all those years ago. Port is from the Douro Valley in Portugal. Tawny port is made from red grapes that have been allowed to oxidise, producing a brown or tawny must or juicy mix. Distilled grape spirit (brandy without the name) is added to port and brings the alcohol content up to 20 per cent. It also stops the sugar in the original grape juice turning to alcohol – hence it tends, in most but not all cases, to be sweet.

Colour: Deep, genuinely tawny, like an autumn sycamore leaf or well-aged, cured leather.

Nose: Roast hazelnuts and almonds, with sultanas and raisins, honey and figs.

Palate: Plums, prunes and brown sugar mixed with a deep alcoholic edge. You can sense the slow-moving River Douro and the *barcas* (sailing barges) taking the barrels downriver on the tide.

Finish: Long and complicated, sweet and low. But with tannins adding the bitterness necessary to provoke another swallow. Or two.

CHAPTER 2

TO BE A PILGRIM: WHISKY'S COMING HOME

Scotland (the Kingdom of Fife)
Lindores new make, aqua vitae and single malt whisky

Holy Flight
- *Lindores Abbey New Make Spirit Drink 2021 (63.5 per cent alcohol)*
- *Lindores Abbey Distillery Aqua Vitae (40 per cent alcohol)*
- *Lindores Lowland Single Malt Scotch Whisky MCDXCIV (46 per cent alcohol)*

Columba was not so much a pilgrim as a spiritual invader and conqueror, with his followers the "soldiers" spreading both a Christian Gospel that would become politically triumphant and the variety of knowledge they brought with them. From reading and writing to distillation. As we shall discover, monks and monasteries are crucial to the development of alcohol as spiritual elixir, social lubricant and economic enlivener. And there is a pilgrimage you can make in Scotland to what may not be the very beginnings of whisky, but claims to be the location where its manufacture, or that of a very close relation, was first recorded.

Mystic Kingdom

Fife is not a county; it's a kingdom. Its ancient stature is reflected in the way history peeks out at you everywhere you go in this vast lump of north-east-central Scotland: the academic, liturgical and political importance of Dunfermline, Culross and especially St Andrews, where the most senior bishop in Scotland sat in his cathedral from the 10th century until the Reformation. It is a place of contrasts, from the decaying industrial coastlines just north of Queensferry to the glorious fishing villages of the East Neuk. And it has always been reached by ferries across the mighty expanses of the Tay and Forth, latterly replaced by some of the most famous bridges in the world.

I have travelled through Fife by bicycle, train, bus, car and motorcycle, and something of the place's strange past always rears up unexpectedly, sometimes overwhelmingly. Perhaps this is nowhere more true than Dunino Den, just 10 minutes from St Andrews. The Dunino kirk looks small, perky and strangely secretive, perhaps because it is the gateway to mysteries much older than Christianity: a wooded glade, a descent from the airy everyday into something ancient and strange. The Den.

It is still used for pagan ceremonies, formal and informal, and modern tokens for healing and contact with fairies, spirits and other elemental beings abound. It is undoubtedly an ancient pre-Christian holy site with an "altar stone", a well and the shape of a footprint carved into the rock. There's a more modern wheel carving, too. If you can find it deserted, it's a place of great tranquility and power, despite the accoutrements of spiritual tourism.

In Fife, there are names scattered across the landscape like Cash, thought to be the original home of that famous country singing family. There is the vast and intimidating Dunfermline Abbey, where some of Scotland's greatest medieval kings are buried. And always something new to find, such as the mysterious and threatening tower that sits in the neat little village of Abernethy with an iron punishment collar and chain, which give every appearance of being recently used, firmly attached to its base.

Magic and ritual stalk this rich farmland, while ruins mark skirmishes and full-on battles rooted in religion, politics and sheer tribal greed. The great estuaries of the Forth and the Tay brought international trade, royal visits and invasions both mercantile and military. Parts, however, now feel bypassed, not exactly forgotten but separate. After all, it is and always has been a kingdom in its own right. And it is a place of pilgrimage.

For 400 years, St Andrews was one of the main pilgrimage destinations in medieval Europe. Rich and poor flocked to be near what were promoted as the bones of St Andrew, the bones of someone who walked and talked with Jesus Christ. St Andrews became as important a destination for the faithful as Santiago de Compostela and Rome. And this was long before the invention of golf.

St Andrews may have been the main draw, but pilgrims also headed to Dunfermline to visit the shrine of St Margaret inside the abbey, and many other saints lurked along the road to St Andrews, in wells, chapels and in handy places for rest and refreshment. Today there are various pilgrimage routes still taken by those seeking spiritual enlightenment. My favourite is the Three Saints Way from Killin in Stirlingshire, the saints concerned being St Fillan, St Serf and St Andrew himself. St Fillan, patron saint of the mentally ill, was reputed to have a glowing arm that lighted the darkness for any benighted unfortunates. However, if you were even more unfortunate and suspected of being mentally ill, you would be bound hand and foot and dumped in St Fillan's Holy Pool on the River Fillan near Auchtertyre. If during this process your bonds were loosened, you were thought to be cured. The pool's power, however, apparently vanished forever when a wild bull was thrown into it and now it's a spot for wild swimmers to immerse themselves instead. St Serf (dragon slayer, associate of Adamnan of Iona and therefore a possible whisky drinker) has such a colourful and bizarre array of stories attached to him that I will mention only one. His pet robin died, but St Mungo brought it back to life. Who was St Mungo? Never mind, we can make that pilgrimage another time.

Pilgrimage has left its mark on the Fife landscape, with many of its ferries, bridges and buildings originally serving the needs of pilgrims on their way to St Andrews. Such was the effect on the place and the people – whose own road to heaven was considered less hard-going if they offered succour to pilgrims – that Fife became known as the Pilgrim Kingdom.

While St Andrews is no longer quite in the Santiago de Compostela league when it comes to footsore pilgrims (other than those golfers cramming in up to 54 holes a day on that holiest of turf), there are other spiritual reasons for taking a leisurely – and perhaps chauffeured – trip around Fife: Daftmill, Kingsbarns, Cameronbridge, Inchdairnie, Aberargie … distilleries ancient and modern, industrial and microcrafting. And of course, there is Lindores Abbey.

I first encountered the town of Newburgh when a group of threatening teenagers chased me down the main street. I was cycling, they were on foot, so I managed to avoid whatever they undoubtedly had in mind for me. Or so it felt at the time. Newburgh is a strange, sprawling place. Its medieval origins are very evident; the industries that once saw it thrive – linoleum and oilskin manufacturing, salmon fishing, a harbour when the Tay was that much nearer – gone. It began, though, with an abbey: "the church by the water".

Travelling from Perth, you're through Newburgh quickly and then you see the white letters painted on the side of an enormous black shed: LINDORES ABBEY DISTILLERY. It's immediately opposite a shop selling candle-making and beekeeping supplies – appropriately enough, for mead was once made here. Lindores was one of the most important stopping-off points for pilgrims. Now it's becoming a holy destination in its own right.

The Spiritual Home of Scotch Whisky

"It's the staff party tonight," says Drew Mackenzie Smith, "Mexican-themed." He shakes his head ruefully and levers himself past the enormous oak banqueting table, made from a single, freakishly massive tree, that dominates the Lindores Abbey Distillery Visitor Centre. The rubber tips of his crutches squeak on the stone floor as we walk past lumps of 12th-century sandstone, remnants of the original abbey ruins recovered during the building of the new, state-of-the-art distillery. An injured leg is causing him some discomfort and making tonight's party loom threateningly. He may be a little slower getting around than normal, but his steps are careful and assured like the measured and highly successful revival of whisky production that he and his wife Helen have overseen in what he calls, with absolute sincerity, "the spiritual home of Scotch whisky".

It sounds too good to be true, a tag line from a brand evangelist's dream. But it's based on one interpretation of a simple piece of accounting: an entry in the Exchequer Rolls of Scotland for 1494 that states "To Brother John Cor, by order of the King, to make aqua vitae VIII bolls of malt." This is the first written record of alcoholic spirit – aqua vitae, the water of life, a flavoured precursor to whisky – being made in Scotland, and by a monk, probably an apothecary on loan to James IV. From which abbey, though? The likelihood, according to Janet P Foggie's book *Renaissance Religion in Urban Scotland: The Dominican Order, 1450–1560*, is that John Cor was a Dominican from Stirling, as that name is recorded in the annals of the striking establishment. But there's another argument, that the John Kawe who is documented as a monk at Lindores at the time was actually John Cor, his second name mispronounced and mistranscribed.[1] And on that the current status of Lindores as the home of Scotch whisky is based. Would a Scot hear "Kawe" and write "Cor"? Awe or or?

---

[1] Foggie, Janet P, *Renaissance Religion in Urban Scotland: The Dominican Order, 1450–1560*, Brill digital publishers, https://brill.com/view/title/8182

The abbey, which is now a picturesque set of ruins, was established in either 1178 or 1191 as one of a network of monasteries operated by the Tironensian order, Benedictines from Thiron in France, with an outpost in Kelso that supplied the original Lindores monks. The so-called "Church by the Water" was funded by David, Earl of Huntingdon, and built on land given to him by his brother, King William I of Scotland.

It was constructed with local red sandstone and covered a very large area. The site was chosen due to the availability of timber and stone, and for the nearby fresh drinking water from the stream called the Pow of Lindores.

Earl David was either looking for heavenly recompense for his investment or paying back a favour from the Blessed Virgin. Sir Walter Scott, in his book *The Talisman*, made famous the tale that Earl David was returning home from a crusade when his ship ran into a severe storm. It's said that he promised to found a large church in honour of Mary if he survived. He did.

The Tironensians were masons, distillers, brewers, carpenters, blacksmiths, sculptors, painters, gardeners, beekeepers, musicians and farmers, and they were proud of their manual labour and technical skill. Due to the abbey's strategic site on the Tay and importance to pilgrims, it became one of the major religious and political sites in Scotland.

At its peak, the abbey owned property across England and Scotland, and it was wealthy, both from rentals and from the Crusades, when knights and noblemen paid the monks to pray for their souls and those of their families for eternity, keeping a candle alight in perpetuity. One of the first things you see on entering the distillery visitor centre today is a candle, kept alight in honour of the monks and the men and women they were paid to remember.

Everyone from Edward I of England to William Wallace (one of the leaders fighting for Scottish independence in 1297) visited, though not at the same time – in Wallace's case, he was taking refuge with 300 of his men. And it's possible that spirits had been distilled there far earlier than 1494.

"We're not making a big fuss about it, but excavations on the abbey site have found what appears to be the base of a kiln still," said Drew. An archaeological survey prior to the building of the distillery revealed two pits that had strong similarities with kiln bases, as well as evidence of large flues running from the pits. They've been preserved and the similarities are remarkable, though professional archaeologists are hedging their bets.

The idea for a distillery on site – Drew's family has owned the land for several generations – was kindled some 20 years ago when his father saw an unusual figure wandering about the abbey ruins one day. It was the legendary whisky writer Michael Jackson (not the one with the glittery glove), who had come on what he called "a grateful Dionysian pilgrimage" to view the place where John Cor may (or may not) have plied his trade and given birth to the whisky industry. But the journey from that moment to the availability of "proper" whisky has been long and at times tricky. And John Cor's or Kawe's aqua vitae has been crucial to the process.

The rules on producing Scotch whisky are strict: when a distillery starts producing spirit, that spirit must be aged for at least three years in oak casks, within the borders of Scotland, before it can legally be called Scotch whisky. The slew of new, "craft" distilleries that have emerged in recent years have all faced the time lag between construction and being able to sell their whisky in different ways, but most have used the raw spirit from their stills to make something that does not require ageing and can be sold immediately or produce much-needed profits, such as gin or vodka.

Not Lindores, whose stills began gushing in 2016. "Gin was an obvious thing to produce, but I just said, no, it's not part of our story," says Drew. "Call it taking the moral high ground if you will, but we decided to stick to our origins and produce aqua vitae, using the same botanicals that would have grown on the site back in the 15th century, and been used by Brother John Cor." In fact, it would be five years, not three, before the Mackenzie Smiths felt sufficiently comfortable with their product to bottle it and sell it as a finished single malt. And again, there was an ethical decision to be made – should that first release be at an exorbitant price, with the subsequent "flipping" of bottles at ever-increasing surcharges to collectors – or should it be available to everyone? The conundrum was solved by producing "The 1494" limited edition in a special bottle and bottling the same liquid in straightforward packaging for wider sale "but through independent retailers". That was released to great acclaim just a few weeks before my visit. And comparatively cheaply, at £45 ($60) for 75 centilitres. Along with the finished whisky, the aqua vitae and the "new make" spirit (straight from the stills) are available to taste and buy on site.

"There will be special finishes and releases in the future," Drew says. "We have sourced some oak from wood grown at Thiron in France, and there will be limited edition whisky aged in casks made from that wood, with some malt obtained from the fields surrounding the monastery there. Normally, we source our malt from two local farms near the abbey here in Fife."

The great glass hall containing the Lindores stills looks out over the remains of the abbey, and attached is the Legacy Bar, which is open to the public on some weekend evenings. There you can try not just the mature whisky, but the aqua vitae and associated cocktails. If you wander downstairs you can take in the great affirmation of aqua vitae's – and by association, whisky's – power, taken from the famous *Hollinshed's Chronicles*, published in 1577 and a source for Shakespeare, Marlowe and Edmund Spenser. And also for Drew Mackenzie Smith, who cheerfully appropriated a section originally written about Irish spirits.

"I know it's not about Scotland," he says, gazing up at the massive display with some reverence, "but I liked it." Written in hard-to-decipher old English, which I have roughly paraphrased, it includes a long list of ailments that aquae vitae can purportedly treat, cure or prevent.

"Being moderately taken … it slows age, it strengthens youth; it helps digestion, cuts phlegm, abandons melancholy, relishes the heart, lightens the mind, quickens the spirits, cures the dropsy [water retention]; it heals choking, clears kidney stones, expels blockages, cures wind; it keeps and prevents the head from whirling, the eyes from being dazzled, the tongue from lisping, the mouth from being muffled, the teeth from chattering, the throat from rattling, the reason from being stifled, the stomach from rumbling, the heart from swelling, the belly from itching, the guts from rumbling, the hands from shivering, the muscles from shrinking, the veins from crumpling, the bones from aching, the marrow from soaking. … And truly it is a sovereign liquor, if it be orderly taken."

Aqua vitae was essentially diluted distilled spirits flavoured with plants and botanicals, and the version available at Lindores has the herbal tang of bitters. It uses plants such as sweet cicely, grown in the Lindores gardens, as well as Douglas fir, basil flowers and dried fruit.

"We've tried our best to authentically recreate what John Cor's recipe would have been," explains Drew, a trained Cordon Bleu chef with many years of experience in top country houses and hotels. "We've reimagined the aquae vitae and it's distilled in pot stills, then infused with a blend of spices and herbs – including cleavers and sweet cicely – which grow in our gardens in the grounds of the ancient abbey. The product is entirely natural, with no added sugars."

The aquae vitae is delicious, as is the five-year old whisky, which is remarkably mature for such an early bottling. That extra two years of ageing beyond the legal requirement has been well worthwhile. But you can taste the origins of its quality in the new-make spirit also available to buy from the distillery. At 63.5 per cent alcohol, even neat it has a delicacy that leads, after years in oak, to something special. Something spiritual. Brother John Cor would be proud.

I wonder what John Knox would make of it all. It was he, after all – that legendary pioneer of Protestantism – who once led an inflamed crowd from St Andrews following the murder of Archbishop George Beaton, helped to ransack Lindores and apparently encouraged the working folk of Newburgh to take its stones for their own houses.

By the end of the Reformation, the Abbey was beginning to be dismantled (with the abbey clock purchased by Edinburgh Town Council), but by the 17th century, the deserted ruins were nothing more than a quarry, with slate, stone and carvings being taken and used in the building of many houses in neighbouring Newburgh. So, John Knox had his way in the end. But did he, I wonder, ever partake of some of the aqua vitae pioneered there by John Cor/Kawe? We know that his mentor John Calvin was partial to a glass of wine, but surely the water of life would have been attractive to the great reformer Knox after a bout of monastery-dismantling? Alas, on this the stones are silent.

I leave Lindores, heading not for the bones of St Andrew but the great angel's wing of the Queensferry Crossing, which will take me across the Forth and then west to Glasgow. Drew wishes me a safe journey, his crutches already being tested for the *jarabe tapatío* (Mexican Hat dance) and *danza del diablo* at the staff party tonight in the shadow of the dully shining copper stills, with the ghosts of John Knox and John Cor/Kawe doubtless watching. One in approval, one possibly not.

Holy Flight – Tasting Notes

Lindores Abbey New Make Spirit Drink 2021 (63.5 per cent alcohol)

Colour: Clear.

Nose: This drink smells of a working distillery, one where alcohol is being produced and is running in that beautiful stream through the glass and brass "spirit safe" (locked and accessible only with customs and excise permission). Fresh and clean, with a hint of ozone and glacé cherries, hospital laboratories and dentist's surgeries. Pears and violets.

Palate: Don't drink this neat. It will burn and deactivate your tastebuds. A little water will make it tastable, and as a raw spirit goes, this is very good indeed. Assured, with hints that, once aged, the associated whisky will be worth waiting for. As it is, good vodka with a slight herbal tang, the cardboard fruitiness of unripened strawberries in a punnet, the maltiness of pre-whisky and old stones from a mountain stream sucked on a dry day.

Finish: Long and fragrant. Not in any way aggressive and abrasive. Springwater with a touch of aniseed and newly mown grass.

Lindores Abbey Distillery Aqua Vitae (40 per cent alcohol)

Colour: Straw or a dawn sky just as the sun comes up in winter.

Nose: When I was a boy, my mum would take me to an old herbalist's, and this is the smell you get when you open a bottle. An apothecary from *Harry Potter*! Ginger, the kind of cinnamon balls you used to get in big glass jars. Fruitcake and Christmas trees.

Palate: Angostura bitters in Coke, or Underberg with American cream soda. A sweetness that never overwhelms. Dark chocolate gingers with parma violets and strawberry liqueur. You get the sense that it's doing you good, or that it ought to do you good as long as you don't drink too much. Best neat.

Finish: Victory V (liquorice) or Fisherman's Friend (menthol) lozenges and ginger wine, fading gently into a fireside glow. Logs crackling, probably well-seasoned pine. Outside, the snow is beginning to fall and the forest darkness is closing in comfortably.

Lindores Lowland Single Malt Scotch Whisky MCDXCIV (46 per cent alcohol)

Colour: Lightly golden. Wedding rings and precious things.

Nose: And here we are – five years old and matured in wine barrels, sherry butts and bourbon casks, but the new-make spirit overtones are readily evident: that blue-sky windswept freshness, the Kirsch overtones and whiff of the sea on a stormy day.

Palate: The aroma does not prepare you for the taste, which is amazingly mature and defined. Those extra two years in wood have paid dividends. There's sherry, but not cloyingly so, with a lightness of touch coming from the Bourbon barrels. Vanilla, caramel and a range of fruits, but there's a gingery burst of heat and preserved figs.

Finish: Fades away over a long period of time, all apple pie and vanilla cream with a touch of warm, firelit libraries. For a five-year-old whisky straight off the starting blocks in a new distillery, it's very impressive. Mind you, they did have 500 years of a head start.

Important Note

In March 2022, some 10 days into the Russian invasion of Ukraine, Lindores was the focus of questions about its ownership. According to a major article[2] by the doyen of whisky experts, Dave Broom, up to 75 per cent of the distillery's shares were owned by two major Russian investors. A few days after publication, it was announced that both had resigned as non-executive directors of the company, and that the Mackenzie Smiths were taking steps "to try and agree a situation whereby the Mackenzie Smith family will acquire their shareholding, thus moving the company to 100 per cent Scottish ownership and control."[3]

As *Holy Waters* went to press Drew Mackenzie Smith told me: "We have a number of very credible people/businesses looking to replace the Russians and would hope to have concluded that by November, but can't 100 per cent guarantee it will happen as quickly as that. I think the main thing is that they understand they have to go, even though technically/legally they don't as they are not sanctioned."

---

[2]   https://thewhiskymanual.uk/scotch-in-russia-russia-in-scotch/

[3]   https://foodanddrink.scotsman.com/in-the-news/lindores-abbey-distillery-severs-links-with-russian-investors/

CHAPTER 3

THE "OLD MOOD-ALTERING"

The Netherlands, Scotland, France
Gin, Cognac, wine

Holy Flight
- *North Uist Distillery Downpour Scottish Dry Gin*
- *Courvoisier VS Cognac*
- *Châteauneuf-du-Pape 2014 (Marc Perrin for the Co-operative Society, UK)*

I think it was the late Gaelic-speaking Scottish musician and comedian, Norman Hector Mackinnon Maclean, who called alcohol "the old mood-altering". And as such its function can be seen as similar to religion. After all, what does faith actually do? It seeks to alter minds, emotions, behaviour. It wants to change your mood at the very least.

And much, much more. Books – indeed, whole libraries – have been written and even sometimes read on the subject of religion's function. Basically, how is faith built and what does it do for human beings? A lot of this thinking is rooted in the work of French sociologist David Émile Durkheim, who argued that all religions both celebrate and worship human society, and the individual's place within it. He suggested that a religion does three things:

1. By its rituals and theology, it brings people together to provide a structure and cohesion in society through rules to live by and feeling part of something.
2. It gives a society the spiritual backup needed to enforce social control and morality. So, you get the benefits of being part of a tribe, but you have to conform or God (via lightning strike or the church elders) will get you.
3. On an individual level, faith answers those big existential questions. You want meaning and purpose? Stick with us, pal.[1]

In the 21st century, the idea of the religious nation state may have diminished in some parts of the world, but in others it has become uncompromising and brutal. But fundamental to all religious groupings, operating on the micro (that Wicca coven in the woods round the back of your house) or macro (Afghanistan) scales, is the individual experience that becomes collective and unifying.

Again, the literature on this is absolutely vast, and this is a book about alcohol's role in religion, not a work of theology, so I'm going to distil – appropriately – things down through my own experience.

Religion is about belonging to a group of people who adhere to the same or similar beliefs, and that depends on a shared acknowledgement of those beliefs, usually in public. Many faiths work simply by geographical location, family connections or cultural prominence, and in my own case this was working-class Scottish evangelical Christianity of the gospel hall, shouting-on-street-corners sort.

But to belong to our wee Brethren Church, to really be "a Christian", you had to be converted, you had to undergo the experience of being "born again". And this was more than an intellectual assertion or attendance at meetings. It was emotional. It was sort of mystical. It was a change of heart and

---

[1] https://revisesociology.com/2018/06/18/functionalist-perspective-religion-durkheim/

mind from a life of sin and degradation to one of holiness and absorption with things divine.

I was 11 years old when this happened to me. I was 16 when I was baptised and was then eligible to join the "meeting", consume of communion (see page 34) and partake of that super-strong fortified wine I talked about in the last chapter. And when I sipped that warming liquid it reminded me of two things. One was being given a teaspoon of brandy to try to alleviate violent vomiting aboard a storm-tossed ferry crossing the English Channel. The other was how I felt that night when my uncle David preached a sermon and I asked to be spared the fires of hell and made into a new person.

Because just as religion changes minds and hearts, affects emotion and infects you with a sense of the numinous, so does alcohol. Just as ecclesiastical architecture (not gospel halls, those little tin huts or converted cast-off kirks; I'm talking about cathedrals and high church style here) with its stained glass and flying buttresses, its enormous spaces and violently echoing acoustics, seeks to manipulate those cowering inside its grandeur, intoxicate them with splendour, so does alcohol. Just as alcohol stimulates and then depresses, religion – or specifically, my experience of the type of Christianity I was reared in – lifts the heart and inflicts a sense of unworthiness, of worthlessness. Then it inflates self-worth through connection with the divinity and the divinely inspired through congregation, membership, belonging. It gets you high, it brings you low. But there is always the possibility of more, either through another service or, a cynical functionalist might argue, via several additional visits to the pub.

Dependence is, for some, inevitable. And I'm talking both about drinkers and spiritual disciples here.

Now you may find this a little simplistic. My own drive from childhood conversion through teenage commitment to adult submergence in a charismatic community, speaking in tongues, prophecy and even – and I know this will shock some of you – dancing, was fuelled by a search for convincing, unarguable religious experience. I never found it, although I did encounter some very strange and sometimes inexplicable things. But it was all paralleled by a curiosity and then experimental obsession with alcohol, which ended up with a series of books and films about the whisky industry and a continued involvement not just in drinking, but making, blending and bottling the Water of Life. But that's another story.

What I want to suggest to you is that the way ethanol, which is a psychoactive drug, works is similar to the way religious experience works. Both can provoke mysticism, the seeing of visions, the dreaming of dreams. They both alter your emotions, affect the brain and body. They are intoxicants and provide reassurance. They are social, provoking and encouraging human interaction, sympathy, friendship, even love. And you may see visions and dream dreams. Your mood could be well and truly altered by either. Or both. As William James says in *The Varieties of Religious Experience*, "The sway of alcohol over mankind is unquestionably due to its power to stimulate the mystical faculties of human nature."[2]

By way of comparison, in Mayan religious practice in the Yucatan, the local brew – a kind of mead called balché – is used to produce altered states of consciousness among those participating. And in Haitian voodoo ceremonies, *kleren*, or clairin – white organic rum – performs the same function. In both religions, alcohol-induced transformation of perception is strictly ritualized and controlled. In Japan, Shinto ritualizes sake, rice wine, in very precise ways, but always recognizing its capacity to alter consciousness. It is seen not only as a blessing, but also the most valuable type of offering a human can provide to the Divine. It is used in all the varieties of religious thankfulness and celebration, as it conjoins the human with the Divine, notably in marriage, where a couple drink three cups of sake, symbolizing Earth, heaven and humanity.

In Scotland, the practice of drinking whisky from a quaich,

---

[2] James, W, *Varieties of Religious Experience*, Mentor, New York, 1985, p.307 (first published 1905)

or two-handled silver cup, by a marrying couple (and their families) has a more practical origin. It means you can't use your weapons to spring a surprise attack on the family of your bride or bridegroom's intended.

If You Want to Get Ahead …

Let's talk about the God Helmet.

Now, there are various alternatives, but you can order something that calls itself the God (Shiva) Helmet online, for around £500 ($649) plus £30 ($40) international shipping or $20 delivery within the USA. And importantly, this is a product fully endorsed by Dr Michael Persinger of Laurentian University in Sudbury, Ontario, Canada, who first came up with the idea, along with colleague Stanley Koren (it's sometimes known as the Koren Helmet or, confusingly, the Koren Octopus) during his work as a neuroscientist.

What is it? Well, try this magnetic hat on for size: it's basically a helmet fitted with electromagnets, which aim to stimulate the brain's temporal lobes. These are the parts of your brain that sit in the skull just behind your ears and are most involved in processing memory and audio signals. However, these particular chunks of brain matter have for a long time been thought to be involved in religious experiences. The Koren/Persinger/Shiva/God Helmet stimulates the temporal lobes as fairly weak electromagnetic signals pass through the skull, and there are a range of scientific studies that have shown the consequent products of "a presence" in the consciousnesses of some blind-tested subjects. Buy your own, plug it in to a computer and see if you encounter God, or something mildly divine. One word of warning. The God (Shiva) Helmet I looked at "is not guaranteed to run on Mac computers. Shiva runs on Windows XP, Windows 7, Windows 8, Windows 8.1 and Windows 10. You can use it on most older PCs. Tech support is free."[3]

There has been much discussion of the God Helmet's various

---

[3]   https://www.god-helmet.com/wp/shiva/order_shiva/shiva_location.htm

manifestations on TV and in the media over the years. All kinds of interesting characters have become involved. Even arch-atheist Richard Dawkins had a go. All he felt was a bit dizzy.[4]

There is, however, one experiment I simply find irresistible, involving various wondrously attractive components. Namely, alcohol, rock music and a selection of the kind of people who would attend an open-air rock festival in the Netherlands.

This is all contained in a paper which, unlike most studies of its kind, is both riveting and hilarious. "The role of alcohol in expectancy-driven mystical experiences: a pre-registered field study using placebo brain stimulation", by David L R Maij, Michiel van Elk and Uffe Schjoedt of the University of Amsterdam, was published in 2017 in the journal *Religion, Brain and Behaviour.*

They were interested in the roles that alcohol might play in religion:

"It could be, for instance, that in the right suggestible ritual context, alcohol intoxication facilitates mystical and quasi-mystical (i.e., extraordinary) experiences. Alternatively, ritual experts such as shamans and witch doctors may benefit from the liberating and mind-altering effects of alcohol as they often display interactions with the supernatural realm following alcohol consumption."

In addition, alcohol could play a part in religious ritual by making participants less critical. They also suggest that shamans, witch doctors and presumably priests) "may benefit from the liberating and mind-altering effects of alcohol as they often display interactions with the supernatural realm following alcohol consumption."

But how to demonstrate any of this?

---

4   https://economictimes.indiatimes.com/opinion/vedanta/god-helmet-a-head-for-religion/articleshow/18026396.cms?from=mdr

The team of researchers wanted to look at suggestibility in particular. Could alcohol play a part in making people more open to religious experience? Enter not the God Helmet itself, but the God Helmet *placebo*. In other words the fake God helmet. The God Helmet suggestion.

What these researchers – I'm tempted to call them fiendish researchers – did was set up a booth at the three-day, 50,000-attendance Lowlands Music Festival. The study was advertised in the festival programme as "Tripping with the God Helmet: Researchers of the University of Amsterdam will electromagnetically stimulate your brain to elicit spiritual experiences." A total of 193 people came forward to try this out. As the researchers state:

> "We set out to test whether alcohol could increase participants' susceptibility to the God Helmet suggestion ... Participants reported a wide range of extraordinary experiences associated with mysticism, including out-of-body experiences, involuntary movements, and the felt presence of invisible beings."

The entire study is available to read online. It is like a sustained student comedy routine.[5]

But basically, what they did was blindfold people, put a fake God Helmet on their heads, having told the participants what it was supposed to do (stimulate their brains magnetically), pump white noise at them through headphones then get them to press buttons indicating spiritual experiences of various kinds. And they did.

What effect did alcohol have? And, seeing as this was a festival in famously drug-tolerant Holland, what about dope? Well, this is where the study, in my opinion, stumbles. The would-be travellers in divine interspace were asked to indicate how much they'd had to drink since getting up that morning. Or smoked

---

[5]   https://www.tandfonline.com/doi/full/10.1080/2153599X.2017.1403952

or otherwise imbibed. Which would be a casual and inaccurate method of assessment at the best of times, as years of court reporting has taught me ("My client has little memory of the events in question, My Lord, having consumed approximately one and a half pints of lager ..." Later witness, a barman: "To my memory the accused drank 14 pints of beer and 10 pepper vodka shots ...").

But there's worse: the study notes that "unfortunately, due to a programming error, these subjective questions were not seen by the participants and had to be obtained retrospectively, in a follow-up questionnaire." At a rock festival. Which for me renders the percentages reported, well ... somewhat questionable: "Of all participants, 73.2% consumed alcohol on the day of testing, 16.8% consumed alcohol and at least one other type of drug on the day of testing, 7.4% did not consume alcohol or drugs, and 2.6% used at least one type of drug without consuming alcohol." And indeed the conclusion that while the fake God Helmet seemed to cause a wide range of extraordinary experiences, "the data did not provide support for the hypothesised relation between objective and subjective alcohol measures, executive control and frequency and intensity of extraordinary experiences." Basically, if you were predisposed to have a spiritual experience, feeling those spiritual vibes, man, the "God Helmet" would help you have one.

But let's face it, most of the participants were drunk or at least a bit inebriated.

I would humbly suggest that at its most basic, what this "study" tells us is that if you apply music, alcohol or other drugs in the context of sensory deprivation and the idea that spiritual stimulus is being applied, you will most likely have a spiritual experience, especially if you're the kind of person who is interested enough in something as attractive to the religious questing as a "God Helmet".

It's like going to church, basically, isn't it? The people who go to church are drawn to the building and the services that happen there because of background, interest, bias or desire.

While there, the intoxicating effect of architecture, sound, colour, music, hymnology, preaching and the presence of other people will combine to have an effect and possibly provoke some kind of spiritual experience. And if they're drunk, half-drunk or off their heads on acid or weed, well …

I have never been to church drunk or high, unless you count a cheese and wine party at St Meddan's Parish Church in Troon, Ayrshire when I was 16. I have come close to some kind of inner encounter with the Divine, or what I perceived as being one, while involved in charismatic dance worship at Overtoun House in Dunbartonshire. I have been bludgeoned by rock music and blinding lights in the service of an evangelical God and been moved, if not ecstatically. I have taken communion where the "wine" was actually Ribena, a blackcurrant cordial (see page 91), and once, after a mass Christian festival communion (of several thousand people), involving very real Bordeaux or Beaujolais (I can't remember which for all-too-obvious reasons), I helped the worship team finish off that leftover red and staggered into the Easter light of Pontins Holiday Camp in Prestatyn, quite transformed.

Holy Flight – Tasting Notes

North Uist Distillery Downpour Scottish Dry Gin

Norman Maclean did not live long enough to taste this product of the islands he loved and is buried on, though he was born of an island family in Glasgow. Eventually, there will be North Uist whisky, but the gin reflects the islands with its overtones of heather, extracts of which it actually contains, as well as the more common citrus notes and spiciness. It's very herby and aromatic, with the usual juniper and orange notes. But don't drown it in tonic. Drink it neat over ice or just the way it comes, with touch of rain …

Colour: Clear as seawater.

Nose: Citrus and spiciness, with lots of aromatic herbs.

Palate: A touch of heather and moorland bogginess.

Finish: A blast of the generic gin tastes of juniper and bitter orange.

Courvoisier VS Cognac

This is the actual brandy bought by my desperate dad from the duty-free shop aboard the Thoresen Ferries cross-channel ferry in 1967, amid violent vomiting from his entire family in a force-eight gale. The brandy undoubtedly helped. I remember (I was 11) the burning warmth as being surprisingly, no astonishingly, redemptive and enlivening. It was the first alcohol I'd ever tasted.

Nowadays, well … VS stands for Very Special (as opposed to the more expensive VSOP Very Special Old Pale), but it's still warming, and it's very reasonably priced. Good for some cocktails if you like that sort of thing.

Colour: Edwardian gentleman's club furniture; leathery brown. A well-seasoned wallet.

Nose: Light, all spring daffodils.

Palate: Apples, peaches and the hint of woodiness in the mouth.

Finish: A wee touch of pepperiness.

Châteauneuf-du-Pape 2014, Marc Perrin for the Co-operative Society, UK

Note that this is not the wine we guzzled so greedily after that mass communion service. I mean, what were we to do? Pour it down the drains? Give it to the lurking Pontins Bluecoats?

I chose Châteauneuf-du-Pape to accompany this chapter because gazing sternly at the quaffing, badly behaved guitarists and tambourine players was the worship band leader, whose name was Dave Pope. And because this is an exceptionally good, very reasonably priced example of what is a great and, after all, religiously named wine.

A classic robust red wine with great maturity and depth from the southern Rhône.

Colour: Inky reddy-black in the bottle. Deep ruby when held to the light in a glass.

Nose: The aroma is all dark fruits, cherry and a touch of oakiness.

Palate: Soft on the palate and smooth, its fruitiness is controlled and never overbearing. The mouth-drying tannins don't turn to bitterness.

Finish: Spicy and intense with a long, pleasurable finish.

CHAPTER 4
THE INDIAN ENIGMA: EAT, DRINK AND BE MURREE

India and Pakistan
Whisky and beer

Holy Flight
– *Amrut Peated Single Malt Whisky*
– *Cobra Premium Lager*
– *Murree Beer*

If you're going to have a god, and you like a drink, then you might as well go for a divinity that enjoys a tipple too. Christianity can offer Jesus as someone who was accused by the moral arbiters of his day as being a bit too fond of the booze (see Luke 7:34: "The Son of Man is come eating and drinking; and ye say, Behold a gluttonous man, and a winebibber, a friend of publicans and sinners!"). But the general tone of the New Testament gospels, gallons of water being turned into wine at the wedding in Cana notwithstanding, is of moderation and a very sober mission. Jesus had bigger things on his mind.

However, head to the city of Ujjain in the central Indian state of Madhya Pradesh and you will find a Hindu manifestation of Shiva who doesn't just like the occasional dram, but thrives on and indeed demands alcohol from worshippers. This is

Kaal Bhairav, who represents Shiva as the annihilator, fierce but forgiving. And nice to animals. He is portrayed in idol form sitting on or sometimes in the form of a dog, and his kindness to stray dogs, which is not necessarily commonplace in the subcontinent, is seen as a tribute to him. He is widely worshipped throughout India because he is usually propitiated quite easily with simple offerings, such as free puri, and there are many temples to this god as well as special days of feasting and worship. But it's in Ujjain that Kaal Bhairav is exclusively into ethanol in all its potable forms. Or at least when there is no worldwide pandemic to cope with. Kaal Bhairav went teetotal, or appeared to, during the Covid-19 outbreak.

In normal times, there are stalls all around the temple selling alcoholic drinks. And every form of whisky and whiskey you can imagine, as the hard stuff is definitely this god's preference. Wine is acceptable though, as are the usual, less alcoholic offerings of coconut and flowers and garlands. The idea is that you approach the temple with a bottle, very much as if attending a party, and half of the contents are poured into a bowl and fed by a priest into the enormous mouth of the god. Turmeric and the red powder called *kumkum* are smeared over the deity's face and his silver head is adorned with a *pagri*, or turban. The alcohol disappears, and no one, despite much speculation and many investigations, appears to know what happens to it. I'm tempted to suggest that like the angel's share in malt whisky maturation – the portion of alcohol that evaporates from oak casks during ageing – it just disappears to heaven. But there is no Hindu concept of heaven. Life is a cycle of reincarnation. However, hold your head up to the Ujjain rain, and maybe you'll taste something very special …

The remainder of the bottle goes back to the worshipper for their own consumption in exactly the same way offerings of food made to other Hindu gods are partly consumed by the devotee as *prasad*. But watch out for the local monkeys, which abound and are fearless. They may be thirsty too.

It will be evident from the tastes of Kaal Bhairav that alcohol and Hinduism are not mutually exclusive. The use of alcohol as a sacrament does happen but is relatively unusual, and Hindu teaching on drinking tends toward caution: moderation in all things. Remember that Hinduism is not a tradition that depends on systematic theology so much as an understanding of the dharma, that evasive concept that can mean duty, morality, ethics and goodness, but is also the power that upholds the entire universe. It's both eternal and very personal. Human actions produce karma, and basically you sow what you will later reap, in this life or the next or the one after that. As for alcohol, the question is, how does it – and indeed any intoxicant or stimulant – fit in?

Some Hindu monastic orders would suggest – not require, but perhaps expect – various restrictive vows such as celibacy and the renunciation of any mind-altering substance. But there are Hindu tantric groups, such as the one in Ujjain, that use alcohol as an offering or for ritual consumption. So-called Reform Hinduism is more relaxed in its attitude toward alcohol consumption, though there is a general recognition that alcohol is a powerful drug capable of being abused. This is perhaps highlighted within Ayurvedic medicine, where the potential for physical and mental damage is counterbalanced by an acceptance that alcohol is essential for making certain ayurvedic herbal remedies – just as in western medicine – and that, as St Paul told Timothy, a little (herbal) wine might be a good idea if you have a stomach problem.

There is, however, as in most faiths, a fundamentalist strain of Hinduism that tolerates no nonsense from brands keen to advance their popularity with reference to the Divine. Amrut, for example, is a distiller in Bangalore, India, founded in 1948, which now sells its acclaimed single malt whisky throughout the world. In the domestic Indian market, it produces a huge variety of drinks, but its single malt – much praised by top whisky writer Jim Murray – has become popular even in Scotland, where tastes in the hard stuff tend to be a mite parochial.

The Golden Pot

Amrut is a big, serious company but its very name offends some elements within Hinduism. The company's website once proudly proclaimed that "...when Gods and Rakshasas – the demons – churned the oceans using the mountain Meru as churner, a golden pot sprang out containing the Elixir of Life. That was called the 'Amrut'..."[1] Nectar of the gods in Sanskrit. Not so different from the water of life, as mentioned at the start of this book. By the Pope.

The Indian subcontinent is a glorious melting pot of faith and culture, and alcohol plays its part, both negatively and positively. The recognition of alcohol's dangerous power is there in the absolute ban on consumption you find either overtly in many mainstream faiths or tucked away in their more fundamentalist corners. In Jainism, for example, alcohol is completely out of the question, as it is seen as doing violence to the soul and body. In Islam, though, things are a little more complicated. The Sikh attitude is firmly against intoxication, but different branches of Sikhism and, for that matter, stages of devotion have contrasting attitudes toward alcohol. Nowhere is it seen as a sacrament and yet you will find plenty of non-practising and unbaptized Sikhs who do drink or who have a relaxed attitude toward handling alcohol in their businesses.

Bring Your Own Bottle

The general notion that Muslims don't drink was something drilled into me as a university student, and it all came down to a single Glasgow thoroughfare, Gibson Street in the West End of the city, and a desperate need on my part for a particular food – curry.

This was the 1970s and we are not talking about sophisticated varieties of sub-continental cuisine. Gibson Street at the time catered for a student clientele who wanted large quantities of

---

[1] https://www.houseofmalt.co.uk/product/amrut-single-malt-indian-whisky/

very hot, spicy food. Vegetarians weren't common in meat-pie Glasgow, so mutton was the order of the day in your madras, vindaloo or mythical tindaloo. Twenty pints of beer and a curry to top it off, one medical student told me, and the resultant stomach haemorrhage could kill. He had seen this, he claimed, in casualty units like the one at the Glasgow Royal Infirmary, the busiest accident and emergency department in Europe, and the only one with its own 24-hour manned police station.

The restaurants were mostly Pakistani (advertised as Indo-Pak) or Bangladeshi and, with the exception of the Sikh-owned Ashoka in then-dodgy now uber-trendy Finnieston, mostly Muslim. So none of them were licensed to sell beer. And let's face it, with curry you needed beer.

You would arrive with your carry out ("kerry-oot") tins of cheap and weak Tennent's Lager. The days of strong German beers like Furstenberg were yet to come. Mr Ali at the legendary Shish Mahal and his colleagues in places like the Shalimar may not have been drinkers, but they were happy to let their non-Muslim customers drink. They would even provide glasses. Corkage? We'd never heard of such a thing.

And in most, if not all, functioning Islamic states, at least those dependent on tourism, incoming expertise and finance or with strong colonial backgrounds, that remains the case. Local followers of Islam cannot or should not drink. Foreigners or followers of other religions can. Perhaps the most obvious example of this is in the state of Qatar, where the hosting of soccer's World Cup tournament in 2022 meant a relaxing of the country's notoriously strict Islamic laws on alcohol – up to a point. Drinking was permitted only in regulated hotels, bars and cruise "party" ships anchored offshore. And woe betide the fan who behaved as football supporters sometimes do and took on the local police in a loudly abusive drunken state. They were, to use a Scottish word, well and truly huckled.

Some Muslims, however, do drink. Just not officially. The late Minoo Bhandara, chief executive of the legendary Pakistani company Murree, brewers and distillers, admitted to the

Guardian newspaper in 2004 that "99 per cent of our customers are Muslims."[2] But, then, so is 97 per cent of Pakistan's population. Sometimes we forget that not all followers of a religion do so entirely faithfully or consistently.

The consumption of alcohol is forbidden in the Quran, where it is portrayed as an evil habit that turns an individual away from God. But that ban was not introduced as a kind of hard-and-fast sledgehammer rule, at least not initially. The holy book's first mention of the subject forbids Muslims from attending prayers while intoxicated (4:43). There's even an acceptance that alcohol can be a vehicle for good (Islamic medicine would have used it as a solvent, as in Ayurvedic practice). However, it cautions that "the evil is greater than the good" (2:219).

After that, things get a little more forthright. And don't forget gambling. "Intoxicants and games of chance" are "abominations of Satan's handiwork", which draw drinkers away from God and prayer. Abstinence is essential (5:90–91). Avoidance of inebriation is the key, and it applies not just to drink, but other drugs too.

The Prophet Muhammad warned against involvement in alcohol production, cursing "the wine-presser, the one who has it pressed, the one who drinks it, the one who conveys it, the one to whom it is conveyed, the one who serves it, the one who sells it, the one who benefits from the price paid for it, the one who buys it and the one for whom it is bought." But then Mr Banderas and his descendants who still run Murree, the oldest operating company in Pakistan, are Parsis, descendents of the Persians who fled Iran for India, and therefore Zoroastrians. This is, in my opinion, possibly the best-named religion in the world. And it is comfortably liberal on alcohol: "Drink wine in moderation, for whoso drinks wine immoderately falls into many a sin," say the Counsels of Adarbad Mahraspandan.[3] Many of Murree's employees in Rawalpindi are Muslim and

---

2   https://www.theguardian.com/world/2004/aug/30/pakistan.declanwalsh

3   http://www.avesta.org/mp/adarbad1.htm

have never let the products they make – everything from gin and brandy to whisky, rum and a bewildering variety of beers – pass their lips.

On 6 June 2012, Scout Willis, daughter of Hollywood legends Bruce Willis and Demi Moore, was arrested in New York City for allegedly drinking in public while (at 20 years old) under age. (It's illegal to drink under the age of 21 in New York.) She had an open can of beer in her hand, but, astonishingly, it was a tin of Murree (there is uncertainty over whether it was an 11- or eight-ounce can). How it even got to the USA is unknown, as there is a ban on exporting Murree alcoholic products from Pakistan.[4] My own strenuous efforts to obtain some, especially the Murree "Islay malt whisky" that has so enraged the Scotch Whisky Association, the body that actively seeks to protect the identity of Scottish whisky, have all proved fruitless. However, I did receive an email from Major Sabih-ur-Rehman, Special Assistant to the Chief Executive, Murree Brewery Group of Companies. He said, "It is heartening to know that the Murree Brewery Company is also known in the remote corners of Scotland. Since sale of alcoholic beverages outside of Pakistan is not allowed, we do not have any stockist of our alcoholic beverages anywhere in the UK. However, if you need any information, we are ready to assist you. Thank you and best of luck!"

The Willis incident did lead to a worldwide upsurge in interest in Murree's products and there have been attempts in the past to have the beers specially made under licence in the UK, with the aim of marketing them to Indian restaurants in much the same way as Cobra. It hasn't happened, at least not yet, so that irresistible slogan, "Have a Murree with your curry", remains unused. In Pakistan itself, the almost equally brilliant company motto "Eat, drink and be Murree" is known but unadvertised – advertising alcohol is illegal.

---

[4]   https://nypost.com/2012/07/07/scout-willis-fights-drinking-charges-pakistani-beer-isnt-sold-here/

But the ban on alcohol sales and promotion in Pakistan is not that old. It goes back only to 1977, when the then military leader Zulfikar Ali Bhutto (fond of a drink himself, but keen to appease the religious right) imposed an alcohol ban on Muslims. Christians, Zoroastrians, Hindus and tourists could, however, and still can, drink it. In 1979, under the regime of General Zia-ul-Haq, drinking alcohol was declared "un-Islamic" and severe punishments were imposed for selling alcohol to Muslims.

But Pakistan's oldest company and biggest drinks (alcoholic and non-alcoholic) manufacturer continues to exist and thrive. It all goes back, inevitably, to the British Raj and the establishment of a brewery in Ghora Galli, in the Pir Punjal range of the western Himalayas, not far from present-day Islamabad. At 6,000 feet (1,830 metres) up, the nearby hill station of Murree was a favourite resort for the British forces, providing a cool, refreshing climate, and indeed was at one time the seat of government. The Murree Brewery, started by Edward Dyer and Edward Whymper, was one of the first modern breweries in Asia, and was born out of a need to slake the British colonial army's thirst. Sales reached an all-time high in World War II, but there have been major local difficulties. An earthquake wrecked Murree's Quetta brewery in 1935 and the company is not immune to Islamic fervour: the original building was attacked by Muslims in 1947 and burned down. Nowadays, a workforce several hundred strong works in the Rawalpindi headquarters.

With a population of 226 million and growing, Pakistan has a tiny number of legal outlets for alcohol in specific areas, particularly the southern state of Sindh. Ironically, Sindh is known as Bab-ul Islam, or the Gateway to Islam, as it was the first area in the Indian subcontinent to come under Islamic rule. All these "wine shops" are owned and run by non-Muslims, and no Muslim is supposed to shop there. However, some do.

There is an enormous black market. So-called "beer quotas" for Christians and people of other religions can be bought up and resold. Imported booze is smuggled into Pakistan through most of its borders.

According to the *Guardian*, "Chinese vodka is spirited across the northern mountain passes, while ancient dhows carry crates of western beer and Scotch from the Gulf states to Pakistan's west coast. In the capital Islamabad diplomats at some central Asian and African embassies are known to offer a discreet take-away service from their diplomatic compounds, in return for a hefty mark-up." In addition, as is the case throughout the world's rural outposts, people make their own, brewing and distilling in the face of dangers such as blindness and even death.

In Islam the consumption and production of alcoholic beverages is seen as wrong. Although there is the promise that things will be different in heaven. There is no use of alcohol in Islamic worship to increase fervour or ease the connection with the Divine. But "rivers of wine" will be available in the hereafter: "Therein are rivers of water unpolluted ... and rivers of wine delicious to the drinkers" (Surah 47:15) and "Surely the pious will be in bliss ... their thirst will be slaked with pure wine sealed." (Surah 83:22, 25)

Why, then, is alcohol apparently forbidden to Muslims while on Earth, yet according to the Quran Muslims will be allowed to drink wine while in heaven? Well, basically God has told Muslims not to drink alcohol during their earthly existence and this is a test of their obedience. If they obey, they will find they can enjoy a drop of the not very hard stuff after death. And besides, the wine in Paradise will not be the same as your average Buckfast Tonic here on Earth.

According to Shaykh Abd al-Azeez ibn Baaz:

"The wine of the Hereafter is good and does not cause any intoxication or harm. As for the wine of this world, it is harmful and causes intoxication. In other words, in the wine of the Hereafter there is no ghawl (intoxication) and the one who drinks it will not become intoxicated; it does not cause him to lose his mind and it does not cause physical harm. As for the wine of this world, it is harmful to mind and body alike. None of the harmful effects in the wine of this world will be found in the wine of the Hereafter. And Allah is the source of strength."[5]

The key is that absence of intoxication. It's not the alcohol, it's what the alcohol does to human beings that Islam – and, indeed, many if not most faiths – finds fault with. It reminds me of a conversation I once had with international wine expert Jancis Robinson, who said that one of the biggest problems for connoisseurs engaged in tasting, comparing and rating wines was the alcohol and its effect on perception. "It would all be so much easier if it wasn't alcoholic," she said.

Buddhism's enormous range of forms and variations makes pinning down one attitude toward alcohol difficult, but it's clear that, as with Zoroastrianism, caution is advised. Again, it's not the ethanol itself, it's what the ethanol does.

The Buddha, before he became the Buddha, was Siddartha Gautama, a Hindu prince, allegedly devoted to the good life in all its forms, including drinking alcohol. At the age of 35, he became enlightened and, in acknowledging suffering as the inevitable course of life, began preaching his Middle Way of detachment from material things and a renunciation of ignorance and illusion through his Four Noble Truths, the Wheel of Becoming and the Eightfold Path.

At the monastery of Tashichho Dzong in Bhutan, the Institute of Mind and Science offers one interpretation of what the Buddha had to say on the subject. Lopen Tashi Tshering, a lecturer at the institute, wrote, "Intoxication can lead to the loss of wealth, increased unnecessary confrontations, illness, disrepute and weakening of wisdom. 'Intoxicant' includes anything we ingest, inhale or inject into our system that distorts consciousness, disrupts self-awareness, and that is detrimental to health." He added, "One is to refrain from drinking even a drop of alcohol and taking intoxicants because they are the cause of heedlessness. If any Buddhists succumb to the lure of

---

[5] *Majmoo' al-Fatawa of Ibn Baaz*, 23/62

intoxicating drinks, they shall not consider me as a teacher."[6]

I love the notion of heedlessness. And yet there are religions where that absence of concern, that willingness to suspend awareness, seems to be part of the approach to worship. Forms like the aforementioned charismatic Christianity, with its dancing, glossolalia, swooning and apparent chaos spring to mind. And not just to mine. In the New Testament, Acts Chapter 2 covers the coming of the Holy Spirit to Christ's disciples at Pentecost. Suddenly, they were speaking in tongues of all varieties. Confusion among the spectators reigned:

> "And they were all amazed, and were in doubt, saying one to another, 'What meaneth this?' Others mocking said, 'These men are full of new wine.' But Peter, standing up with the eleven, lifted up his voice, and said unto them, 'Ye men of Judaea, and all ye that dwell at Jerusalem, be this known unto you, and hearken to my words: For these are not drunken, as ye suppose, seeing it is but the third hour of the day.'"[7]

You have to love Peter's grasp of the nitty gritty here: look, I know you think we're drunk, but it's too early, boys.

Back to Buddhism, though. Its flexibility as a faith means it has adapted to different cultures and indeed, different attitudes toward alcohol. Different climates. Today in, say, San Francisco you will find guys in bars debating the notion of "mindful drinking" (and in some ways this book is all about mindful drinking – the awareness of the wonders of what you are consuming as opposed to diving in only for the effect). In many monasteries in Tibet and India, Vajrayana practitioners will incorporate alcohol as part of their meditative practice. In fact, it was this which led to the original concept of urban "mindful drinking". It happened, unsurprisingly, in Scotland.

---

[6] https://kuenselonline.com/buddhism-and-intoxication/

[7] Acts 2:12–47

Chögyam Trungpa Rinpoche was one of the most important teachers in Tibetan Buddhism, and after his escape from Chinese-occupied Tibet, he spent time at what became the Samye Ling monastery in Dumfriesshire. I have been there. It has an excellent cafe, which is unlicensed. I was friendly with the late Colin Betts, author, teacher, musician and retired drug dealer, and Colin's commitment to the precepts of Tibetan Buddhism never really interfered with his taste for marijuana and (to a lesser extent) Grey Goose Vodka.

Rinpoche, who was sometimes accused of being an alcoholic, renounced his monastic vows; he smoked and drank and encouraged his students to do so. He was one of the proponents of Vajrayana tantric practices (so-called "thunderbolt" Buddhism), and some would argue that his encouragement of students to drink was a kind of spiritual provocation; others are less generous. Rinpoche leading his Vajrayana students into "mindful drinking" led to confusion and uncertainty. Some reacted well to the application of ethanol, with the experience of drunkenness "loosening the ties to the material world". Others were ill. One student said that they were encouraged to drink just enough to relax, to appreciate their situation and to help their ego go to sleep. The idea was to watch how the alcohol affected them and see how it could relax their mind: "When you feel that loosening inside you, then you stop."

And there is this, from the *Treasury of Precious Qualities* by Jigme Lingpa:[8] "Alcohol, the taking of which is a downfall according to the Shravaka Pratimoksha and constitutes a fault in the bodhisattva discipline, is regarded in the Mantrayana as a substance of samaya that must always be present. The Guhyagarbha-tantra states:

Meat and alcohol must not be lacking
For they are substance of accomplishment,

---

[8]   Lingpa, Jigme, *Treasury of Precious Qualities*, commentary by Longchen Yeshe Dorje, Kangyur Rinpoche, foreword by HH the Dalai Lama

Food and drink, essences and fruits
And all that is a pleasure to the senses."

I have a friend whose name I'm not able to provide here who spends a lot of time in India, at the Tibetan Buddhist outposts there, and he confirms that this approach to the use of alcohol is common. It is not, however, constant. On a purely practical level, those of us who have been around drink know how easy it is to slip from justified drinking ("I only had a couple of pints to be sociable") into destructive and sometimes terminal consumption. Who can forget the blunt advice of Proverbs, Chapter 1:20: "Wine is a mocker, strong drink is raging: and whosoever is deceived thereby is not wise."

On the other hand, the occasional small libation is all right. Probably. If taken in the right spirit.

Holy Flight – Tasting Notes

Amrut Peated Single Malt Whisky

I first came across an older expression of Amrut in Glasgow in the 1990s, and I think the city was the brand's first point of contact in the UK. Himalayan whisky sounds as if it ought to work well – what could be more Highland? It did then and it does now, only better. There is a superb cask-strength version available, but this tasting is of the more moderately priced 46 per cent bottling – higher than the old expression and giving some added weight. A lot of hard work and care has been put into production for a worldwide market.

Colour: Classic burned caramel-gold. Not to infer that burned sugar has been used. Similar colour, though.

Nose: Smell it (best add a teardrop of water) and you will pick up smoke from the peat used to malt the barley, some toasted caramel and hot honey.

Palate: On swilling it around the mouth, malt extract and fruit emerge.

Finish: After swallowing, you will get the impression that you've just drunk a cup of strong tea while sitting at a peat fire. On the foothills of the Himalaya. With chilli in the vicinity.

Cobra Premium Lager

Cobra beer is readily available worldwide in Asian restaurants, and you'd expect that as Cobra is now majority-owned by US conglomerate Molson Coors and mostly made in the UK, in the beer heartland of Burton-on-Trent. Its story is fascinating. The company was founded in Britain by Karal Bilimoria and Arjun Reddy after (now Lord) Bilimoria found that British and German lagers didn't work well with Indian food. Some £20,000 ($26,500) in debt after graduating from Cambridge University, he managed to borrow enough cash to commission a brewery in Bangalore to produce a softer, less carbonated lager, called it Cobra and began distributing it to Indian restaurants from the back of an old Citroen 2CV car. Cobra took off like a rocket. If you've eaten Indian food in the UK, you've probably been offered it or its competitor Kingfisher as an accompaniment.

I have drunk Cobra often and always with spicy food. It is a classic lager with the rounded-off lack of bubbles that makes it work so well with curries ranging from jalfrezis through vindaloos to the scariest phaal. It also tends not to come back down your nose even if you apply it rather too enthusiastically to a thirst.

Colour: Clear, bright and yellow. Not much of a head; inviting.

Nose: Breakfast cereal before the milk goes on, with slight hoppiness.

Palate: Light, easy drinking, a bit malty but a perfect curry accompaniment.

Finish: Inoffensive, which, for a with-food beer, is a good thing generally.

Murree Beer

As I have said, despite contacting Major Sabih-ur-Rehman in Rawalpindi and gingerly tapping various contacts in the licensed trade in Scotland, I have been unable to obtain any Murree for personal assessment. The few reviews available online stem from the brief relationship Murree had with a brewery in the Czech Republic, a variety of beer which briefly emerged in the wake of the Willis incident described above.

A drinker in Oslo came across a can of the basic Murree beer (Czech version) in a restaurant there (doubtless at vast expense; Norwegian alcohol prices are horrendous) and described it as being clear and golden, like most lagers, with "a fairly decent white head". The overall impression was of blandness and low carbonation, which would indicate the beer had been designed to work well with spicy food.

There may be a few tins still lurking on shelves throughout the world, and one can only hope that someday Murree will be available to accompany curries outside of Pakistan, in its original form, whatever that may be, given the amazing range of liquids produced by the company.

CHAPTER 5
WINE THAT MAKETH GLAD

Italy (Rome), Scotland (Kirkcudbright), Israel, The Lebanon
Cordial and wine

Holy Flight
— *Chateau Musar 2015*
— *Ribena (Blackcurrant cordial)*
— *Kool-Aid (Grape drink)*

Wine, then. Made from grapes. Traditionally, all you need do is
tread them down into a mush, and the wild yeasts in the air and
on the grape skins will produce a form of wine.

Wine is everywhere in the Bible (it makes 130 appearances
in the Old Testament alone), and is thus, in practical drinking
terms and symbolically, running like a river through Judaism
and Christianity. In terms of sheer pragmatism and direct
instruction, you can't beat Deuteronomy 14:26:

> "And thou shalt bestow that money for whatsoever thy
> soul lusteth after, for oxen, or for sheep, or for wine, or
> for strong drink, or for whatsoever thy soul desireth: and
> thou shalt eat there before the Lord thy God, and thou
> shalt rejoice, thou, and thine household."

In Judaism – with the proviso (as in all religions where drinking is permitted) that over-indulgence is wrong – wine is seen as essential to worship on particular occasions and desirable at other times in membership of the faith community. It's regarded as holy and is the only drink prayed over. Wine must be drunk at Passover, and on the Sabbath: Rabbi Eitan Webb, a Jewish chaplain at Princeton University, says this: "To welcome the Sabbath with a glass of wine is to meld together our spiritual and material existences. It is a meeting of body and soul."[1]

The root of all this is the benefit brought by wine during its moderate consumption in context. And the context is, yes, ceremonial, but nearly always linked to the notions of gathering for a meal. The Passover feast, or Seder, eaten in Jewish households across the world in memory of the deliverance of the Jews from slavery in Egypt, is perhaps the most complete example of this. Every adult participating will drink four cups of wine to illustrate God's saving of His chosen people from imprisonment and servitude. The four cups represent four kinds of redemption. There is the cup of sanctification, the cup of judgement, the cup of redemption and the cup of the kingdom. A fifth cup is kept for the prophet Elijah in the hope he will arrive as an unknown guest during the celebration, representing future redemption and heralding the imminent coming of the Messiah. That cup is left undrunk.

While the Passover meal was always celebrated, it was not always as formalized as it is today. Under the influence of Greek "symposia" or philosophical discussions, it was not until the 2nd century that distinct rules, regulations and rituals were put in place for the Seder. So, when Jesus and his disciples celebrated the Passover it would have been a more casual, ordinary meal, though unleavened bread and wine would have been crucial. The ultra-formal, even magical ritual of Christian communion – the Eucharist – is based on what must have seemed to the disciples

---

[1] https://vinepair.com/wine-blog/the-evolution-of-alcohol-across-the-three-monotheistic-religions/

a relatively normal celebration of an annual feast – even a fairly relaxed and informal gathering in that upper room in Jerusalem.

It was a meal. Noisy, full of side conversations, feuds, worries, jokes; some drinking too much, some not very much at all. Concerns about what was due to happen next day. Suspicions about what Judas's agenda might be. Or, for that matter, Jesus's. There was almost certainly mutton as well as bread. Hungry men, eating messily. And then …

> "And as they were eating, Jesus took bread, and blessed it, and brake it, and gave it to the disciples, and said, 'Take, eat; this is my body.' And he took the cup, and gave thanks, and gave it to them, saying, 'Drink ye all of it; For this is my blood of the new testament, which is shed for many for the remission of sins. But I say unto you, I will not drink henceforth of this fruit of the vine, until that day when I drink it new with you in my Father's kingdom.'"[2]

Suddenly, everything got very, very serious. The stakes were being well and truly upped. This was food and drink that symbolized death, regeneration and salvation. But the food and wine they'd all been enjoying, which sealed their companionship and community, now meant the death of their leader and friend. Here are the roots of the Eucharist.

Grumpy old St Paul, writing much later to the early Christians at Corinth, was concerned that their celebration meals had got out of hand, and too many were gorging themselves and rolling about like gluttons and drunks. So, he called for a separation between the celebration of "the Lord's supper" and communal dining. In other words, no getting inebriated during communion. The philosopher Alain de Botton in his book *Religion for Atheists* suggests that what we now call the Eucharist started off as simply a chance for early Christians to gather for a meal, very much like

---

2   Matthew 26:26–29

the Jewish Sabbath gathering for food … in the understanding that it's when we ruminate over food and drink that we can turn our thoughts to the needs of other people.[3] De Botton is of the opinion that this (relatively simplistic) interpretation of early Church life could be reintroduced on a secular basis to the social and psychological benefit of everyone.

In 1 Corinthians 11:26–29, Paul provides the branch of the early Christian church in Corinth with a detailed pattern for communion that would, in the glorious, sonorous language of the King James Version of the Bible, become memorized by the English-speaking millions and provide a pattern for Church practice.

I make no apology for reproducing those verses here. Apart from anything else you can sense the petulance of Paul, I think ("Can't you lot eat and drink and get drunk in your own homes?"), and the stern admonitions about damnation at the end are aimed at those who were using the availability of wine in large quantities to get roaring drunk:

"When ye come together therefore into one place, this is not to eat the Lord's supper. For in eating everyone taketh before other his own supper: and one is hungry, and another is drunken. What? have ye not houses to eat and to drink in? or despise ye the church of God, and shame them that have not? what shall I say to you? shall I praise you in this? I praise you not.

For I have received of the Lord that which also I delivered unto you, that the Lord Jesus the same night in which he was betrayed took bread: And when he had given thanks, he brake it, and said, 'Take, eat: this is my body, which is broken for you: this do in remembrance of me.' After the

---

3   Botton, Alain de, *Religion for Atheists: A Non-Believer's Guide to the Uses of Religion*, Penguin, London, 2012

same manner also he took the cup, when he had supped, saying, 'This cup is the new testament in my blood: this do ye, as oft as ye drink it, in remembrance of me.' For as often as ye eat this bread, and drink this cup, ye do shew the Lord's death till he come. Wherefore whosoever shall eat this bread, and drink this cup of the Lord, unworthily, shall be guilty of the body and blood of the Lord. But let a man examine himself, and so let him eat of that bread, and drink of that cup. For he that eateth and drinketh unworthily, eateth and drinketh damnation to himself, not discerning the Lord's body."

This is very strong stuff and forms the roots of the various rituals of communion celebrated throughout Christianity. The formalization of communion into a symbolic act of great theatricality and dramatic power begins here. But it is symbolic. The wine is still wine, yet, just as the wine in the Seder symbolizes the sheep's blood painted on Jewish doorways and lintels during the exile in Egypt to protect against avenging angels, the communion wine symbolizes the protective and redemptive blood of Jesus that will be shed for the salvation of the world.

An Ordinance

In the Church of Jesus Christ of Latter-Day Saints, commonly known as the Mormons, water is used in the weekly communion service known as an "ordinance" (sacrament). This was not always the case. When the founder of the church, Joseph Smith, introduced the sacrament, fermented wine was used and indeed drunk socially by members.

In 1830, Smith received a "revelation" that wine should not be bought by members from "enemies", meaning the non-Mormons who either persecuted or simply disagreed with his beliefs. But this "Word of Wisdom" was not church law, rather it was seen widely more as an unbreakable rule. However, it was one of the motivations for Brigham Young in developing agriculture in Utah, along with the realization that brewing and winemaking were major economic drivers.

And so vineyards owned by Latter-Day Saints spread throughout Utah and California, and wine produced by members was used in the ordinance.

Then, church members and leaders became part of the temperance movement in the late 19th and early 20th centuries, and this led to changes in interpretation of Smith's 1830 pronouncements, which included warnings about the effects of alcohol. Eventually the well-known church-wide ban on drinking came into force, and fermented wine was no longer used in communion. But that meant the essential biblical symbolism disappeared, or, at the very least, was watered down. Unlike in the Roman Catholic tradition.

A Sacred Mystery

The question of what happens during the Eucharist is, to say the least, a matter of contention. In traditional Roman Catholicism, the doctrine of transubstantiation clearly states that the bread and wine, as blessed by the priest and presented during the Mass, becomes the actual body and blood of Christ during that ritual. This is a "sacred mystery" (though there have been attempts using Aristotelian metaphysics to explain it philosophically) and one which of course is crucial to the divide between Catholicism and Protestantism. Orthodox Christianity in its various forms wavers on exactly what transubstantiation means. Not just books, but whole libraries have been written on this subject, but as this volume is about alcohol and religion, I do not propose to go any further down the road of theological speculation and, it must be said, division. Remembering that I come from a country where, to this day, the issue causes bloodshed and death on a regular basis, I can still feel the spittle landing on my green St Ronan's blazer on that terrible first day at Troon Primary School.

But I am interested in the wine. What is this wine that can become so divinely special? Does it intrinsically have to be of a particular kind, prepared in a certain way? And what do you have to do to turn wine into the actual blood of Jesus?

Canon 924 of the present Roman Catholic Code of Canon Law (1983) states that "The most holy Sacrifice of the Eucharist" must be celebrated in bread, and in wine to which a small quantity of water is to be added. The wine should be natural, made from grapes that are "not corrupt", which means that the wine must be naturally fermented. It shouldn't have anything added to it but, in fact, it can be fortified and sulphites can be added to preserve it.

Most, if not all, communion wine is made from bulk grape juice, which is then fermented and fortified, like so-called tonic wines. It should not be more than 18 per cent alcohol. In fact, non-alcoholic wine is sometimes used, and even gluten-free wafers can be obtained. Top supplier in the UK for this sort of thing is the company Frank Wright and Mundy of the Isle of Wight, who cover the entire waterfront in ecclesiastical hardware and software, new and "preloved". From holy water sprinklers to my absolute favourite: individual miniature plastic sealed communion cups with built-in removable communion wafer.[4]

The product is described on the company's website as a "refilled communion cup with individual unleavened wafer and Concordia grape juice. The elements are pre-packaged, with both wafer and Non-Alcoholic Communion Juice in a single two-part recyclable container. Designed to fit standard communion trays. Twelve-month shelf life. No refrigeration required. Sold in boxes of 10 cups."

The world of ecclesiastical supplies is seductive. It was all I could do, while browsing the catalogue of Grace Supplies in Hull (not Hell, though you can see how mispronunciation could lead to problems), not to order a few clerical collars and shirts just in case ordination beckons. And they do their own-label 15 per cent alcohol communion wine at £110 ($143) for a case of 12, with free delivery. There is also the Poterion

---

[4] https://www.frankwrightmundy.co.uk/shop/

Fair Trade communion wine, also 15 per cent, slightly more expensive and made in South Africa. You can get it in red or amber, from either Cabernet Sauvignon or Muscat grapes, with sugar added to give it the necessary potency. And sweetness, presumably. The added sugar allows each (unconsecrated) bottle "to last weeks once it has been opened."[5] I don't know where exactly the Vatican gets its supplies (though the present Pope's family have a background in winemaking in Piedmont and His Holiness is reported to be a connoisseur and expert sommelier himself). However, Vatican City, with a population of just 825, is reported to have the highest annual consumption of alcohol per head in the western world – 74 litres per person per year – seven times the amount drunk in the USA.[6]

You receive communion by either intinction (the dipping of the bread into the wine by the priest, who then places it in your mouth) or by direct sipping from a silver – it must be precious metal – chalice. This is known as the "common cup". There are variations in other churches involving a fistula – a metal straw, basically – or a spoon. Individual glasses are often used in Protestant churches. In the past it was common, particularly in countries such as Ireland where wine was not produced, for only the priest to receive the blood of Christ, his parishioners only taking the bread.

After a Roman Catholic Mass, any wine left over that has been consecrated as the blood of Christ must be drunk either by the priest, those attending the Mass or those helping to distribute communion. In these post-pandemic days, the issue of disease is on many minds and indeed lips, and communion was impossible during the peak of lockdown, at least officially. Disease is nothing new as a threat to the Eucharist, as Anthony Cazalet reported in the *Catholic Herald* in April 2021: "Perhaps the first academic study into contamination was carried out by

---

[5] www.church-supplies.co.uk/

[6] https://blog.xtrawine.com/en/the-vatican-tops-the-list-of-heaviest-wine-drinking-nations/

Howard S Anders of Chicago University in 1897," he wrote, "Found in the dregs of the chalice was tubercle bacilli – the cause of TB and leprosy – pus and, perhaps less surprisingly, mucus ... during the Spanish flu epidemic, hundreds of thousands of people died as a result of drinking from the common chalice."[7]

But how does the wine become the blood? We all know Jesus changed water into wine at the wedding at Cana in Galilee (gallons of it, if my childhood lessons on the capacity of those great amphora were correct). But how does a Catholic priest, simply be praying over it, change wine into blood? How is this explained? In truth, the answer is it is a matter of faith. The doctrine of the Real Presence goes back a long, long way and really hinges on a fundamentalist interpretation of scripture.

In his book *Early Christian Doctrines*, (Protestant) church historian J N D Kelly writes, "Eucharistic teaching, it should be understood at the outset, was in general unquestioningly realist, (that is) the consecrated bread and wine were taken to be, and were treated and designated as, the Saviour's body and blood."[8]

He also says that the second-century Christian writer Ignatius of Antioch[9] roundly declares that bread is the flesh of Jesus, the cup his blood. Clearly, he intends this realism to be taken strictly, for he makes it the basis of his argument against the Docetists' denial of the reality of Christ's body. The roughly contemporary Bishop Irenaeus[10] also teaches that the bread and wine are really the Lord's body and blood.[11]

The present Pope may enjoy a bottle of whisky and have a background in viniculture, but he is uncompromising on transubstantiation, adhering to the Mysterium Fidei (Mystery

---

[7]   https://catholicherald.co.uk/wine-for-the-masses/

[8]   Kelly, J N D, *Early Christian Doctrines*, Continuum Publishing, London and New York, 2000, p.440

[9]   Ignatius of Antioch, also known as Ignatius Theophorus, Christian martyr, early writer and Patriarch of Antioch

[10]   Early Greek bishop

[11]   ibid., 197–98

of the Faith) as spelled out in 1965 in an encyclical of Pope Paul VI: "In the investigation of this mystery we follow the Magisterium of the Church like a star. The Redeemer has entrusted the Word of God, in writing and in tradition, to the Church's Magisterium to keep and to explain. We must have this conviction: 'what has since ancient times been preached and received with true Catholic faith throughout the Church is still true, even if it is not susceptible of a rational investigation or verbal explanation' (Augustine)."[12]

So there you have it. Believe it. Or believe it not. Not every Roman Catholic, by the way, accepts the doctrine of the Real Presence, just as not every Church member will choose to take communion at the Mass.

It's a long way from the rowdy Corinthian meals St Paul so bluntly criticized. But as Alain De Botton says, there are benefits from the ceremony, the ritual of the Mass. If participants manage to remain awake for the Mass and the lessons it provides, he says, the ceremony should at the very least take us out of our own narrow selfish experience. And it should help us take on board some notions of community and collaboration.

I was speaking to my wife, an avowed rationalist, about the strangeness, the otherworldliness of this belief. How, I mused, could anyone taste the wine and believe that while tasting of wine (though a good red wine may well have overtones of iron and bloodiness), it was the actual blood of Christ?

"But why not?" she said. "If you believe in God, if you believe in divine miracles, heaven, hell, all that stuff … then why not?"

Ribena, Kool-Aid and Flavor-Aid

I was given the drink called Ribena in large quantities when I was child, thanks to its massive popularity during and after World War II. Ribena's origins are all about warfare, about sea blockades

---

12 www.vatican.va/content/paul-vi/en/encyclicals/documents/hf_p-vi_enc_03091965_mysterium.html

and submarines. German U-Boats prevented the importation of most citrus fruits during much of World War II and Britain's children needed a native source of vitamin C. Hence, the planting of blackcurrant bushes by the tens of thousands and the advent of Ribena. It was sweet, dark and glutinous (it still is), named after the blackcurrant plant *Ribus negrum*, and it was *wrong* to drink it neat. You were meant to dilute it, but that didn't stop us sucking the blue-black-purple nectar straight from the bottle.

Now, I know that readers in the USA will find references to Ribena somewhat puzzling, and even the very idea of drinking blackcurrant juice. This is because blackcurrants were banned in the USA for a long time, and the flavour is almost completely alien to American tastebuds. According to the magazine *Business Insider*, "probably fewer than 0.1 per cent of Americans" have tasted a blackcurrant.[13]

Until the late 19th century, blackcurrant production was extensive in the USA, along with gooseberries and white currants. These are all of a single species called *Ribes* (as in Ribena), but it was discovered that they carried a fungus that attacked white pine trees, a main source of industrial timber in the USA at the time. So the Federal Government passed drastic laws that led to the complete eradication of all *Ribes* plantations – thought to be about 7,400 acres – in the USA, and by the early 20th century, there were almost none left.

However, times change and since 2003 the cultivation of blackcurrants has been permitted in New York State. There is now some cultivation of blackcurrants not just in New York's Hudson Valley, but in Connecticut, Oregon, Washington and also in Canada.

Ribena is important in my life. It was used as communion wine (slightly diluted, but not by much) in the gospel hall at Kirkcudbright in Galloway, one of the least touristy corners of Scotland. I loved – still love – Kirkcudbright, a beautiful village

---

[13] www.businessinsider.com/blackcurrant-america-vs-europe-2016-10?r=US&IR=T

that for decades has been an artists' colony and is the focus of a famous novel by Dorothy L Sayers featuring her detective hero Lord Peter Wimsey in *Five Red Herrings*. Oddly, I once was in a position to open a cupboard in said Gospel Hall and found stored therein perhaps 50 or 60 partially empty bottles of Ribena. Despite the Brethren's staunch adherence to communion-as-mere-symbolism, the idea of dumping those half-empty Ribena bottles obviously offended someone's idea of holiness.

The drink was reformulated in 2018 to conform to regulations regarding the amount of sugar in soft drinks (that used to be colossal and was infamous for its effect on children's teeth). It's still sweet, slightly slick and jelly like (if you drink it neat, which you shouldn't), and according to the *Guardian*, it tastes "like a robot's armpit".[14] I disagree. I quite like it.

But as I say, Ribena, whether in the less-sugary or full-fat form, and for that matter blackcurrants, remain mysteries to the average American. As a consequence of all this, candy or soda marketed in the USA that is coloured purple or deep red is usually labelled as made from grapes or at least having grape flavour or characteristics. As in, for example, that staple of American soft drinks, Kool-Aid (albeit supplied in powder form and diluted with iced water). Or its slightly cheaper, Chicago-born relative, Flavor-Aid. Both available in "grape" varieties.

It was grape Flavor-Aid, mixed with cyanide, promethazine, diazepam and chloral hydrate, that over 900 people took, or had forced upon them, on 18 November 1978 in Jonestown, Guyana, at the behest of Jim Jones, leader of the People's Temple commune. It was the biggest example of cult murder-suicide in modern history. There have been many books and films about Jones and the People's Temple, with another in preparation: a major Hollywood production featuring Leonardo Di Caprio both as a producer and the actor playing Jim Jones.[15] But at

---

[14] www.theguardian.com/lifeandstyle/shortcuts/2018/mar/16/why-ribena-fans-have-been-left-with-a-bad-taste-in-their-mouths

[15] https://deadline.com/2021/11/leonardo-dicaprio-jim-jones-mgm-jonestown-1234869994/

its simplest, Jones led almost 1,000 Americans to Guyana to begin a new life as a pseudo-Christian, radically socialist community, following accusations of abuse in the USA. US Congressman Leo Ryan, along with a TV news crew and others, flew to Guyana to investigate accusations of abuse and imprisonment by Jones, who by this time was addicted to drugs and dangerously erratic in his behaviour. Ryan and several others were murdered by Jones's elite guards and, in anticipation of an armed response from US law enforcement, Jones ordered the entire community to take the poisoned Flavor-Aid and die with him. However, he is thought to have shot himself in the end, having seen the terrible effects of the concoction he administered to his followers, including around 300 children.

This happened in a dreadful parody of the Eucharist, a so-called "white night" of feasting and drinking leading to death that the Jonestown residents had rehearsed, using non-toxic Flavor-Aid.

The appalling episode has given rise to a phrase now commonly used to indicate someone who has so completely absorbed and accepted an opinion – even one completely without foundation – that they believe it utterly and act upon it. Such a person is said to have "drunk the Kool-Aid" (though there is also an argument that this usage first pops up in Tom Wolfe's exploration of 1960s LSD use by Ken Kesey and his Merry Pranksters, *The Electric Kool-Aid Acid Test*). This is an absolute nightmare for the marketing department of Kraft Holdings, who now own and sell Kool-Aid. Worse, it wasn't Kool-Aid but Flavor-Aid that was used at Jonestown, though there are indications that some Kool-Aid may have been present on the site.[16]

I have never tasted Flavor-Aid. I did try Kool-Aid for the first time when I was 12, thanks to an American boy who came

---

[16] www.theatlantic.com/health/archive/2012/11/stop-saying-drink-the-kool-aid/264957/

to live in our town and brought some with him. His name was Kurt Everard and his father had the biggest car anyone had ever seen. We wouldn't drink it, though. We ate the powder direct from the packet. I remember thinking it was a bit like solid Ribena. There were, as I recall, no ill-effects.

Holy Flight – Tasting Notes

Château Musar 2015

There is something wonderful about the fact that Musar has been produced all the way through some of the most turbulent times in Lebanon's history, despite the making of alcoholic drink being, to say the least, something of a religious issue in the region.

Musar's vineyards are in Lebanon's fertile Bekaa Valley, and vines have been grown here for millennia. There is a temple in the ancient city of Baalbek (once known as Heliopolis, or Sun City) that was built in honour of Bacchus, Roman god of wine, and Lebanon's wines are mentioned several times in the Bible, for example in Hosea 14:7:

> "Those who dwell under his shadow shall return;
> They shall be revived like grain,
> And grow like a vine.
> *Their scent shall be like the wine of Lebanon*"[17]

The Phoenicians are thought to have taken winemaking from the Lebanon to Egypt, Greece, Italy and Spain over 4,000 years ago. Jesuit monks brought strains of the vine from France to plant in the Bekaa Valley, originally to produce altar wine. Gaston Hochar founded Chateau Musar in 1930 and the business is still in the Hochar family.

Musar is or was a favourite wine of certain authors, notably the late novelists Iain Banks and William McIlvanney, both, perhaps

---

[17] www.biblehub.com/hosea/14-7.htm

not coincidentally, Scottish. And it is one of my favourite wines, though I admit to being entranced by its origins.

Generic Bekaa Valley reds are sometimes available through supermarkets' own-brand bottlings and should be investigated with caution, though at the time of writing Aldi in the UK are offering one that is quite palatable.

These notes refer to the 2015 vintage of Chateau Musar.

Colour: A deep, earthy red.

Nose: Berries like brambles and blackcurrant, black cherry and then a deep, spicy earthiness.

Palate: Vanilla and oak, with a kind of powerful softness that embraces and then gives you a sense that this may be worryingly drinkable in quantity. But be discriminating and take it easy. There is a character in a William McIlvanney thriller who makes the (terminal) mistake of thinking this is a much weaker wine than it appears. It has a freshness and that balances that school-desk oakiness and leathery world-weariness that makes the wine work well with fattier foods like mutton. One of my all-time favourite wines.

Finish: Tannins and an earthy, stewed tea aroma. But deeply satisfying.

Ribena Blackcurrant Cordial

Colour: It looks like a mature red wine. It certainly does not taste like it, though.

Nose: Childhood, but only in Grangemouth, or Motherwell before they closed the steelworks.

Palate: Let's say you take it with the same amount of water thoroughly mixed in. Sweet, sticky, fruity but in a weirdly aspirin-like way. Somehow goes up your nose and really that's not at all pleasant.

Finish: Wash your mouth out with soapy water. Then brush your teeth. Or crack open a bottle of Chateau Musar (see above) …

Kool-Aid
Grape flavour, as remembered from 1969
Eaten dry: An explosion of intense, purple flavour.

Grape flavour, caffeine-free, unsweetened 2022 version, diluted with water as per instructions and with added sugar
Colour: Purple. Ish.

Nose: Cremola Foam (a now-deceased British equivalent, which was fizzy, not still) or something chemical that comes close to grapes or oranges. Or cherries. Fruity. Fruit gums, or fruit pastilles, melted and sprayed.

Taste: It tastes … purple. More purple than purple. For many Americans, I know this is the taste of childhood. For me, it's the mystery of big Kurt's vast collection of baseball bats, gloves, electric games that wouldn't work on UK voltage and his sudden departure for home, leaving it all behind in a playground pile for us to squabble over.

Finish: Somehow, you want … more.

CHAPTER 6

MONKS, NUNS AND TROUBLE IN THE STREETS

England (Buckfastleigh, Devon), France and Spain
Wine (fortified and naturally fermented)

Holy Flight
– *Buckfast Tonic Wine*
– *Dom Pérignon Vintage Champagne 2010*
  (Cheaper alternative: Freixenet Cordon Negro Cava)
– *Green Chartreuse*
– *Barr's Irn Bru (1901 edition)*

When I was a newspaper reporter, one of my favourite duties was to attend Monday morning sittings of our local court, watching the perpetrators of the weekend's misdemeanours strut their weary stuff in front of the forbidding, gowned nemesis: the judge, known in Scotland at this level of the judiciary as the sheriff.

The duty legal aid solicitor would have visited the assortment of sorrowing, sore and generally regret-ridden men (mostly men) and women and persuaded the majority to plead guilty. Ninety per cent of the time, they'd been drinking before committing acts of violence, vandalism, theft or crazed and dangerous driving. Their memories were often vague or non-existent. "My Lord, my client would in mitigation plead that he has very little recollection of Saturday night's events. He recalls going to the Excelsior public house and there partaking of a pint, perhaps

97

two pints of beer. After this establishment closed, he may have been inveigled into attending a party at the victim's house where more beer and possibly the fortified wine known as Buckfast were consumed …"

Buckfast Tonic wine. Known in Scotland and Northern Ireland as Buckie. "Wreck the Hoose" juice. Electric soup. Extremely popular among football supporters in central Scotland, allegedly first springing to popularity because its sweet heaviness and 15 per cent alcohol content, made as it is from South African grape juice or mistella, reminded supporters of Glasgow Celtic FC of altar wine. This is almost certainly nonsense. What really makes Buckfast the ideal street (and domestic) fighting drink is the large amount of caffeine it contains. Combined with disinhibition from alcohol, you have a message in a bottle that spells trouble. It is the Espresso Martini of the hooligan classes.

It is not a drink I have ever cultivated an affection for. It tastes somehow both cloyingly sweet and aggressively bitter, with a forbidding treacly stickiness that prophesies both a horrendous hangover if you take more than a couple of gulps, and a kind of promise that it will lead you very quickly astray. It makes dark and sinister threats. Particularly if teamed up with a couple of cans of Carlsberg Special Brew.

I did once almost acquire a taste for its relative, Sanatogen Tonic Wine. When I was 16 and sitting my senior exams at school, my mother would for some reason send me off on a daily basis, having consumed after breakfast a glass of this beetroot-red libation, which was reported to be full of iron and other vitamins as well as a large dollop of alcohol. I passed all my exams with the exception of art, which I somehow managed to forget all about. I have no idea why.

My very religious mother would also have been praying for me, which may have added some holy sparkle to the secular substance of Sanatogen. But with Buckfast, prayer comes built in, because this concoction is made by and for the benefit of monks, namely those residing at Buckfast Abbey on the edge of Dartmoor in south-west England.

It makes sense for monks to make wine or beer, and often to distil either or both into spirits. These establishments have always been repositories of technical knowledge; the theory and practice of producing alcohol have travelled across the world in the libraries and memories of monks and priests. Extensive monastic landholdings meant agriculture was always going to provide the basic grapes or grain necessary, and the need to support both the spiritual mission of the monks and the necessarily grand architecture of worship led to the development of profitable sidelines.

Just as you can trace the influence of Greek philosophy through Christianity, you can follow the trail of Greek winemaking expertise into and throughout Christendom. It had been generally thought that the Romans took viniculture with them in the wake of their conquests, but a 2009 Cambridge University study[1] concluded that the Greeks got there first, arriving in the port of Marseilles (then called Massalia), grape seeds in hand, around 600 BC. There they established a community and interbred with the local Celts. Eventually, glasses containing Cotes de Rhône began clinking merrily.

That's one view, anyway. More recently (well, a mere 1,660 years ago or thereabouts) there was a clothes-ripping act of charity by a Roman soldier called Martin. He offered a beggar a piece of his cloak. This led, the story goes, to him having a vision of Christ and his conversion, baptism and eventual manifestation in France as St Martin of Tours. Roman soldiers, handily, underwent training in viniculture so they could sort out some refreshments during long postings in faraway locations, so it seems St Martin's early military service proved useful.

You can visit the Chateau St Martin in Provence, which is built on the site of a Roman villa. In the 12th century, monks from the islands of Lérins off the coast of the French Riviera established a priory and built underground cellars that are still used there today. Martin himself is thought to have made major

---

[1]   https://www.cam.ac.uk/research/news/greeks-uncorked-french-passion-for-wine

contributions to winemaking technology in France, including developing the Chenin Noir and Chenin Blanc grape varieties, planting vineyards at Vouvray and accidentally discovering the need for pruning when his donkey ate the tops of some vines. This allegedly infuriated the local monks who owned the vineyard – until harvest time when the vines produced a greater yield than ever before.

Martin established the abbey of Marmoutier just outside Tours in AD 372. It was one of the biggest and most powerful monastic settlements in medieval France, but hardly a trace of it remains today – there were frequent burnings, sackings and general disapproval down the centuries. Yet as a source of both mysticism and winemaking knowledge in France, it remains crucial. As does St Martin, his donkey and that legendary act of apparel-tearing love for a beggar. Incidentally, the Hungarian wine industry also pays tribute to St Martin, as he was born in what is now that country.

The Benedictine order was key in the establishment of monasticism and for that matter winemaking, not just in France but throughout Europe. St Benedict of Nursia is in fact the patron saint of Europe, which must be something of a tricky business given the current state of the European Union. St Benedict was Italian and lived until AD 548. He founded 12 monastic communities near Lazio before establishing the massive monastery of Monte Cassino in southern Italy. The Rule of St Benedict became enormously important and influential as monks and their habits spread, focusing on work and prayer, and instructing followers to make vows of obedience and commitment. The need for monastic communities to be self-supporting and the consequent development of winemaking was part and parcel of this. In France, Cluny Abbey was founded thanks to the cash that William, Duke of Aquitaine, donated to the Benedictines in 910 and, through its strict adherence to the Rule of St Benedict, it became a major force in the development of monasticism in Europe. These days, only a tiny part of the original abbey remains as a public museum, which has no religious connection. That's what happens when you have a full-on revolution of the French sort. In 1790, most of the abbey was burned to the ground.

For 500 years the Benedictines were key players in the French wine industry throughout almost every part of France, from Champagne and Bordeaux to the Mediterranean. The order grew rich and, in the eyes of some, a bit too fond of its own wealth and luxury – a little bit lax and louche. There was a split, and out of the Benedictines came a more fundamentalist group, the Cistercians, who applied the Rule of St Benedict even more strictly. They were serious to the point of asceticism. But they made wine (and, later, beer: the Tynt Meadow Trappist beers made in England are products of the Bernardine order of Cistercians). They worked hard, those Cistercians, and soon began to outdo their father sect in wine production. Notably, the Cistercians are thought to have pioneered that curse of the bourgeois partying classes, Chardonnay. (I'm joking. A good Chardonnay such as Cloudy Bay is a joy and a true taste sensation. But you may have to go to New Zealand to get a good one. Or pay a lot of money.) Anything But Chardonnay? I don't think so.

Monks were crucial to the development of many classic French wines, including Pouilly-Fuissé, Châteauneuf-du-Pape (the clue is in the name) and Chablis. Pick a chateau in Bordeaux and it's more than likely you will eventually find the name of a lost, razed revolution-ravaged abbey. Those monks got everywhere. And there is one name, one monastic appellation so to speak, that everyone is familiar with, which remains a brand like no other: Pierre "Dom" Pérignon. Father of the cork. Inventor of champagne. The man who first slurped some fizzy "method Champenoise" wine and exclaimed, "I am tasting the stars!"

Except he wasn't that man and he didn't say that he'd been tippling astronomically. A 19th-century advertisement for champagne did put those words into his cartoon mouth, but fizzy wine was happening long before Pierre Pérignon encountered secondary fermentation. It was an accident and not caused by the practice of adding sugar to trigger that starburst of bubbles.

Pierre was born in Champagne in 1638. Well, in the town of

Sainte-Menehould in the province of that name, the youngest of seven children. His father's family owned several vineyards. At 17 he entered the Benedictine abbey of Saint-Vanne near Verdun. Prayer, reading, instruction and hard manual work outside became his lot, as befitted followers of the Rule. But Pierre had already proved his abilities in the field of not just growing vines, but also maturing them, and it was as a cellar master that he moved in 1668 to the Abbaye de Saint-Pierre d'Hautvillers, where he would stay for the rest of his life, helping to double the acreage of its vineyards and developing its wine production massively.

The fizz in the wine coming out of Hautvillers was in fact a problem. It was caused by accidental refermentations, and it was all due to the weather. Wines bottled in the summer and laid down in the cellars would still be fermenting due to active yeast, and when autumn brought cooler climes, fermentation would often stop before all the sugars had turned to alcohol. Come the warmth of spring, the yeasts would be re-activated and fermentation would begin again. Corks would come out of bottles or, worse, there would be an explosion and whole racks of wine could be lost in a chaos of broken glass and flowing liquid.

There had to be a way of controlling this and indeed making fizzy wine as a deliberate end product. Aristocrats had discovered it and it carried a premium due to all those explosions. It wasn't, as some have argued, just a case of adding sugar, using cork stoppers and wire to retain them and ordering in toughened glass from England. It was a great deal more subtle than that.

In 1718, Pérignon's colleague Canon Godinot published a set of wine-making rules widely considered to be dictated or at least influenced by Pérignon.

These included the instructions that:

- The process should be as natural as possible, without the use of additional chemicals.
- Only (red) Pinot noir grapes should be used, as they were less likely to cause refermentation.

- Small crops were preferable and vines should be pruned down to less than a metre.
- Harvesting should be done just after dawn when conditions were cool and moist, with the grapes treated extremely gently to avoid damage. Grapes should be consistently small and any aberrations should be disposed of.
- No bare feet should be used for crushing the grapes. Modern, gentler Coquard presses were to be used – one of the techniques that enabled red grapes to produce white wine.

As for that business about the corks ... it is part of winemaking myth that Dom Pérignon was the first to apply cork to sealing the necks of wine bottles having noticed Spanish travellers using tree bark instead of the traditional hardwood stoppers. According to George Taber, author of the book *To Cork or Not to Cork*, champagne corks were being used on the Duke of Bedford's estate in England from 1665 – several years before Pérignon became chief bottle-minder at Hautvillers.

And this brings me to the English scientist Christopher Merrett. Because it is a matter of historical record that he was the one to first work out how you could put the bubbles into wine and keep them there. Merrett presented a paper to the Royal Society, describing how English winemakers had been adding sugar to wines to give them a bit of zing, several years before Pierre Pérignon even became a monk.

"Our wine coopers of recent times use vast quantities of sugar and molasses for all sorts of wines to make them drink brisk and sparkling and to give them spirit," he wrote, in the first use of the term "sparkling".[2]

But those Champenois monks knew a good story when they saw it, and one of Pérignon's successors at Hautvillers, Dom Groussard, ran with the Dom Pérignon myth. As 1896 dawned, the local "Syndicat du Commerce" produced a pamphlet called *Le Vin de Champagne* that lauded Pérignon as the progenitor

---

[2] https://www.bbc.co.uk/news/uk-england-gloucestershire-39963098

of champagne, albeit by adhering to "ancient traditions". This served two purposes. It gave champagne a very specific geographical location and made it the intellectual and spiritual inheritance of good old, stern, hard-working Benedictines. The Rule triumphed. Sort of.

Nowadays, the brand Dom Pérignon is made by Moët et Chandon (it was first brought to market in 1921) and is promoted in a way I doubt Pierre Pérignon would recognize or approve of. It has been given a new, metaphorical form of fizziness, that of ultra-hipster celebrity, with limited-edition bottlings designed in collaboration with stars such as Lady Gaga, Lenny Kravitz and the editors of the uber-cool style magazine *Toilet Paper*. As the website states: "Lady Gaga and Dom Pérignon, two creators who believe in the power of absolute creative freedom, invite you to a fabulous, exuberant, exhilarating celebration – a joyful convergence that rewards the inspiration to create, to reinvent ourselves and write our own story."

Pierre's corks would be well and truly popping.

The Elixir of Life

Let's talk spirits. To make eau de vie (the water of life, as in Chapter 1) that can be matured into cognac or brandy, depending on where and how you do the maturing, you need to distil wine. This means, as when making whisky out of what is essentially beer, that you heat the wine until the alcohol, which boils at a lower temperature than water, turns to steam. You then condense it, usually using what is called a "worm" – a coil of narrow pipe cooled in water. And hey presto: the hard stuff.

Cognac is brandy made in the Cognac region of France. Benedictine is something else again – a herbal liqueur made by adding a concoction of plant extracts to distilled spirit. The recipe is, inevitably, secret, allegedly known to only three people at any one time (like the recipe for that non-alcoholic Scottish wonder, Irn Bru). By its name, you'd think Benedictine was rooted in the monastic tradition. But you'd be completely wrong.

What happened was this. In 1863 a man called Alexandre Le Grand, aided by a pharmacist, came up with a recipe for a herbal liqueur. It was based on old medicinal formulae Le Grand had acquired from some kind of religious foundation to which his maternal grandfather was connected. How to sell it? Call it Benedictine and pretend it was invented by monks! That might work.

Le Grand claimed the drink had been produced at the Benedictine abbey of Fécamp in Normandy until the abbey's destruction during the French Revolution. To give some credence to his religious claims, the letters "D O M" were printed on each bottle, standing for "Deo Optimo Maximo" ("To God, most good, most great"). This is a phrase used by the Benedictine order as a dedication of their hard work. One can only surmise what St Benedict would have thought of this imaginative misappropriation.

Monks do, however, make medicinal spirits. And there are always great stories. Imagine if someone offered you not just eau de vie, aqua vitae or a way of making brandy, but a formula for *the* elixir of life. Something that would bring people back from the dead. Something like, I don't know, the aforementioned Irn Bru, "Scotland's Other National Drink". Or maybe not. (If you're a stranger to the delights of Barr's Irn Bru, there are tasting notes at the end of this chapter.)

Some Carthusian monks at Vauvert, near Paris, were offered an apparently death-defying recipe around 1600, or so the story goes, by François Hannibal d'Estrées, one of King Henry IV's Marshalls. It was an alchemical formula meant to extend life, and these Carthusians were specialists in medicinal plants. However, they couldn't make it work, or possibly became fed up with waiting around to see if it had worked. Either that or they all died young, thus proving that the recipe wasn't working.

So, the formula for everlasting life was locked away and forgotten. Then, after 125 years or so it came to light once more and was sent to the Carthusians' headquarters near Grenoble in the Chartreuse mountains, a place with plentiful plants and monastic expertise on how to use them. It took almost 150 years apparently, but what emerged, courtesy of one Brother Gérome Maubecas in 1737, was certainly a reviver, assuming you were suffering from a really deathly hangover. After much tinkering, the monks decided to release their concoction into the world. There's no doubt that overindulgence in the resulting 142-percent proof Elixir Végétal de la Grande-Chartreuse would send you to an afterlife of one kind or another.

The story of Chartreuse then becomes tangled in the extreme. The monks – indeed all religious orders – were expelled from France in 1793 and the formula for Chartreuse both went with them to exile in Catalonia *and* fell into the hands of a Grenoble pharmacist. Some monks returned to Grenoble in 1816 and were gifted the formula by the pharmacist's heirs, and by 1842 the Green and Yellow Chartreuses we all know (and very possibly dislike) today had emerged. Green is 110 per cent proof, with the milder, yellow version just a tongue-tickling 86 per cent.

However, things did not go well for the Carthusians. They were expelled from France again in 1903, and production of the elixirs began in earnest in their Catalonian refuge. Back in France, a commercial group began producing a similar drink under the Chartreuse name but, after they faced bankruptcy in 1929, some local businessmen of a spiritual bent bought up the shares and gifted them to the monks. Despite a French Government ban, religious production of Chartreuse began again. It wasn't until after World War II that the expulsion order against the monks was officially lifted.

These days, you are likely to find Chartreuse used not in a medicinal way, but as a minor component on cocktails such as a Jabba the Hutt (vodka, lime, cider, Green Chartreuse) or, if you dare, a Trump's Golden Cowlick: gin, cider, prosecco, maraschino and Green Chartreuse.

Perhaps you'd rather just have a glass of monastic wine instead ... and for that you can go right back to the start of winemaking in France.

At the beginning of this chapter I mentioned the Chateau St Martin in Provence, and how 12th-century monks from the

Lérins Islands established a priory there. Today you can take a short boat ride from Cannes to Saint-Honorat, one of the Lérins islands. The spectacular Abbey de Lérins on Saint-Honorat is home to just 21 monks, but they produce much-praised organic wines from their eight hectares of vines. These are monks with access to the highest realms of media moguldom and political movers and shakers. They produce seven vintages, including Saint Salonius, which is often served to the jury of the Cannes Film Festival, and can be found in the glasses of bigwigs at the more prestigious state dinners in Paris. Let's face it, it wouldn't be a monastery without some secret recipes for herbal liqueurs. There is the aromatic Lérina, made with 44 herbs and seeds, and Lérincello, which sounds and tastes very like limoncello. Yes, there are lemons in it.

And it's not just monks who make wine.

You will find the last winemaking nuns in France at Notre-Dame de Fidélité, in the Provençal village of Jouques, not far from Aix-en-Provence. This is not an ancient establishment, dating back only to 1967 and the arrival of 15 sisters from Paris. There had been a vineyard on the site and, with local help, the nuns began making wine. In 2016 they achieved the "Origine Coteaux d'Aix". It's a pretty *vin de sud* "ordinaire" by all accounts – I haven't tried it – but give the sisters time.

Back to Buckfast

Let me take you on a trip to the absolutely glorious Buckfast Abbey. It's hard to miss, dominating the small Devon town of Buckfastleigh, which is set in a pleasant valley on the edge of Dartmoor. Maybe, like me, you're obsessed with old steam and diesel railway engines, and you've come to take a ride on the South Devon Railway Trust's line. Perhaps, again like me, you enjoy open-air swimming. There's a pool. Buckfastleigh looks prosperous, well preserved, pleasant, and in no small measure that's due to the main attraction, the abbey. Not to mention the fact that the abbey's Charitable Trust takes a keen financial interest in the town's wellbeing, supporting local charities and sometimes businesses, such as the local post office, which it helped save from closure.

Because Buckfast Abbey is not poor. It's incredibly wealthy, in fact, and that wealth is built, essentially, on Buckfast Tonic Wine.

Buckfast Abbey is a collection of spectacular, if not particularly old, buildings. The first Abbey was founded in 1018 and was taken under the Cistercians' wing in 1147. Becoming an important religious centre, it grew until 1539 when Thomas Cromwell and Henry VIII did their usual stuff, expelled the monks and closed it down, seizing assets merrily as they went. Buckfast was left in ruins.

Exile and expulsion, as you'll have noticed, is a recurring theme in the story of monasteries, abbeys and monastic orders. In 1882 a group of just six Benedictine monks were expelled from France, arrived in England and settled at Buckfast. They began the rebuilding process and today Buckfast is the only medieval Benedictine Abbey to have been restored and returned to its original use. It now serves not just as home to a community of monks, but as the local Roman Catholic church. It is truly at the centre of this lovely, well-groomed, civilized community.

It's a glorious place to visit today. Its gardens are spectacular, and the Abbey church, despite only being finally completed in 1938, has the stillness and glamour of somewhere much older. It is ornate, glittering and sometimes overwhelming. The huge, modern, stained-glass window of the Last Supper in the Blessed Sacrament chapel is rightly hailed as a masterpiece and is the work of Buckfast's own Father Charles Norris. His craft techniques, perfected at Buckfast, have been used in over 150 churches and chapels.

There is a restaurant. There are beehives, paying tribute to the Abbey's long tradition of beekeeping, a nod to the Cistercians of the Middle Ages. The "Buckfast Bee" – the name is trademarked – was developed by Brother Adam, who was beekeeper at Buckfast's modern manifestation for over 70 years.

It's recognized worldwide as a gentle, disease-resistant and good honey-producing bee.

It's all rather wonderful. As the Very Reverend Dom Francis, Prior and Novice Master says in a specially produced video welcoming visitors:[3] "From this still and holy centre, our purpose – to give glory to God and to walk in His ways – radiates out. And affects all that we do. So that in all you see we hope you will find a reflection of the beauty and tranquillity and loving kindness of God."

But all of this loveliness, all of this rich spirituality and community mindedness, comes at a price. And that price is paid by sales of Buckfast Tonic Wine. "Wreck the Hoose Juice", aka "Commotion Lotion" and, in certain parts of West Central Scotland, "a bottle of What the Hell Are You Looking At?" The Abbey, needless to say, does not appreciate this informal nomenclature, and is keen to point out that there are other means of support for its spiritual activities. There is a conference centre and hotel. You could, a few years ago, even be welcomed as a delegate to your hosted conference with a "Buckfast's Fizz" – tonic wine, fruit, mint, orange juice, soda water and crushed ice. As Jonathan Deacon, the finance director, says: "The Abbey pays for the upkeep of its buildings and the monastery by its commercial activities." Key to that is "a blend of fortified wines that arrive at the Abbey from Southern Europe." That wine is fortified with large amounts of caffeine, sugar – more for the version sold in the Republic of Ireland – and various standard emulsifying and stabilizing chemicals. The recipe was tweaked in the 1920s after the Abbey entered into a distribution deal and was told the original product – that secret recipe from France – was too medicinal. It's sweet, potent and – see the tasting notes at the end of this chapter – to me, not particularly pleasant. Though, to be fair, I am someone who detests Vermouth and therefore

---

3   https://www.buckfast.org.uk/vocations
    https://www.youtube.com/watch?v=Ls7KMtr9B-o

have a glaring absence in my life when it comes to the much-vaunted Martini.

It is exported globally. An acquaintance working in Kenya recently saw a roadside billboard advertising it as "the new sensation". However, in parts of Scotland and Ireland it is both loved and hated with a vengeance. Because from some points of view, the peaceful glory of Buckfast Abbey is built on misery, death, injury, destruction, addiction and violence.

You could of course say that alcohol of any sort taken in the wrong context and to excess would have those effects. But Buckfast is special. Between 2010 and 2012, for example, Buckfast was mentioned in no less than 6,500 crime reports from what was then Strathclyde Police. In one 2013 incident in Glasgow, Tracey Meikle, 33, murdered Lorraine Foy, 36, in front of her two teenage daughters by stabbing her to death in what was called a frenzied knife attack. She was jailed for life. Her defence lawyer Gordon Jackson QC told the court his client had taken valium washed down with Buckfast Tonic and cider and could remember little of the attack: "She never really denied that she was the person involved in this but doesn't know how it happened or why it happened. It was just something out of nothing."[4]

Let me take you to the so-called Buckfast Triangle, which I know well, as my family comes from there. Three towns in Lanarkshire, once at the centre of Scotland's heavy industry but which have struggled with social and economic decline for many years: Airdrie, Bellshill and Coatbridge. There, Buckfast is not a blessing but a curse.

The author Damian Barr was born and brought up in Bellshill (which has an interesting history as a brewing ground for artists and writers – the likes of Teenage Fanclub, the Soup Dragons, BMX Bandits and Sheena Easton come from there) and in 2014 he wrote memorably in the *Guardian* newspaper about the effect of Buckfast Tonic on his upbringing:

---

[4]   https://www.bbc.co.uk/news/uk-scotland-glasgow-west-25944139

"It's the sickly-sweet scent I remember on the breath of every angry man in my life before he raised his hand. It's the poisonous green bottles smashed all over the streets of the estate I played on – the evil emeralds I picked out of my knees."[5]

In 2015, Catherine Stihler, Labour Member of the European Parliament, claimed that Buckfast Tonic "causes untold misery in communities across the country",[6] and former First Minister Jack McConnell described the brand on BBC Scotland's *The Politics Show* as "a badge of pride among those who are involved in antisocial behaviour". It was, he added, "a seriously bad drink".[7] The litany of criticism has never stopped, with the monks being very reluctant to respond. Their distributor, J C Chandler, or their public relations representatives tend to do so in their stead.

In 2013, Alex Neil, Member of the Scottish Parliament and then Scotland's Cabinet Secretary for Health, Wellbeing and Sport, told Buckfast Abbey that they should stop making Buckfast Tonic Wine, provoking Abbot David Charlesworth to make a rare response to the media: "If you ban Buckfast, ban Scottish whisky. It's alcohol, much stronger. But oh no they wouldn't do that. So, they are picking on a particular thing as a conscience salver."[8] This prompted MSP Elaine Smith to say that Buckfast Tonic Wine was more problematic than Scotch whisky because of Buckfast's caffeine content.

Jim Wilson, from J C Chandler, responded, "It's been there for over 80 years. Why should we go about changing the recipe of something just to satisfy somebody's whim?"

The Abbot, understandably, is unhappy about the association between his godly repository of grace and spirituality and

5   https://www.theguardian.com/society/shortcuts/2014/feb/03/buckfast-triangle-alcoholic-drink-monks-west-scotland

6   https://www.glasgowtimes.co.uk/news/12656589.mep-in-push-for-ban-on-buckfast/

7   https://www.scotsman.com/news/politics/mcconnell-joins-war-words-buckfast-seriously-bad-drink-2507806

8   https://www.bbc.co.uk/programmes/b03lbygl

mayhem on Scottish (and Irish and Northern Irish) streets. "I don't want Buckfast Abbey to be associated with broken bottles and drunks, but is the product bad? No." To which Damian Barr responded, "That's like Kalashnikov feeling sad about the way his rifles are used. It is unholy water."

The fact is that the monks are not going to stop treading the grapes of wrath into tanker loads of heavy-duty profit which they can, as they say, channel into good works and prayer. It's worth anything between £5 and £8.8 million ($6.5 and $11.5 million) a year to them. The fact is they do recognize the damage that it does. Otherwise, why would Buckfast Tonic be available in plastic half-bottles (the use of the glass containers as weapons was a huge problem) and now cans? And the liquid is not advertised or marketed in Scotland and Northern Ireland.

But then it doesn't have to be. The cult of Buckie is a meme on the internet, a joke to some, a tongue-in-cheek celebration to others. There is a World Buckfast Day (8 May), Facebook groups, and at buckfast.com, run by the distributors not the monks, lists of dishes you can make using the wine (for example "Buckfasted Chestnuts and Chestnut Mushrooms") as well as cocktails that read like desperate attempts at civilization. There are T-shirts, caps, jackets, all kinds of merchandise available on the web, little of it official. And there's even a kind of Buckfastian hipster trend. Not so much "Wreck the Hoose" juice as modify the Farrow and Ball wallpaper. In nice patterns.

Over to David Charlesworth again, who told BBC News, "We don't make a product for it to be abused. That's not the idea. We make a product that is a tonic wine. It annoys me to think that these problems, all the social deprivation of an area of Scotland, is being put on our doorstep. That's not fair. I'm not producing drugs, which I know are going to be used abusively. If I say I don't feel any responsibility, that makes me sound like a heartless so-and-so. That's not the case. Am I upset about how tonic wine is used? Of course I am. It would be ridiculous to say otherwise."[9]

---

[9] https://www.bbc.co.uk/news/uk-england-devon-25236076

A Papal Blessing

The mixing of chemical stimulants with alcohol is neither new nor uncommon. A Café Correto is an espresso with added grappa or Sambuca, or sometimes brandy. Red Bull and vodka may not give you wings, but it will lend a bit of effervescent stimulant ying to a depressive alcoholic yang. And then there's rum and Coke, in the days when Coke had both caffeine and cocaine in it. But perhaps the most fascinating and religious use of booze-with-a-lift is Vin Mariani.

You can still buy Vin Mariani, but it's had its teeth drawn. It's now a mixture of red wine and "de-cocained coca", but in its vintage days, it was a full-throttle, cocaine-laced tipple. It all began with Corsican chemist Angelo Mariani, who was interested in the medical effects of coca leaves, having been influenced by the anthropologist and neurologist Paolo Mantegazza.

Mantegazza, a 19th-century thorn in the side of the Roman Catholic Church, believed in the potential of some drugs and foods to alter human perceptions, physiology and psychology, and saw cocaine as a bit of a miracle drug, having come across it during a trip to South America. He observed natives using coca leaves, tried it himself and carried out extensive, ahem, testing, again on himself, during 1859. He then wrote a scientific paper called *Sulle Virtù Igieniche e Medicinali della Coca e sugli Alimenti Nervosi in Generale* ("On the hygienic and medicinal properties of coca and on nervous nourishment in general"). The benefits of cocaine, were, he thought, obvious:

"... I sneered at the poor mortals condemned to live in this valley of tears while I, carried on the wings of two leaves of coca, went flying through the spaces of 77,438 words, each more splendid than the one before ... An hour later, I was sufficiently calm to write these words in a steady hand: 'God is unjust because he made man incapable of sustaining the effect of coca all life long. I would rather have a life span of ten years with coca than one of 10,000,000,000,000,000,000,000 centuries without coca.'"[10]

---

[10] https://www.bionity.com/en/encyclopedia/Paolo_Mantegazza.html

Well, who could blame Angelo for being interested in trying this himself? And why not add it to alcohol and see what happened? By 1868 Mariani had started marketing a liquid called Vin Tonique Mariani (à la Coca du Pérou), made from Bordeaux wine and coca leaves. Claret with a kick. The alcohol helped extract the cocaine from the coca leaves. Export Vin Mariani contained 7.2 mg of cocaine per ounce and it was claimed that a few sips would restore health, strength, energy and vitality.

Mariani was an energetic salesman – a brand evangelist, in modern parlance – and solicited testimonials from all kinds of celebrities, which were used in memorable advertising campaigns. The actress Sarah Bernhardt proclaimed it "the king of tonic wines" and Thomas Edison praised it for helping him stay awake longer – a real lightbulb moment. Ulysses S Grant drank it while writing his memoirs and there are dozens more celebrity endorsements. The ones that interest me most, however, are those of Pope Leo XIII and Pope (later Saint) Pius X. This letter from Cardinal Rampolla in Rome must have been a delight for Angelo:

"Rome, January 2 1898

It has pleased His Holiness to instruct me to transmit in his august name his thanks to Monsieur Mariani and to testify again in a special manner his gratitude. His Holiness has even deigned to offer M Mariani a gold medal bearing his venerable image."[11]

There's no question that Pope Leo appreciated Angelo's tonic. He carried a hip flask full of it "to fortify himself when prayer was insufficient." It helped him in his amazing output – 88 encyclicals, more than any other pope. And he was alive and kicking until the age of 93.

All of this and Vin Mariani was also the inspiration, so it is said, for Coca-Cola. Or to be precise, for Coke inventor

---

[11] https://www.drugtimes.org/recreational/cardinal-rampolla.html

John S Pemberton's original product, which came out in 1885 – Pemberton's French Wine Coca. This was similar to Vin Mariani, but included extracts of kola nut, which provided extra oomph in the form of caffeine.

Later in 1885, some counties in the USA passed prohibition legislation and Pemberton's response was to develop a non-alcoholic version of his French Wine Coca with a certain carbonated fizz. He called it Coca-Cola.

Holy Flight – Tasting Notes

Buckfast Tonic Wine

I once conducted a book festival reading and tasting that involved some of the less upmarket alcoholic drinks. There was Scotsmac, a ferocious combination of cheap whisky and cheaper South African sweet white wine, the favourite of some of my schoolmates when I was growing up; two of the other west of Scotland "electric soups", Lanliq and Eldorado (known as Lanny and El-D, both sweet, fortified street wines); and Buckfast Tonic, aka Buckie. No one would drink the Buckfast. At least, not after a first fateful sip.

Its supposed similarities to altar wine notwithstanding, the addition of caffeine gives it a strange, bitter aftertaste you might not expect if you're not a Buckfast fan (or Buckieroo, as the saying goes). Some have described the taste as being like flat Coke mixed with burned toffee, and there's some truth in that. Medicinal notes come through, along with intense sweetness and cherries.

At 15 per cent alcohol, you may think this is not that much stronger than a robust Australian Cabernet Sauvignon, but the large amounts of sugar and caffeine turn it into a powerful, punchy (often literally) package.

In Scotland and Ireland you will find restaurants making Buckfast puddings, flavouring ice cream with it and generally trying to soften its hooligan image. The same is true at the

Abbey itself. But the fact remains that for most people it's not a pleasant drink. It delivers a heavy hit of alcohol and backs that up with sugar and caffeine. A tonic? I beg to differ.

Colour: A worryingly malevolent brown.

Nose: Something burning there beneath that cloyingly sweet bitterness. You know you're about to get mugged.

Palate: Both very sweet and overpoweringly bitter. Bubble gum and Cola with a hint of cloves and paraffin.

Finish: You've been siphoning petrol or diesel or worse from a vehicle and accidentally swallowed some because the police have noticed and you've had to beat a hasty retreat.

Dom Pérignon Vintage Champagne 2010
(Cheaper alternative: Freixenet Cordon Negro Cava)

And of course, Dom Pérignon (always vintage) is one of the world's great champagnes. The absolute minimum you will pay in the UK for a bottle of the 2012 vintage is £155 ($200), and those prices will do nothing but rise. The sky is the limit for older bottlings.

I would be lying if I said I'd tried it. Well, I think I'd be lying. There was a night, a television industry party many years ago, where the executive producer was retiring and was on his last expense-account piece of work-related entertainment. There was brandy at £50 a glass, so there could well have been Dom Pérignon. Or something more expensive if it was available. But if there was, I can't remember what it tasted like. There were probably bubbles. I'm certain there were bubbles.

So, as I have no tasting notes of my own on this champagne, I'll offer instead the description made by Dom Pérignon's cellar master, Vincent Chaperon, at the launch of the 2012 vintage:

> "As soon as you smell it and come back to it the nose is
> full and varied, mingling flowers with fruit, and the vegetal
> with the mineral. The bouquet is tactile, subtly enticing
> us along a trail of powdery white flowers and nectareous
> apricot, followed by freshness of rhubarb, and mint and

then the vegetal appears – what we like to underline – then you feel the minerality of ash. White pepper. On the palate it is quite clear there is one word – energy. The attack is rounder, welcoming but very quickly it is starting to vibrate and then explodes in your mouth with a surge of effervescence and tonicity. Focused by acidic and bitter notes, the finish brings a penetrating tautness marked by ginger, tobacco and toasted accents."[12]

I, on the other hand, will go for the cheap and cheerful Spanish fizz I've been drinking since my rock'n'roll days (when it was used as a chaser for Absolut Vodka), and still rate. I always enjoy the slightly seedy air of faded glamour that comes with the opaque black bottle and the gold labelling. All for around £10 ($13) or less.

It comes from Catalonia, is made using the same method as Dom Pérignon, and is very good indeed, ice cold and drunk on its own or as the basis for cocktails (see below). You could mix it with Buckfast Tonic, but I do not recommend this. A bar in Glasgow was providing Buckfast cocktails at one point – a favourite was a picture of gin, lemon juice, egg white and Buckfast called … Breach of the Peace.

Freixenet (pronounced *Fresh-ay-net*) leaps tingly out of the bottle or glass straight down (or up) your nose if you're not careful.

Colour: A kind of limestone off-white; creamy, but coming from that opaque black bottle there is something wonderfully mysterious about it.

Nose: Lots of lemon sherbet, apple and peach as you sniff it.

Palate: In the mouth it's all lemon- or grapefruit-flavoured San Pellegrino mineral water but with a kind of wet sandstone mineralogy.

Finish: The celebratory lift and sparkle only champagne and its derivatives can bring. And all the time, you're thinking: *At least I didn't pay £200 ($260) for this.*

---

[12] http://www.the-buyer.net/tasting/wine/dom-perignon-2012/

Green Chartreuse

The Carthusians use 130 herbs and spices to make this. Basil and caraway are discernible amid the alcoholic kick. Oh, and it's green. There's a degree of embrocation oil as you swallow, and sweetness. It's pungent. It's fair to say I am not a fan and have not tried the yellow stuff. There are limits.

A shot of the green mixed with the Freixenet described above will provide you with a Cava Chartreuse cocktail. A Chartreuse Champagne cocktail is a more expensive option. You should, if you insist (and I don't), use Yellow Chartreuse, add some gin, cider blueberries, a maraschino cherry, and you are well on the way to the infamous Donald Trump cocktail known as the Golden Cowlick. Green Chartreuse, by the way, at 55 per cent alcohol, is much stronger than Yellow, which comes in at 40 per cent.

These are my tasting notes on Green Chartreuse, which I hope never to encounter again.

Colour: A sickly, frankly disturbing green.

Nose: An old-fashioned herbalist's shop, distilled into something medicinal that your mother has told you will do you an immense amount of good, but you know, in your heart of hearts, is going to be disgusting.

Palate: And you were correct. Mint, spices like caraway and perhaps basil, but mint more than anything else. It reminds me of a patent medicine called Life Drops my mother used to administer to the Morton children when they were sick. Perhaps the association is unfortunate.

Finish: Eventually, it will fade. Minty, that sense you have done your duty and may not die imminently.

Barr's Irn Bru

This carbonated soft drink (soda) was launched in 1901 in Scotland by A G Barr. There are several versions of it in these health-conscious days, most struggling to remove as much unhealthy sugar as possible from what must be a few of the company's much-vaunted "secret" recipes.

The firm's official line is this: "In 1901, steel workers working on the re-building of Glasgow Central Station were drinking too much beer to quench their thirst. So, a local soft drinks manufacturer named A G Barr brought to them a tonic-like drink made with caffeine and sugar that could get the workers through a hard day's graft. 'Iron Brew' was born and a long history of it getting Scots through tough situations began."[13] This is not necessarily the whole story. There were a variety of "iron brews" made throughout Scotland by different companies, and A G Barr is the one that triumphed, through years of brilliantly inventive advertising. It is the west of Scotland's favourite hangover cure, and during the 2021 COP26 Climate Change Conference in Glasgow, Barr's managed to gain a monopoly on soft drink sales at the venue. Suddenly everyone had to at least taste Irn Bru. Once …

The "1901" version comes closes to the heavily sugared drink I grew up with. Though, oddly enough, the company claim it contains no caffeine. What can I tell you? It's fizzy, sweet and has a kind of metallic orange taste. When I was a child, like Popeye with spinach, I would imagine it making me stronger and more energetic. Today, I can sense the imminent arrival of diabetes if I ever touch the sugared stuff. And yet Diet Irn Bru just seems … wrong.

It's popular in Islamic countries, apparently, as it's seen as the unAmerican anti-Coke drink. Religion. It gets in everywhere.

Colour: A virulent, glowing, nuclear orange.

Nose: Metallic, as it should be. Girders! Or just that fizz of carbon dioxide mixed with sugar and a touch of pepper.

Palate: Actually, it seems to reach right up into your frontal lobes. A kind of bittersweet eruption of rusty oranges mixed with cloves and burned sugar.

Finish: A desperate need to finish the entire bottle – and very quickly.

---

[13] https://www.agbarr.co.uk/about-us/news/irn-bru-1901-makes-sweet-return/

CHAPTER 7
THE BREW THAT IS TRUE

Ireland, Germany, England
Beer

Holy Flight
– *Murphy's Stout (canned)*
– *Weihenstephaner Hefe Weissbier*
– *Weltenburger Kloster Dunkle Weissbier*
– *Tynt Meadow English Trappist Ale*

Beer has been described as the midwife to civilization. Although anyone who has been on Glasgow's Byres Road or Sauchiehall Street just as the pubs are (finally) shutting may tend to disagree.

The fact is that when humans began to settle into agrarian societies and started sowing, cultivating and harvesting grains – around 12,000 years ago – they began encountering fermentation. Get grain of any variety damp and it will begin to sprout, producing sugar. Wild yeasts are everywhere. Leave grain to steep and it will become alcoholic. Drink enough of that and you may become an alcoholic. But before that dependence develops, you – early human – will find that you become, as they say, a bit tiddly. You will dream dreams and see visions, talk a lot of nonsense and possibly behave immoderately.

As the process of turning grain into alcohol grew more scientific and financially rewarding, that process became central to the development of socialization, trade, medicine and, for that matter, religion. The society that drinks together worships together.

No one likes beer. Not to begin with, not when you're a child. That first taste, no matter if it's a dark stout, a pale pilsner or a golden ale, is unpleasant in the extreme. It's not even strong enough to provide the warming glow of spirits. The overwhelming bitterness is perhaps a warning that the effects of drinking too much beer can be, well, unpleasant. And explosive …

Beer is bitter, even its sweetest of manifestations. Wine, or most wine, tastes horrible to a child, too. A friend told me his first encounter with a straightforward red table wine had put him off the stuff for life. "It looked like Ribena," he said, "like lovely blackcurrant juice or something. And then it tasted like sick." In later life he became a lover of Baileys Cream Liqueur and other intensely sweet substances, along with mixed drinks like rum and Coke or vodka and almost anything sugary. He was a little too old to be seduced by the fiendish commercialism of alcopops, which are essentially alcoholic soft drinks.

My late dad, who was from a teetotal religious background, first tasted beer during his national service in the Royal Air Force. Only toward the very end of his life did I find out about the enormous influence his Uncle Robert had had on him. Dad was one of three children brought up by a mother widowed very young after my grandfather, a mining engineer, was killed in a pithead accident. Uncle Robert, my granny's brother, was a flamboyant and glamorous figure who ran a chain of shops, a wholesale vegetable business and other, rather less reputable businesses including, during World War II, the unofficial manufacture of cigarettes. "He used to sleep with a gun under his pillow," Dad told me in his last weeks of life. "And he kept dogs for security."

Uncle Robert would travel to wherever Dad was serving in the RAF and take him out to bars, hotels and restaurants. "Robert taught me about life," Dad said. Which was why, as a child, I would occasionally see Dad taking a half pint of local ale during one of our holidays in the Lake District in Cumbria, northwest England, far away from the prying eyes of the Brethren elders. I still remember the look on my Uncle Jim's face when Dad offered him a sip of his Jennings Bitter or whatever it was. Uncle Jim was all grown up and still his face twisted in disgust. It was the first beer that had ever touched his lips, and I prided myself on the fact that my expression of horror had been less obvious when, sometime earlier, Dad had given me a taste. "How anyone can drink this for pleasure, I really have no idea," said Jim.

You have to learn to like beer. Jim had never done so, never would. For myself, the revelation occurred one night in Cork in Ireland, in what I remember as the Station Hotel, where they had Murphy's Stout on draught. I had tasted Guinness and disliked it. Brief encounters with what was termed "Heavy" in Glasgow and the tinny, metallic tang of Tennent's Lager had not appealed. I had been a good, Christian, near teetotal boy at university and only now, a young and gauche journalist, was I learning to drink, away from home and with no Uncle Robert to guide me. I ordered a half pint of Murphy's, reasoning that as I was in Cork, I had better try the local brew.

I distinctly remember the experience as taking place while the TV in the bar's corner showed an episode of a then new show called *Bless Me Father*, about an Irish priest played by Arthur Lowe. So God, or at least a televisual facsimile of one of His representatives, was in the house.

That first sip of Murphy's was like nothing I have tasted before or since. Creamy, not bitter, or with just a slight edge of pungency, but not sweet either. A kind of dark perfection. Before I knew it I had moved on to a full pint and only as I drained that glass did I feel any effects from the alcohol. On the corner TV, Arthur Lowe in full priestly garments was taking Mass. I looked at the barman and said: "Murphy's ... is that the same as Guinness?"

It was like that scene in *An American Werewolf in London* when two young American students enter a strange pub called the Slaughtered Lamb. The entire bar fell silent, apart from the tinny drone of Arthur Lowe's voice. The barman leaned in toward me. "That is Murphy's Stout, son, and be blessed that you tasted it here in its home, its birthplace, Cork. And never mention the word Guinness again."

I went home with six strangely shaped bottles of Murphy's, but they didn't taste the same in Glasgow. Gradually, in those pre-craft beer days, I moved on to discover ferocious and palatable German brews like Furstenberg, the first of the strong lagers to take Glasgow by storm, as well as wonders such as Theakston's Old Peculiar, which was only available on draught in one Glasgow pub, the Bon Accord. There were all kinds of beers, even all sorts of stouts. Murphy's crossed the Irish Sea and eventually became almost as ubiquitous in Scotland as Guinness, but it never tasted the same as it had on that astonishing night in Ireland. Not even when I rode my motorbike back to Cork just to try and find the Station Hotel bar (it had disappeared) and order a pint of the stuff. In the end, I had to settle for a pint of Murphy's in my new hotel, in a bar all plastic and velour. It tasted just like Guinness.

A love for beer continues down the generations of my family. Now, one of my sons has written two books on beer and is a partner in a brewery. But that's (yet) another story.

A Pint with Ninkasi

Beer's association with religion is ancient. Fancy a pint with Ninkasi? Well, you'll have to go back to search for the pub culture of the Sumerians, in Mesopotamia, anytime between 4100 and 1750 BC. We know that those Sumerians liked a beer or several and that Ninkasi was the goddess responsible for making sure they got their daily dose. How are we sure of that? Because there's a recipe discovered on a clay tablet from around 1800 BC. It's in a poem of praise to the goddess called "The Hymn to Ninkasi". Here is some of it, translated by Miguel Civil, Professor of Sumerology at the University of Chicago, in the early 1960s.

"[…] Ninkasi, your father is Enki, Lord Nidimmud,
Your mother is Ninti, the queen of the sacred lake.

You are the one who waters the malt set on the ground,
The noble dogs keep away even the potentates,
Ninkasi, you are the one who waters the malt set on the
ground,
The noble dogs keep away even the potentates,

You are the one who soaks the malt in a jar,
The waves rise, the waves fall.
Ninkasi, you are the one who soaks the malt in a jar,
The waves rise, the waves fall.

You are the one who spreads the cooked mash on large
reed mats,
Coolness overcomes,
Ninkasi, you are the one who spreads the cooked mash
on large reed mats,
Coolness overcomes,

You are the one who holds with both hands the great
sweet wort,
Brewing [it] with honey [and] wine
(You the sweet wort to the vessel)
Ninkasi, […] (You the sweet wort to the vessel)

The filtering vat, which makes a pleasant sound,
You place appropriately on a large collector vat.
Ninkasi, the filtering vat, which makes a pleasant sound,
You place appropriately on a large collector vat.

When you pour out the filtered beer of the collector vat,
It is [like] the onrush of Tigris and Euphrates.

Ninkasi, you are the one who pours out the filtered beer
of the collector vat,
It is [like] the onrush of Tigris and Euphrates.[1]

Inspired by this, in 1991 Fritz Maytag of San Francisco's Anchor Brewing Company had a go at brewing "Ninkasi Beer" and brought the resultant liquid to the annual general meeting of the American Association of Micro Brewers. The translator of that ancient recipe, Miguel Civil, reported that the beer had an alcohol concentration of 3.5 per cent and was like cider, dry but not bitter.[2] Possibly a bit like that pint of Murphy's I had in Cork.

Once you had a goddess of beer, you obviously considered that she had certain obligations to you. The Sumerians expected Ninkasi to provide beer for them every day and so presumably there were Ninkasi-blessed brewers who did her bidding and had the expertise to keep the pints pouring.

Moving swiftly through history some 3,000-odd years, Ninkasi had a lot in common with Arnold of Soissons, patron saint of hop-pickers and Belgian brewers. His Saint's Day is 14 August and so if you're looking for an excuse to quaff some Belgian ale, that is the day to do it. Or indeed, any other day of the year.

Mojo Filtering

Arnold of Soissons is also known as Arnulf of Oudenburg, but must not be confused with any number of Arnulfs of Oudenarde, who were barons and not as saintly. He was born around 1040, in Brabant, west of Brussels, and, like so many of our favourite saints and monks, was a soldier in Henry I of France's army in his young days. There are tales that he was

---

[1] https://samorini.it/doc1/alt_aut/ad/civil-a-hymn-to-the-beer-goddess-and-a-drinking-song.pdf

[2] https://www.openculture.com/2015/03/the-oldest-beer-recipe-in-history.html

a keen amateur brewer even then, keeping his fellow soldiers refreshed with his brews. He then repented of his warlike ways and entered the Benedictine monastery of St Medard in Soissons. Three years as a hermit ended with him being nominated as abbot of the monastery, which he desperately tried to avoid. According to his official biography, he tried to flee the monastery but was chased back by a wolf and, seeing this as a sign from God, reluctantly assumed the role of monastic boss.

Other honours assailed him. He became a priest, then a bishop (again, he tried to turn this down) and it was only when his bishopric was seized by a more aggressive servant of the Lord that he, with some relief I think, headed off without a whimper to a quiet life as a brewer.

He became the founding abbot of St Peter's in Oudenburg, Flanders, and it was there that he came into his own as a beer cheerleader and brewing maestro. The peasants in the surrounding area were encouraged to drink beer at any time of the day – even breakfast – for health reasons. There was good reason for this – the weak or so-called "small" beer may not have been particularly potent, but its degree of fermentation was sufficient to kill the germs found in river water. He apparently encouraged the locals to make their own beer and, in times of plague, gave them monastic beer to drink and thus saved many lives.

It was St Arnold who realized you could filter beer, getting rid of spent yeast and other pollutants, by passing it through basketwork. This idea came to him while he was weaving the traditional small beehives called skeps for the monastery's honey production.

Which seems intensely practical. However, prayer and beer went together and one of the miracles that led to his later canonization involved him praying that the beer production at the monastery should increase, after a building collapse had caused stores of booze to be destroyed. And lo and behold, the beer flowed in even greater quantities than before. All was well.

Arnold died young, in 1087, aged just 47. His saintly status was confirmed in 1121, and since then, he has often been depicted on beer labels and posters wearing armour, carrying a mash rake (used in the brewing process) and standing near a beehive.

Oddly enough, another St Arnold, or Arnulf, lived about 400 years before St Arnold of Soissons or Oudenburg. He was St Arnold (or Arnulf) of Metz in France. If that sounds confusing, even more confounding is the fact that he too is portrayed as the patron saint of brewers and brewing and is often pictured holding a mash rake. Frankly, you begin to wonder if someone, after a few drinks too many, was getting a trifle confused with their Arnolds. Or Arnulfs. This one (who lived from 582 to 645) has less written documentation about him, but a great story, known as the Legend of the Beer Mug.

It was a very hot day in July, 642. The good folk of Metz had decided to carry out a bit of officially blessed tomb-raiding – they had headed off 160 kilometres (100 miles) or so south to the town of Remiremont to dig up the body of their former bishop and bring him back to their (and his) home parish. They were exhausted, very thirsty and there wasn't a pub or even a decent stream in sight. As they were just about to leave Champigneulles, one particularly thirsty Metzian, Duc Notto, prayed that "by his powerful intercession the Blessed Arnold will bring us what we lack."

In a flash the small amount of beer remaining at the bottom of a pot expanded massively and there was suddenly enough for the entire squad of pilgrims. So much, in fact, that it lasted them all the way to Metz.

I can't help feeling it was no mere coincidence that this happened in Champigneulles. The village is famous for its spring water and is now home to a brewery that produces "La Reine des Bières". The blessings of St Arnold the First seem to have started there and then spread far and wide.

By Ass to Bavaria

Whether or not Arnold the First's influence led St Corbinian to take the secrets of brewing to Bavaria is unknown, but this particular saint arrived in the Bavarian town of Freising in 720, aboard a bear. Not beer, bear. Another great saintly tale. On his way to Bavaria from Rome, whence he had been sent by the pope, his donkey was attacked and killed by a bear. Not taking this lightly, Corbinian detained said bear, removed the saddle and pack with all his belongings from the dead donkey and strapped all of it onto the bear, who clearly knew when he or she was beaten.

The bear duly bore Corbinian and all his stuff to Freising, then was set free and packed off back to the mountains, having presumably learned that attacking and eating a saint's donkey is never a good idea. Corbinian went on to found a church dedicated to St Stephen, along with accommodation for a group of monks, although the first fully-fledged monastery was established by Bishop Hitto von Freising between 811 and 835, and dedicated at first to St Vitus, then to St Stephen and St Michael. It was an Augustinian monastery until about 1020, when it turned Benedictine. And the Benedictines sure liked to brew.

Now we have reached the beginnings of Bavarian brewing, and the advent of the world's oldest continuously operating brewery – what is now the Weihenstephan Brewery. You can order their beer today from anywhere in the world, and I can thoroughly recommend it (see Tasting Notes, page 136).

The Weihenstephan Brewery has a document from the year 768 that clearly indicates brewing there was underway in that year. It refers to a hop garden paying a tithe (a proportion of income) to the monastery. The City of Freising licensed a brewery in 1040, and that date appears on every bottle from Weihenstephan. There is something thrilling about pouring a beer with a history that long. Also widely available is bottled beer from Weltenburg Abbey brewery, which also claims to be the oldest brewery in the world. It's an interesting one, as though there is little doubt that Weltenburg did not start brewing until 1050, a decade after Weihenstephan, there is still a functioning monastery on the site and the brewery is run by the monks. Weihenstephan is owned and run by the Bavarian state and has been since the monasteries in Bavaria were closed in 1803. Weltenburg closed, too, but reopened as an abbey and a brewery under the authority of King Ludwig I in 1842. Ludwig was very interested in beer, though it nearly cost him more than cash. The so-called Bavarian beer riots took place between 1 May and 5 May 1844 after Ludwig announced a tax on beer. Bands of students and workers attacked the police. The Bavarian army was not keen to become involved and order was only restored when Ludwig reduced the price of beer by 10 per cent. Wisely.

Since 1923, the Bayerische Staatsbrauerei Weihenstephan has been operated in conjunction with the Technical University of Munich as both a state-of-the-art production facility and a centre for learning. Which in many ways continues the monastic tradition. Beers without bears.

Caught in La Trappe

Many will associate beer with the Trappist orders and "Trappist" has become a synonym for "very strong and likely to get you very drunk very quickly". Stag and hen party outings to the Trappist breweries of Belgium have become commonplace, but in fact it all goes back to France and the Cistercian monastery of La Trappe in Soligny-la-Trappe.

In 1664 the Abbot of La Trappe felt that the Cistercian order was becoming too liberal. He introduced strict new rules in the abbey, which was the beginning of the so-called Strict Observance. Fundamental to this was the notion that monasteries should be self-supporting. And as we've already seen, what better way to do that than by first, producing all the alcoholic beverages you might need and then selling them to the public at large to fund the whole monastic enterprise?

By 1685 La Trappe was making its own beer (and it still does, though with Dutch brewing expertise), and as the Strict Observance and the Trappist order grew and spread throughout Europe, so did brewing. The French Revolution in 1789 and other forces of secularization closed many monasteries, but the Trappist order remains a force in the world, as does its beer. But how to prevent just anyone calling themselves a Trappist and starting to produce beer under that name? It was really only in the 1930s that Trappist beers started to become available first to local buyers and then to a global market

In 1997, eight Trappist abbeys – six from Belgium (Orval, Chimay, Westvleteren, Rochefort, Westmalle and Achel), one from Holland (Koningshoeven) and one from Germany (Mariawald) – agreed to found the International Trappist Association (ITA), with the aim of securing the precious Trappist branding and stopping any old brewer donning a habit and making some "monastic" beer. The rules, which were to be strictly observed, are as follows:

1. Beer must be brewed within a Trappist monastery, either by the monks or guided by them.
2. The brewery must not be the main activity of the monastery and the business practices associated with it should reflect the values of a monastic way of life.
3. Brewing should not be primarily for profit. Income should cover the living expenses of the monks and maintenance of the buildings and grounds. Whatever remains should go to charity, for good works or for those in need.

By 2021, the number of Trappist breweries had grown, as monasteries throughout the world recognized the economic and presumably spiritual benefits of making beers. At the time of writing, these are:

– Gregorius and Benno from Stift Engelszell in Austria
– Chimay from Abbaye Notre-Dame in Belgium

- Orval from Abbaye Notre-Dame d'Orval, Belgium
- Rochefort from Abbaye Notre-Dame de St Remy, Belgium
- Westmalle, made by Abdij der Trappisten Westmalle, Belgium
- Achel, brewed by St Benedictus-Abdij, Belgium
- Westvleteren, from St Sixtus Abdij (very small quantities available), Belgium
- Mont des Cats, brewed at the Abbaye Notre-Dame de Scourmont in Belgium in partnership with the Mont des Cats monastery in France
- La Trappe – a wide range of beers brewed by Abdij Onze Lieve Vrouw van Koningshoeven – the Dutch concern owned by the major conglomerate Royal Swinkels Belgian. It's still classed as Trappist because the operation takes place within the monastery walls and under the monks' supervision.
- Zundert, produced at the Zundert Maria Toevlucht Abbey in the Netherlands
- Tre Fontaine, brewed by Abbazia delle Tre Fontane in Italy
- Spencer, brewed by Saint Joseph's Abbey in Spencer, Massachusetts, USA
- And just before Spencer came the advent of Trappist beer in the UK thanks to some extremely far-sighted monks at the St Bernardine Abbey at Tynt Meadow.

Back to Burton-on-Trent

It was in fact a Tibetan Buddhist who introduced me to Tynt Meadow, which only arrived on the drinking scene in 2018 as the twelfth official Trappist beer in the world and the first in the British Isles. Roger Protz, esteemed beer writer, told the BBC at the launch of the beer in 2018 that not only did he love the beer itself ("I'm stunned. It's absolutely gorgeous") but that its arrival was "a great moment for both English beer and English history". Father Michael, the youthful head brewer, said, "I was worried that I was going to brew a beer I didn't like, then I really liked it. I think it's something special, something different but very English."[3]

The Cistercian Mount Saint Bernard Abbey was founded in 1835 in the English Midlands, halfway between Leicester and Burton-on-Trent, the absolute epicentre of British brewing. On Michaelmas Day, 29 September, Brother Augustine Higgs moved into a semi-derelict cottage in Tynt Meadow. He was soon joined by other monks: Luke, Xavier, Cyprian, Placid and Simeon. Their leader, Father Odilo Woolfrey, wrote: "Here we are. I with my little company, already established in a little cottage on this land in Charnwood Forest which we have named "Mount Saint Bernard".'[4]

The monks set about establishing a farm and the first monastery proper was opened in 1837. Seven years later, the beautiful, rather homely buildings you can see today set amid lovely grounds were finished. And they had a local, monastic beer, solely for the use of the monks themselves, though apparently visitors were prone to commenting on how palatable it was. Alas, the recipe was lost, and the main activity at Tynt Meadow became dairy farming.

The monks here have a missionary zeal that extended first to the establishment of a foundation in Cameroon called Bamenda Abbey and led to Bamenda in turn founding the monastery of Our Lady of the Angels in Nigeria. But for a small group of monks in the English countryside, running a dairy farm was neither easy nor profitable, and so the search began to find another way of supporting their work in the 21st century, something that would fit with Cistercian tradition. Why not brewing beer?

The aim was to have an industry that would not only make money but also involve the majority of the monks. There was already a pottery on site, and a flourishing shop. After much research and brotherly discussion, and in the knowledge that

---

[3] https://www.bbc.co.uk/news/uk-england-leicestershire-44581210

[4] http://www.mountsaintbernard.org/our-history

there was a long tradition of Cistercian brewing and there was a history of beer having once been produced on site, they embraced their Trappist heritage and came up with the beer loved so much by Roger Protz and, for that matter, me.

"In 2017–18 we relocated our refectory, kitchen and laundry to provide space for the installation of a new artisanal brewery," say the monks. "We will keep the volume of production relatively small. Just enough to meet our expenses and support our charitable commitments. As of 2018, the brewery is our principal field of labour. All the work, from brewing to bottling and packaging, is done by the monks."[5]

I love the fact that Father Michael and his colleagues use the word "nurturing" to describe their beer. The tasting notes at the end of this chapter will give you some idea of how much I agree with their assessment, and the brothers add, "The monks of old had a saying: '*Patet porta, cor magis*. The door is open, the heart even more so.' By inviting you to taste Tynt Meadow, we offer you a taste of our life." But beware, at 7.4 percent alcohol, this is extremely strong stuff. There is a Belgian Trappist saying that beer should be liquid bread not coloured water, which makes this a very robust wholemeal indeed. Interestingly, one of the items you can buy in the Tynt Meadow shop is "Father Joseph's Tynt Meadow Beer Bread – DIY bread-making kit (not ready-baked)", which, alas, I have not had a chance yet to obtain and try. I imagine it is absolutely delicious.

Father Michael and friends experimented with a range of different beers to acquire experience, which must have added a little extra enjoyment to monastic life. And with the help of a home-brewing kit, the experienced brewing monks at the abbeys of Norcia, Saint-Wandrille and Zundert, as well as local Burton-on-Trent expertise and input from the other Trappist breweries, they tried out various recipes. Finally, they settled on the dark, sweet, strong beer you can buy today.

---

[5] http://www.mountsaintbernard.org/our-history

The brewery is state-of-the-art: glittering in stainless steel and with the wink of computer screens seeming at odds with the monks' white robes, though in another sense, being perfectly appropriate. I said the abbey was somehow homely. Maybe "humble" is another good description. The buildings hunker down in the landscape, the architecture reflecting the Cistercian code of simplicity and humility. But the beer … well, it's a big, proud, strong, dark classic that thoroughly deserves its recognition as the first ever British beer worthy to be called Trappist.

This statement by the Tynt Meadow monks gives a good insight into how they do things and why. "Cistercians esteem the value of simplicity. Simplicity doesn't stand for a thing done simply, or cheaply, but rather represents a distillation of complexity. It is about processing and ordering a rich, varied reality in such a way that the result seems self-evident: 'This is how it has to be!' We see this quality at work in the way the early Cistercians built their churches, composed their music, wrote their sermons, cultivated their land. We hope you'll recognize it, too, in the way we brew our beer."[6]

It's interesting to compare Tynt Meadow with Buckfast. Both plough their profits into supporting their respective monasteries and into charitable and missionary work. But Buckfast do so on a grand and spectacular scale, while Tynt Meadow's approach is far simpler. This is a direct reflection of the orders involved – Buckfast is mainstream Benedictine whereas the Strict Observance Cistercians of Tynt Meadow are following what in effect was originally a breakaway, ascetic group.

I'm sure neither group of monks would want me to assert a preference for one order over another. However, I will say this. I have bought several cases of Tynt Meadow since its launch in 2018. But if another drop of Buckfast Tonic wine never crosses my lips, I will have no regrets.

---

6   http://www.mountsaintbernard.org/our-history

Holy Flight – Tasting Notes

Murphy's Stout (canned)

Not quite the divine revelation that I experienced in Cork, but a reasonable approximation thereof, thanks to the nitrogen widget in the can. Murphy's has 5 per cent of the stout market in Ireland (the rest is Guinness) but 28 per cent in Cork and environs. Worldwide, it's reasonably easy to obtain.

Everyone mentions milk and cream when it comes to Murphy's, and the tinned version is no exception. It's rich and smooth, the nitro widget providing a tight texture in your glass. There are notes of chocolate and milky coffee, with roasted barley and cornflakes.

The intention was always that Murphy's would be milder and less aggressive than Guinness. Even in tinned form, it remains an excellent beer, and at 4 per cent alcohol (it used to be lower) you can have another. If you like.

Colour: Blacker than sin itself, but in a good way.

Nose: Dark malt, the ashes of hurling sticks.

Palate: Dark chocolate and roasted barley, coffee and cream. Rich and smooth.

Finish: A kind of cereal milkiness, tinged with attractive bitterness.

Weihenstephaner Hefe Weissbier

It's a wheat beer, so expect that pale pungent scent and taste of cloves. It pours golden and clear and the pungency might be a little too much for some. Comes in half-litre (just under a pint) bottles, which I frankly find a bit much in this style of beer, so worth sharing with someone. A robust 5.4 per cent alcohol, you can drink it and think of St Corbinian's poor old donkey (see page 129). My part-time-brewer son believes that this is one of the best beers in the world.

Colour: That ginger beer paleness you'd expect from a Weissbier.

Nose: Crinkles the nostrils with ginger and spice.

Palate: Herbal semi-sourness and lemony zest on top of a lager dankness. Not for everyone.

Finish: A kind of thin bitterness.

Weltenburger Kloster Dunkle Weissbier

Another wheat beer but this time a dark chocolate-brown colour. I first tasted a Munich Dunkel in, unsurprisingly, Munich, and the idea of a dark, characterful and yet lager-style beer was completely bizarre to me, used to stouts, "heavies" and weak fizzy lagers.

Colour: Brown as an English ale, though it clearly isn't one.

Nose: It's sweet, with malt and syrup-of-figs notes. A malt loaf that's just been unwrapped.

Palate: And then you drink and it's a slightly odd combination of tangy cloves and citrus fruit.

Finish: Banana bread mixed with unsweetened cocoa.

Again, half a litre (just under a pint) may be too much unless you're both thirsty and in the mood for something quite demanding. Budweiser or Miller Lite this is not.

Tynt Meadow English Trappist Ale

Tynt Meadow is a joy.

Colour: It pours in a dark reddish-black with mahogany highlights, its head Guinness-solid and, well, beige.

Nose: Dark chocolate, fruit and licorice.

Palate: There's an odd mildness at first, but this is a really hefty Trappist ale at 7.4 per cent. You really know you've had a drink, and yet it's only 33cl (a little over half a pint) per bottle, which seems just right. There's cocoa and you could be drinking a stout – a Murphy's as described above. But you're not. It's a seriously full-on drinking experience, sweet and smooth and to be taken very much on its own terms. Can't think of any food I'd want to eat with Tynt Meadow. It is a meal in itself.

Finish: More, please. But limit yourself. This is very strong stuff.

CHAPTER 8
WELL, WELL, WELL

France and Scotland
Water

Holy Flight
– *Perrier*
– *Highland Spring*
– *Whatever comes out of your tap*

I used to drive past it every day, on my way from home in the Scottish Highland village of Cromarty to work in Inverness. Between the hamlet of Munlochy and the Tore Roundabout, where the Highlands' main transport artery, the A9, at last becomes duel carriageway for its long haul south, the edge of the forest looks like a grimy mess of rags, abandoned clothing, weather-bleached textiles. The trees are festooned with ribbons, streamers, baby clothes, adult garments, old bits of unidentifiable cloth.

This is the Clootie Well, one of many such healing springs scattered throughout the Celtic corners of the UK and Ireland. The pieces of cloth are offerings from those seeking healing, either for themselves or others, and the cloth should have been worn or at least been touched by the person requiring help.

The well itself, invisible from the road, is apparently dedicated to St Curetan or Boniface, a bishop of the area during the last days of the mysterious Picts. He was based in the nearby village of Rosemarkie – like many places on the enormous peninsula called the Black Isle, a place steeped in spookiness and superstition. Or maybe that's just me. I kept nearly crashing my car there, distracted by the bad vibes that affected the Ford Escort's steering.

Boniface allegedly came from Palestine and was a descendant of the sister of St Peter and St Andrew. He was supposedly ordained as a priest by the Patriarch of Jerusalem before travelling to Rome and becoming Pope, later resigning and moving to Pictland. As you do.

This part of the Highlands is heavy with New-Age bodhran-playing and woodland wicca, and a great deal of the customers St Boniface gets at the Clootie Well ("clootie" is old Scots for "cloth") are interested in spirits older and more varied than the one Boniface was dedicated to. Springs and wells have always had their mystical associations. The "wishing wells" you sometimes see in shopping malls, replete with coinage and made of plastic, are distant relations. And yet their continued custom proves there is a deep-seated demand for watery wishing.

As far back as the Iron Age, natural bodies of water were regarded as "thin places" – gateways where the natural and supernatural met, where you could penetrate the mysteries of Beyond. Gods dwelt there and were consequently worshipped, asked for help, given offerings. You can still find Iron Age artefacts in the less popular pools and lochans (small lochs or lakes) where such divine beings had their houses or crossover points.

In the 15th century the English chronicler William of Worcester recorded a "holy-hole, or well" in the famous cave at Wookey, in Somerset, England, which had been inhabited since the Palaeolithic era. There are many springs near Neolithic or Iron Age monuments, such as the Swallowhead Springs, near Silbury Hill in Wiltshire, England. As time passed, the reverence for the site continued, no matter who was occupying the land. Partly due to the Romans' obsession with cleanliness, water was a big part of their culture, with springs featuring heavily at temple complexes such as Bath. Once established, the watery tradition of god-haunting was deeply, ineradicably rooted, and as divinities changed, as fairies, elves, trolls and trowies (Scottish trolls) took their place, the wells remained places to encounter otherworldly beings, to seek guidance and succour. They were places of pilgrimage. They were magical.

The island of Unst is not just the most northerly in the Shetland Isles – and therefore Scotland – but it is also one of the most ... I was going to put "haunted". But perhaps it's better to say, as one local historian told me, that it's a place where the barriers between the past and the present, this life and the afterlife, the physical and the spiritual, are exceptionally thin.

Scotland is full of thin places.

If Shetland is remote, Unst can seem unearthly. Beyond the beyond. Far to the north, it's a place where there is little darkness in the summer or light in the winter. It is full of unexcavated tombs, lost churches, burial chambers and the sites of half-forgotten battles. It was where the Vikings first landed in their movement west, where Celtic monks came before their dangerous voyages to Scandinavia could begin.

And their stories. Hundreds of stories.

I could tell you about Madge Coutts, the witch; the Death Bird of Colvadale; the blood-soaked sacred earth of Swinna Ness. But we're talking about water here, and I want to recount something I heard first-hand from a man called Steven Spence, a renowned fiddle player. And I can vouch for the terror that can lurk in the winter darkness of Scotland's northernmost outpost – in the land of the White Wife.

I first encountered the White Wife in liquid form. There was once a delicious beer, brewed in Unst, called White Wife after the island's most famous, most often encountered ghost. And Steven Spence, who worked at the long-dead Valhalla Brewery, wrote a fiddle tune to celebrate its launch. He has met the White Wife.

One dark January night two or three decades ago, Steven was driving his van from Baltasound to Uyeasound. It was 9 o'clock in the evening, and he was coming down the Watlee Brae, near the Watlee Burn (a burn is a large stream or small river), where, perhaps not incidentally, a travelling merchant was murdered several hundred years ago.

Suddenly Steven glimpsed from the corner of his eye what he thought was a shaft of moonlight glittering on the passenger side of his van. And he noticed a terrible, foul smell. But that night there was no moon. And his van was as clean as a newly valeted vehicle could be. He looked around. And sitting in the passenger seat was an old woman. What he noticed, immediately, he told me, was her teeth, which were rotten. That was where the smell was coming from.

He says the sight gave him, as they say in Shetland, a "braa gluff", or a terrible fright. He had to steer the van around a bend in the road, so looked ahead for a moment, and when he turned around again, the White Wife had gone. Steven says that afterwards he was a bit nervous about driving near the Watlee Loch, but he soon got over it, wishing that the White Wife would once again appear to him. He'd like to hear her story, he says. But she has never again made an appearance to Steven. Maybe, he jokes, she didn't like him.

Several other people have met the Wife, always in the same way, appearing as a passenger in the front seat of a car driven by a single young man, always near the Watlee Bridge. Grotesque, yellow, foul-smelling teeth are commonly reported. These sightings continue today, and when I worked for a time in Unst, staying there overnight occasionally, I would often pass that bridge. Someone, as a joke, had painted a stone pillar next to it with a white face. The first time I saw that reflected in my headlights I nearly jumped out of my skin. But I looked at the passenger seat of my car and there was nobody there. Besides, I am no longer young. Nor am I single.

So, who was the White Wife? No one appears to know. But one suggestion – that she was somehow looking for her son – sent me back to the older stories about Unst, and the one about that merchant or pedlar who was murdered and thrown into the burn of Heljabrun, which flows into the Loch of Watlee. Ever since, that Loch and the burn itself have been reputed to possess healing powers, due to being seasoned with the dead man's remains. If you threw white money – silver – or three stones into the water, you would be healed, provided you then drank the water. Heljaburn, after all, means the burn of health.

An old woman looking for her son. Could the White Wife be the spirit of that ancient dead pedlar's mother, eternally checking for any young single man travelling the road he fatally trod so long ago?

If you're single, male and youthful, do you have the courage to come to Shetland, to Unst, and find out for yourself? Oh, and she has a preference for red cars and vans, apparently. Red – the colour of blood.

How did that ancient pedlar die? No one knows, but as he was murdered, you can imagine that his blood flowed red in the burn of Heljabrun, down into the Loch of Watlee. In Unst, that thinnest of thin places.

At first Christianity tried to eradicate these ancient myths, legends and pagan practices. "No one shall go to trees, or wells, or stones or enclosures, or anywhere else except to God's church, and there make vows or release himself from them," stated Theodoris in his Penitentials in the 7th century. And around AD 640, St Eligius ordered that "no Christian place lights at the temples or at the stones, or at fountains and springs, or at trees, or at places where three ways meet … Let no one presume to purify by sacrifice, or to enchant herbs, or to make flocks pass through a hollow tree or an aperture in the Earth; for by so doing he seems to consecrate them to the devil."[1]

Demolish the Kirk

Near my house in Shetland, in fact at the centre of the graveyard where my wife and I will eventually be buried, lie the ruins of a kirk (church) that was razed to the ground by its own minister in

---

[1]   The Penitentials of Theodoris, 7th century AD, http://www.orkneyjar.com/tradition/sacredwater/index.html

the 17th century. He was so angered by his parishioners' habits of laying votive offerings on May Day morning, washing their faces in the dew and generally digging deeper into the place's Pictish history than the stern old kirk, that he had the whole place demolished.

But not quite. The outline of the church still stands. And it's rumoured that people still go there at dawn on May Day to leave some silver and wash their faces in the dew, hoping for riches, or to beautify or refresh their skin.

Mostly, the church (albeit not every minister) acted tactically and absorbed as many pagan habits and traditions as it could without serious compromise. And so St Boniface took over that spring near Munlochy, and cloths or "cloots" started appearing on the nearby trees. Wells became holy wells.

Throughout Europe, Christianity walked if not on water, then certainly wherever it flowed. "Living Water" is a symbol much used in the Old and New Testaments, notably in Jeremiah 2:13 and 17:13, where the prophet describes God as "the spring of living water", who has been forsaken by his chosen people Israel; and in John 7:38: "Whoever believes in Me, as the Scripture hath said, out of his belly shall flow rivers of living water." Moreover, a spring was brought forth by the staff of Moses and then there was the Well of Beersheba, where both Abraham and Isaac dug wells and concluded peace treaties.

Holy wells remain part of the European and Middle Eastern landscape, though there are many fewer than there once would have been. Protestantism did away with a lot, as saints became, quite literally, anathema. The Reformation instigated by Henry VIII and his chancellor Thomas Cromwell saw not only monasteries but the often-adjacent springs and wells removed from at least official sanctification. However, some, like the Holy Well at Walsingham in Norfolk, England, which was once a crucial part of any pilgrimage to the village's shrine to the Virgin Mary, vanished completely.

The Walsingham Holy Well had Norman origins. In 1061 the Lady Richeldis de Faveraches, wife of a local lord, is said to have had a vision of the Virgin Mary, who transported the noblewoman to Christ's home in Nazareth and told her to build a copy at Walsingham. Angels were then involved in its construction, on a site identified by the sudden eruption of two clear streams of water. It was a place of pilgrimage from the start, and a priory was built there in the 1100s. Desiderius Erasmus, visiting in 1511, described it as "a shed, under which are two wells full to the brink; the water is wonderfully cold, and efficacious in curing pains in the head and stomach. They affirm that the spring suddenly burst from the earth at the command of the most holy Virgin".[2]

The priory was destroyed and the Walsingham well was lost until 1931 when it was found during rebuilding work; it has since reassumed its place in the pantheon of welldom. You are supposed to drink the water to achieve healing, but as a metal grille makes access impossible and its state of purity is these days unknown, this is now challenging to say the least. Yet pilgrims still come. And throughout the Victorian and Edwardian eras and into the 20th century, the idea of wells providing benefits grew ever more current.

Water was everywhere in the 19th- and early 20th-century world of inner and outer health; spas and thalassotherapy centres sprang up and many still flourish today. These, like the ones at Malvern and Strathpeffer, offered water with murky, often sulphurous natural content and were essentially secular. And yet you cannot visit a modern hotel spa, such as those found in any major town and city, without wondering about the religious symbolism of all those treatments, the plunge pools, the whirlpool tubs and the attendant gods and goddesses of massage, not to mention the beautifully laundered towelling robes. Suddenly, it's like a Roman or Greek *nymphaeum* or *nymphaion*, a kind of temple consecrated to the nymphs who inhabited the springs such buildings were erected upon.

There is a flourishing "holy well" movement even today, and much discussion and dissension about which particular wells

---

2   https://spartacus-educational.com/NORwalsinghamS.htm

may or may not have with gods, goddesses, saints and, for that matter, sinners. Water is one of those spiritual subjects that seems to get quite literally under people's skin.

A Little Dab'll Do You

Water in a contained form is common to most religions, part of the cleansing and purification rituals that, in using water's cleaning properties, offer symbolic preparation for human communication with the Divine. Only the pure in heart will see God, after all, but how do you wash your heart? When I was a wee boy, lurking awestruck in a fundamentalist Gospel Hall, I would try to work out how you could literally wash your heart free of sin when it was a physical organ lurking within your body, as told to me by teachers (and illustrated medical textbooks – never mind how I saw them). The idea that this was a thought process, an inner occurrence, took a long time to penetrate my metaphorical skull. And the symbolic nature of physical acts involving H_2O as reflecting spiritual renewal and rebirth, longer still. After all, that would very definitely *not* be an ecumenical matter.

The Christian and Jewish use of holy water in the Mass and other services or rituals has its origins in the Old Testament, originally in the application of water to deal with those (and their habitations) who were judged unclean after having been in the vicinity of a corpse. Numbers 19:18 says: "And a clean person shall take hyssop, and dip it in the water, and sprinkle it upon the tent, and upon all the vessels, and upon the persons that were there, and upon him that touched a bone, or one slain, or one dead, or a grave." This is the water of separation or expiation, but I love the Jerusalem Bible's translation of "lustral water". Lustral is a beautiful word referring to something used in a rite of purification, but containing elements of "lustre", which means it reflects light. And surely when we're talking about holy water, that's what we mean – it's water that separates, that cleanses – but that also reflects the light of the Divine.

How do you make water holy these days? Well, the blessing of a priest will do the job, and that happens within the Roman Catholic, Anglican and Orthodox traditions. It is used for blessing people, places and objects, and to cast out demons or get rid of evil. Water features in the Presbyterian and fundamentalist Evangelical traditions too, but it is not considered holy in and of itself. Which is just as well, as the tradition of baptism by immersion would require a very large amount of it and a consequent largesse of blessing.

Sprinkling someone with holy (or Presbyterian unholy) water is the main ritual of baptism, be it of a child or an adult, and signifies the washing away of sin and the separation of that person from evil and their past unregenerate life. It also symbolizes them being embraced by Christ and the family of Christ as a newly born and purified person, dying to sin and being raised again with Christ in new life.

The tradition I come from went for no-holds-barred full-immersion baptism, usually in a tank hidden most of the time beneath the public-speaking platform at the front of the Gospel Hall. I can still remember falling backward at the hands of a leading elder as I was baptized, aged 16, in the name of the Father, the Son and the Holy Spirit, wearing cricket whites. The girls wore white modesty robes which never, as I recall, quite succeeded in preserving the entirety of that modesty once soaked.

But the symbolism of that backward plunge – burial with Christ in death, rising again in resurrection – was simple and profound, though for me the post-baptismal feast with endless home bakes was the main thing to look forward to. You didn't feel any different, spiritually, whatever that was. But you did feel hungry, and then full, thanks to the generous baking of the church's womenfolk (men did not bake in those days, unless they were professionals). And afterwards you were able to join the church and take communion, eating that soft white bread and drinking that strong, fortified Old Tawny wine, Sunday after Sunday.

Later, when I was involved with charismatic house groups and at one point living in a community in an old manor house with several tongues-speaking families, I witnessed baptism in the icy depths of nearby Loch Lomond, the largest lake on the British mainland, and played the guitar to accompany this much more public display of regeneration. And later still, once I had abandoned Christianity, I attended a relative's baptism in a strange fundamentalist church where the baptismal tank was in the shape of a coffin, and the symbolic descent into watery death had overtones of Hammer horror movies or a piece of Manga film.

But as I say, that water wasn't holy. The people were blessed, not the liquid.

In churches where water is deemed sacred, pre-blessed water is usually kept in a font (as in fountain, but not as big) near the church's entrance, or sometimes in an area called a baptistry. People can dip their fingers in and bless themselves as they come into the church. Although this is done mostly in a cursory way, holy water was once considered extremely powerful, and the risk of it being stolen or syphoned off for unholy magical practices meant that many fonts were kept lidded and locked in the Middle Ages.

Infection Risk

In recent years the need to preserve religious congregations from infections has been highlighted by the Covid-19 pandemic, but the risks of open fonts and the possibility of death by holy water were first recognized in the 19th century. Tests at various churches throughout the world have over the years identified a host of contaminants that can and indeed have caused serious problems, including a patient with burns who was badly infected after being sprinkled with holy water. During the 2009 swine-flu epidemic in the USA, Bishop John Steinbock of Fresno, California recommended that "holy water should not be in the fonts"[3] for fear of spreading infections. And an automatic, motion-detecting holy water dispenser was installed in an Italian church.

During the Covid-19 pandemic, local solutions abounded. As an example, in my parents' hometown of Bellshill in Lanarkshire, the Sacred Heart Church, along with the chapel at pilgrimage site Carfin Grotto, installed contactless holy water dispensers, designed and made by a parishioner.

Paul Lawlor and his son, Chris, worked out a way of providing water without the need for anyone touching the container and built two prototypes in a shed. They donated one to the St Francis Xavier church in Carfin and one to the Sacred Heart in Bellshill.

This use of holy water and making a sign of the cross when entering a church reflects a renewal of baptism, a cleansing of venial sin, as well as providing protection against evil. Eastern Orthodox churches do not encourage this use of holy water on entrance, but drinking it, sometimes every morning, is common. There is normally a font near the entrance of a church so that worshippers can drink or take some home to consume later. We've already seen that in the Church of Jesus Christ of Latter-Day Saints (see page 85), water is used in place of communion wine.

Roman Catholic and High Anglican priests will take holy water into homes on various occasions to bless individuals and families. And of course, holy water is available to buy, not just in monastery shops, but online. As I write, Amazon in the UK offers a "Cross My Heart 7cm 40ml Holy Water From Lourdes Grotto, Plastic Bottle Blue Lid, LOURDES Prayer Card and Medal and a 2cm Pewter Love Token Brooch" for £8.99 ($11.79). Although, in fact, the water at Lourdes, as with other holy springs thought to have healing qualities akin to the Clootie Well at Munlochy, is not necessarily holy unless it has been blessed by a priest. There is no indication in the Amazon

---

3   https://www.catholicdoors.com/faq/1500/qu1608.htm

listing that this has happened, but one five-star review states that the recipient "felt better for the use of this".

In other world religions, water's role is crucial. The Golden Temple at Amritsar in the Punjab, India is one of Sikhism's holiest sites and the water surrounding it is believed by many to have healing powers. The ritual cleaning on entrance will feel familiar to anyone who has entered a Gurdwara or temple anywhere in the world. In Hinduism, water represents God, and immersion in the holy Ganges River is, like Christian baptism, a symbol of sin being washed away. The (now illegal) placing of human ashes in the river is thought to hasten salvation and improve karma.

And in Buddhism, my old friend lustral water makes an appearance, offering protection when used within the Theravada tradition during a Paritrana ceremony and is later given to people to take home. Shia Islam also has a tradition of holy water from springs, which can provide healing to those who drink it.

In the Wicca tradition, salt is blessed and stirred into a bowl of water that has also been purified. Some say that this represents the womb of the Goddess, and the source of all life on Earth. The mixture of salt is consecrated and used in many ceremonies and rituals of magic. It also reflects the use of salt in the Anglican and Roman Catholic traditions as an addition to Holy Water, or indeed on its own as a barrier or preventative when dealing with evil.

Of course, as we all know from a multitude of movies, holy water is or can be used as a weapon against vampires and other nasty, hellish creatures, not always with total success. In fact, it's mostly in the movies that holy water is used against the undead. On the ground in Eastern Europe, crucifixes were thought to be more effective. Along with sharpened stakes.

Back at the Clootie Well, I'm remembering an afternoon I spent there in 1988, interviewing a man called Malcolm Dent for a TV documentary about rock music and religion. Malcolm – effusive, funny and sadly no longer with us – was a childhood friend of Led Zeppelin guitarist Jimmy Page, and Malcolm became the resident caretaker (accompanied by his family) at the musician's Highland retreat, Boleskine House in Foyers on the shores of Loch Ness.

The Great Beast

Once owned by legendary purveyor of things magical and founder of the esoteric religion called Thelema, Aleister Crowley, Boleskine's reputation as a place where very strange things happen continues to this day, despite its destruction in a mysterious fire. It is now owned by a foundation that is working to restore the building and has links with the modern Thelema movement. The place retains an international reputation for occult goings-on and among other fundraising activities, its current owners are selling stones from its burned ruins to fund the restoration, along with "a limited, small quantity of Abramelin oil-scented candles", described as being "special to Boleskine House, being the incense described in the early modern magical grimoire *The Book of the Sacred Magic of Abramelin the Mage*.[4] It was this text that inspired Aleister Crowley to conduct a mysterious ceremonial rite at Boleskine House in 1899 to achieve the mystical state of knowledge and conversation with the holy guardian angel."[5] The nearness of water and the essential presence of river sand was part of the magical package, necessary for rites to take place successfully.

Crowley was just 25 when he bought Boleskine in 1899, after searching for the perfect location for a series of rituals from the 14th-century magical manual mentioned above, the *Book of Abramelin*, so central to the Thelema beliefs. He needed a secluded house with a door that opened to the north and a terrace covered in river dust. The idea was to summon demons but keep them outside the house itself. The area around Boleskine – wooded, steeped in local tragedy, and

---

[4] https://www.boleskinehouse.org/product/boleskine-house-abramelin-candle/

[5] Crowley's definition of "the holy guardian angel" changed throughout this life but is generally thought to be a representation of what he called initially "the silent self" or the human unconsciousness.

with all the myths and legends of Loch Ness to boot – has an atmosphere some find troubling, and which undoubtedly attracts occultist tourism.

Malcolm and I talked under the trees at the Clootie Well, surrounded by symbols of belief, need and hope. It was a strange experience, listening to him describe his – generally happy – time at Boleskine with his wife and family. By and large sceptical about occult goings on, he explained that there were nevertheless some things that happened during their time there that he found inexplicable.

Doors would slam all night. "You'd go into a room and carpets and rugs would be piled up." The doors in the house would suddenly spring open, even on calm days or nights, as if someone was running through the house. "We just used to say that it was Aleister doing his thing," Malcom said.

Chairs switching places, friends claiming they'd been attacked by devils and a sense "of pure evil" accompanied by the snorting of an invisible wild animal – none of this deterred Malcolm and his wife from staying at Boleskine and raising their family there. It remains to be seen what will happen at Boleskine now, but you can arrange to visit and, as I say, buy a little bit of burned Boleskine for yourself. Perhaps you could follow Aleister Crowley in one of the many treats he meted out to gullible visitors. These included a "wild haggis hunt". Crowley's capacity for practical jokes may have been underestimated.

Later, after interviewing Malcolm, I travelled north to the Saint Duthac Hotel in Tain, and there, steeped in Glenmorangie, as live music played and a roaring fire heated the ancient bar, I learned of this Highland town's crucial importance in the world of religion.

In August 1513, King James IV of Scotland was preparing for war with England and feeling the pressure of impending bloodshed. He possibly sensed his own doom, as the following month he would be killed, along with the elite of Scotland's army, at the Battle of Flodden. However, he did manage one final pilgrimage, and that was to Tain to the shrine of St Duthac.

It was his favourite shrine and one he had visited many times during his reign.

They were holidays as well as spiritual exercises, these pilgrimages. The king played cards for high stakes, was entertained at most of his overnight stops by musicians, took part in falconry and had young women who came to dance for him, if they did nothing else. There were harpists and organists in his retinue. And when the king and his followers arrived in Tain, they partied, and then pleaded with St Duthac for wisdom, for health, for life. St Duthac was, after all, an 11th-century monk, probably from Ireland, who was buried at Tain despite his body having failed to rot. A fate, alas, King James did not share.

But that night in the St Duthac, as we mourned the loss of our host Jimmy's father and listened to a local band playing, we drank Glenmorangie whisky, made legendarily by "the 16 Men of Tain". We went to bed late. Next morning there was to be a funeral and a trip to another sacred source.

When I think of my own trips to holy wells, there is one that springs powerfully and immediately to mind. It is mostly in the advertising material associated with Glenmorangie whisky that it is referred to as sacred – the history is a bit hazy, unlike the water that flows from it.

It's not really a well, though I have to say that the extraordinarily beautiful Tarlogie Spring, above Tain in Ross-shire, Scotland, does appear truly miraculous, bubbling from the rock with a glorious crystalline purity that somehow tastes unlike any other water. It is the one and only source of the water that magically becomes Glenmorangie whisky, and with a film crew, I spent an afternoon there talking, sipping and enjoying the wonderful location with the distillery management. And yes, more than one bottle of the wonderful distillate that comes from "the Glen of Tranquillity" was opened that day, though it's only fair to admit that for many years the tranquil glen's next-door neighbour was a much-used RAF bombing range.

Happily, there were no bombing raids on the day we sipped whisky, diluted with the water that was its original source. It felt transformational. It felt like magic. It felt like healing.

Holy Flight – Tasting Notes
— *Perrier*
— *Highland Spring*
— *Whatever comes out of your tap (faucet), if it's safe to drink*

Colour? Nose? Palate? I'm not going to classify these three waters (one of which will vary massively depending on the state of your supply) in such a way. With fizzy water, it's all about the bubbles really, despite the supposed chemical differences and mineral content. Perrier's are smaller than Highland Spring's.

In recent years there has been a backlash against the obsessive mineralization of personal water consumption, at least in the wealthy West. Remember when people bought plastic bottles of Perrier or Highland Spring from a machine in the gym? Now you have your own aluminium water bottle and you fill it from your tap. Assuming you live in a country or city where the water supply is safe and pleasant to drink.

When our family first went to France on holiday, we children were warned that if we drank water from a tap, we would surely die a horrid and slow death. So, we drank Vichy and other local mineral waters (we were in a caravan, five of us) and lo, some of it tasted of rotten eggs. This, we were told, was good for us. The idea that drinking "natural" water from underground springs, water that picks up more mineral salts than the stuff you're supplied with by your local council, has its appeal. There may well be good medical reasons for consuming the stuff that comes out of a hole in the wall at Strathpeffer, though I have tried it once and will not be doing so again.

Also, there's fizziness. That can be nice. Perrier is naturally carbonated (though the process is complex: The Vergèze spring that Perrier comes from is indeed naturally carbonated, but the water and carbon dioxide gas are separated, with the water then being purified and the carbonation being re-inserted during bottling. Naturally. Or unnaturally, if you prefer. Most but not all other sparkling "mineral" waters have bubbles pumped in from giant tame dragons. Or possibly cylinders of gas.

The two commercial mineral waters above provide contrasting styles and provenances. If you are really keen to match, for example, whisky with the water from which it was distilled, there are ways of doing this, notably using one table that compares the alkalinity of various proprietary Scottish waters, whisky region by whisky region. You will find it on the Alcademics site.[6]

What I would say is this: if your tap water provider is reliable, and your H_2O safe, drink it. Use it. You are privileged, compared to those in many parts of the world where water, which should be a staple, readily available life-saving commodity, is either polluted or dangerously scarce. If you're concerned that there's a whiff of chlorine from your tap (faucet), pour it into a jug and leave it out or open in your refrigerator. The smell will disappear. It may be replaced by whatever else your fridge smells off, admittedly (garlic, Camembert cheese, rotting prunes), but that is a matter for you and your household.

---

[6]   https://www.alcademics.com/2013/08/bottled-waters-most-resembling-waters-of-scotland.html

CHAPTER 9

HOLY DRINKING IN THE AMERICAS

USA, Mexico, Canada, South America
Tequila, Mezcal, whiskey and wine

Holy Flight
– *Jose Cuervo Especial Gold*
– *Evan Williams Kentucky Straight Bourbon Whiskey*
– *Elijah Craig Kentucky Straight Bourbon Whiskey*
– *Heaven Hill Corn Whiskey 9-Year-Old (That Boutique-y Whisky Company)*

My experience of drinking in the United States of America has been, for the most part, distinctly secular, though my journeys into and across the southern states have occasionally seen encounters with laws on alcohol consumption that can seem obscure. Dry counties, desiccated townships, bars that frown on the sale of whiskey before dark. And locations such as the one celebrated – perhaps that's not quite the right word – by the B-52s on their album *Cosmic Thing* usually have their dryness associated with strong fundamentalist Protestantism, or so a study from 2018 called "Breaking Bad in Bourbon Country: Does Alcohol Prohibition Encourage Methamphetamine Production?" concluded.[1] In Alaska,

1   Jose Fernandez, Stephan Gohmann, Joshua C Pinkston (April 2018), *Southern Economic Journal.* 84 (4): 1001–23. doi:10.1002/soej.12262

concerns over alcohol abuse have led to the prohibition of drink sales in some areas.

Then, of course, there's Utah, with its local ordinances based on the teachings of the Church of Jesus Christ of Latter-Day Saints. There are maximum levels in most parts of the state dictated for cocktails and mixed drinks, among other restrictions that affect not just LDS members, but everyone. However, as we have already seen, Brigham Young and many of the early LDS settlers in Utah were, if not heavy drinkers, then convinced winemakers and brewers who recognized the economic power of alcohol. The church's theology and practice changed over the years to account for the social problems caused by drink and the power of the prohibition movement.

Prohibition – that potent word. The introduction of the Volstead Act in 1920, prohibiting the sale of alcoholic beverages across the nation was fuelled initially by the Christian temperance movement, which was largely Protestant in origin, but it was taken up by progressive elements of all the political parties and aimed to tackle domestic abuse, political corruption and widespread drunkenness. Until 1933, alcohol for pubic consumption was in the hands of criminal elements, with one exception: the Church. Federal legislation opened up an exemption for the production and legal consumption of communion wine.

This led to some extreme vinicultural creativity in California's Napa Valley. Georges Latour, as you would guess from his name, was a French immigrant who began producing wine aimed at the Catholic communion market. A friend of the Archbishop of San Francisco, his wine was soon given a divine stamp of approval – it was to be the only permissible eucharistic product used in the diocese. George Okrent, in his book *Last Call: The Rise and Fall of Prohibition*, writes that Latour tended to look away when his wine was poured into secular glasses. "When a priest took receipt of an order for, say, 120 gallons of Beaulieu (a not uncommon amount), he suddenly had an inventory of 46,000 communion sips, more or less – or perhaps, 10,000 communion sips, with nearly a hundred gallons set aside for members of the congregation. Sometimes the wine didn't even leave the rectory. In 1932, six cases of Beaulieu's best were shipped to Chicago expressly for the use of Cardinal George Mundelein."[2]

It's thought that there was a 700 per cent increase in wine production solely for the Roman Catholic Church during Prohibition. But other faiths benefitted too, and with less need for senior authorities to become involved.

George Latour also produced kosher wine. No need for archbishops to give permission for priests to order it. Any rabbi could order wine for any member of their congregation. Synagogue attendance increased markedly, as did membership, and even the dead somehow became official recipients of alcoholic liquid resurrection. They were convenient names on a list of acknowledged worshippers. The faithful departed. There were rabbis who dealt in sacramental champagne, sacramental crème de menthe, sacramental brandy and various other liquors utterly unconnected to any aspect of Jewish religious practice.

And as the USA's First Amendment blocked most investigations if religious exemption came into play, "any man who dressed in solemn black, possessed a Jewish cast of countenance and wore a beard was automatically a rabbi."[3] The semi-legal libations flowed.

Eventually, as we know from countless films and books, the violence and disorder produced by criminal efforts to circumvent Prohibition led to a shift in public opinion, and the Volstead Act was repealed. No longer was rabbinical or priestly privilege necessary if you fancied a bottle of Napa Burgundy or holy crème de menthe with your dinner.

Prohibition is sometimes seen as the inevitable outcome of settlers from Europe who brought their extreme evangelical

---

[2]   Okrent, George, *Last Call: The Rise and Fall of Prohibition*, Scribner's, New York, 2011

[3]   Ibid.

Protestantism with them, but the truth is that those Pilgrim fathers, often portrayed as stern and starchy, teetotal Puritans, arrived in North American with brandy, port and all the skills necessary to brew beer and make wine. The tavern was just as important a part of early settlements as the church, and often close by. Then of course there was my namesake, the so-called Lord of Misrule, Thomas Morton. But we'll get to him in due course.

It's important, when discussing alcohol in North and South America, to realize that Native Americans – first in the Aztec and Mayan cultures of South America, but spreading north to what is now the south-western USA – had a long culture of producing fermented drinks and using them in religious ceremonies. This historical association has since become something of a marketing tool for modern drinks producers. One recent example is sotol, now mostly sold as a distilled spirit but originating around 800 years ago as a beer-like drink made from fermenting the sotol plant, a cousin of asparagus that grows well in desert regions. The Raramuri people from the Chihuahua region of northern Mexico are generally regarded as its originators. Then in the 16th century, Spanish colonists introduced distillation techniques and produced a spirit. In a similar way, pulque, brewed from the sap of the agave cactus, was an indigenous drink that European distillation techniques transformed into mezcal and tequila (mezcal can be made from any type of agave, tequila only from the blue variety).

There are some archaeological suggestions that Native Americans may have had their own, pre-European-invasion distillation technology, but the spirits we know today as mezcal, tequila and sotol were produced as a result of the Spanish determination to use their technology, blended with traditional Mexican fermented drinks and local ingredients, to make identifiably "local" spirits and corner local markets.

Sotol Raramuri is a trade name, a company based in Juarez that produces distilled sotol and markets it heavily in the USA and elsewhere. There has been controversy over its use of indigenous Mexican and Native American imagery in the brand's social media advertising. One ad shows a woman with a primitively painted face, the sun rising behind her. "*Sagrado Espíritu, sagrada tierra*" – Sacred Spirit, sacred earth, reads part of the associated caption. And if you delve into the marketing campaigns of mezcal and tequila, you will quickly come across Mayahuel, the Aztec goddess of agave and fertility. Historically, she is closely associated with pulque, appearing in various pre-Columbian texts that depict her as an agave plant with 400 breasts filled with pulque. Mayahuel is often touted as "the goddess of tequila".

And so tequila, mezcal and sotol have been represented as aiding and abetting or being a crucial part of ancient Mexican spiritual practice. The truth is that genuinely indigenous drinks like pulque, tepache (made from pineapples) and tejuino (corn) are more likely to have had ceremonial uses.

Henry J Bruman, in his book *Alcohol in Ancient Mexico*, describes various drinks made from mesquite pods, honey and tree bark, as well as corn, pineapple, cactus and asparagus. He identifies pulque as considered sacred, drunk primarily by the elderly, by mothers who were breastfeeding and by the elite of society during festivals and religious ceremonies. It was only in the 17th and 18th centuries that colonists began experimenting with the distillation of what were seen by Europeans as inferior drinks – and, in the case of pulque, was associated with ceremony and ritual – which gave them the potential to fuel social unrest and rebellion against the Spanish overlords. Mezcal and tequila became inextricably linked with the *hacienda* agricultural system of colonial control and industrialization. Pulque fell from favour because it was prone to going off and was thus difficult to transport. And then, as beer became more and more popular and the exporting of mezcal and tequila more profitable, its religious and social significance withered away. Only the advertising copywriters still worshipped at the 400 breasts of Mayahuel.

The Tavern and the Chapel

But what of North America and indigenous drinks in the more temperate zones of the continent? As in any agricultural society, the discovery that rotting fruit or corn could produce mind-altering substances was important, but crucially alcohol was restricted mainly to religious ceremonies and celebrations. It was too powerful to be applied merely as a social lubricant. It's thought that the Creek of Georgia and the Cherokee of the Carolinas fermented fruit and it's possible that the Huron of south-eastern Canada and later north-eastern America made a mild beer to be consumed at tribal feasts. The Kwakiutl of Vancouver Island produced a mildly alcoholic drink using elderberry juice, black chitons and tobacco. So, there was ritualized drinking. And then the Europeans arrived. And, oh, how they drank. They worshipped in their own particular ways on the run from repressive governments on the other side of the Atlantic. If alcohol was not an intrinsic part of their worship, it walked hand in hand with it, and often waltzed drunkenly from tavern to kirk and back again.

In John Hull Brown's book *Early American Beverages*, he argues "the two basic social institutions of Colonial America were the church and the tavern",[4] which he admits "may seem shocking ... and not at all in harmony with contemporary views of the daily life of the Puritans." However, the records do not lie. Worship and quaffing booze went together like Calvin and Predestination for the Pilgrim Fathers.

These taverns or "ordinaries" were not simply pubs. There was an obligation on local settlements to provide lodging houses that also served basic food and drink, and in some cases the drink outweighed everything else. In others, strict licensing by church-weighted authorities meant that clients were limited to two drinks a day and there were restrictions on "immoral" activities such as dancing, singing and playing games. Other communities were much more liberal, and the

---

[4]   Hull Brown, John, *Early American Beverages*, Bonanza Books, New York, 1966

ordinary was a place where the strictures of the Church could be balanced by the relaxed, letting-your-hair-down vibe of the tavern. The ordinaries did not simply pop up at the same time as meeting houses and churches but were often licensed on the condition that they were built close together. In 1651, a Boston landlord was given permission to operate a house of "common entertainment" on the condition that "he keeps it near the new meeting-house."[5]

Sometimes it wasn't just the clientele that was interchangeable. In Cambridge, Massachusetts, the keeper of the first licensed "house of entertainment" was a deacon of the church and later Steward of Harvard College. And buildings could have multiple uses. Governor Winthrop's official residence, the "Great House" in Charlestown, Massachusetts, became a meeting house in 1633 and then a tavern called the Three Cranes. It was here that the seeds of American prohibition were sown, because the first temperance vow had been taken in the building by Governor Winthrop. He "upon consideration of the inconveniences which had grown in England by drinking one to another, restrained it at his own table and wished others to do the like; so it grew, little by little, into disuse."[6] This was the habit of toasting. Actual drinking, moderate or not, probably continued.

And if there wasn't a church, the tavern would do as a place of worship. In Providence, Rhode Island and Fitchburg, Massachusetts it's on record that the tavern served as a meeting house prior to a separate building being erected. Also, elders and deacons would often meet in the tavern to thrash out matters of church discipline, and that crucial aspect of worship – seating arrangements.

It's no surprise that some were drawn more to the pleasures of the public house than filled with desire for the spiritual benefits of the church. And when war came, soldiers definitely

---

[5]   Earle, Alice Morse, *Stage-Coach and Tavern Days*, Macmillan and Co., London, 1900

[6]   Hull Brown, John, *Early American Beverages*, Bonanza Books, New York, 1966

had their preferences. In *Lives of the Signers to the Declaration of Independence*, by Benson John Lossing,[7] Charles Augustus Goodrich quotes Benjamin Franklin's conversation with the Rev Charles Beatty, acting chaplain to his army of 500 volunteers engaged in battling the French and indigenous people. The men were reluctant to attend Rev Beatty's services:

> "Dr Beatty complained to me that the men did not generally attend his prayers and exhortations. When they were enlisted, they were promised, besides hay and provisions, a gill of rum a day, which was punctually served out to them, half in the morning, and the other half in the evening, and I observed they were as punctual in attending to receive it; upon which I said to Mr Beatty, 'it is perhaps below the dignity of your profession to act as steward of the rum, but if you were to deal it out, and only just after prayers, you would have them all about you.'"

It is not recorded whether or not the Rev Beatty took Franklin's advice.

Conditions in the early meeting houses were often bitterly cold, and sermons could be very long. It's no wonder that some parishioners, finding themselves warm both internally and externally in the comfort of a tavern, were reluctant to trudge through ice, snow or mud to the cold and forbidding church. A law was eventually passed in Massachusetts forcing tavern keepers to stop serving while a service was taking place. And tavern keepers were expected to carry out their trade responsibly. There were tavern inspectors whose job it was to enforce the rules, and sometimes they seemed to do so to their own benefit. In the Plymouth community of Duxbury the landlord was found to be getting high too much on his own supply and he was summarily replaced by a Mr Seabury, a tavern inspector. He

---

[7]   Lossing, Benson John, *Lives of the Signers to the Declaration of Independence*, Tales End Press (ebooks), 2011 (reprint)

was appointed in 1678 "to sell liquors unto such sober-minded neighbours as her shall think meets; she as her sell not lease than the quantity of a gallon at a time to one son, and not in smaller quantities by retail to the occasioning of drunkenness."[8]

Another Tom Morton

The drinks sold in these early colonial hostelries would be locally brewed beer, imported wine (often fortified) and the occasional spirit brought over in barrels from Europe. It's obvious that civil authorities exercized control under church and that they expected moderate consumption and good behaviour. Equally, it's clear that sometimes, things could get out of hand. And nobody personifies this more than Thomas Morton. Or as I prefer to think of him, Great-Great-Great-Great-Great-Great Grandpa Tom.

As far as I know, I am not in fact related by blood to Thomas Morton, lawyer, would-be settler and land grabber, Maypole-dancer, arms dealer, libertine, rebel, chancer and "Lord of Misrule", as he was described in 1628 by William Bradford, Governor of the Plymouth Colony, which is a matter of some regret, as he is by some distance the most fascinating, funny and downright shady of the early settlers. It was no wonder that he annoyed the local Puritans so much they moved heaven, earth and every aspect of the law they could muster to get rid of him, shut him up or, at the very least, stop him talking and writing. He is the antithesis of a Puritan: a dodgy, colourful, sometimes apparently deranged figure whose own personal colony of Merrymount stands like a beacon of neopagan licentiousness amid the tightly controlled world of tavern and meeting house. He was also keen on fraternizing with the local natives, trading with them, learning from them and indeed selling them guns. No wonder he terrified the living daylights out of some of his colonial neighbours.

---

[8]   Earle, Alice Morse, *Stage-Coach and Tavern Days*, Dabney Press, Washington DC, 2007 (originally published 1900).

Thomas Morton was born in southwest England into Devon gentry in 1579. His family were landowners and high Anglicans, at the time when Devon was a remote corner of the land if not immune to Protestant reform, then perhaps contemptuous of it. Devon was different, and the kind of Anglo-Catholic worship there also incorporated many aspects of popular folk culture that seemed to many reformers too close to paganism.

Morton's life in England is shadowy and combines what were clearly important social and political connections with a populist, crusading zeal for the rights of the underdog, along with an affection for bad behaviour of all types involving drink and women, and an attitude to litigation that seems at best mischievous and at worst nefarious. He studied law at London's Clifford's Inn, and the hard-living culture of the Inns of Court was very much to his taste. He mixed with the likes of Frances Bacon and William Shakespeare, and the playwright Ben Jonson became a lifelong friend. Despite his Royalist beliefs, he was a strong defender of the principals of common law against the centralizing influence of the Crown. His early legal career involved working in defence of displaced Devon workers, but the crucial business connection of his life was with the colonial entrepreneur Ferdinando Gorges, an associate of Sir Walter Raleigh who had been part of a conspiracy against Queen Elizabeth I with the Earl of Essex. Gorges was heavily involved in the colonial project in New England and would eventually found the colony of Maine.

Morton's marriage to Alice Miller, a relationship which reeks of economic ambition, became embroiled in complex and endless legal wrangling over her father's inheritance, and extremely difficult relationships with her ultra-Puritan son George, involving assaults, beatings and worse. All the time Morton's attentions and ambitious were turning westward. But as this High Anglican with somewhat loose morals and an affection for pagan practices set sail, the violent Puritanism of his stepson may have coloured his attitude toward what awaited him on the other side of the Atlantic.

Backed by Gorges, Morton left his legal hassles in England and headed to America in 1622 for a three-month visit. He returned complaining that he had received an unfriendly and intolerant reception by the Puritan communities. He and Gorges convinced the King, Charles I, that they could succeed in trading with the native tribes and in 1624 Morton left England aboard the ship *Unity* with one Captain Wollaston and 30 indentured servants. Settling on a stretch of coast formerly occupied by the Algonquins – now Quincy, Massachusetts – Morton began dealing with the tribe, selling them guns and alcohol in exchange for furs, food and, crucially, knowledge. Although the weapons were used by the Algonquins against other Native Americans, the Puritan settlers at Plymouth were enraged and frightened. Morton and Wollaston's tiny trading post was successful and expanded into a fully-functioning colony known initially as Mount Wollaston.

Morton's instinct to defend the underdog kicked in when he discovered that Wollaston had been selling indentured servants into slavery on the Virginian tobacco plantations. He encouraged the servants who were left to rebel with him against Wollaston, who fled to Virginia, leaving Morton in total, fairly benevolent control. Morton then renamed the colony Merrymount, declared the indentured servants free men and encouraged co-operation, sexual relationships and economic integration with the local Algonquins, although Morton retained his folk-religion ideal of Devon rural Anglicanism as a set of beliefs he hoped the local tribes could eventually convert to.

Needless to say, the nearby Puritans of Plymouth were aghast. Morton had gone native, the colonists decided, and anyway he was pretty much a heathen to start with. There were rumours of debauchery, including sexual liaisons with native women during drunken orgies in honour of Bacchus and Aphrodite. Governor William Bradford wrote in his history *Of Plymouth Plantation*:

"They … set up a May-pole, drinking and dancing about
it many days together, inviting the Indian women for
their consorts, dancing and frisking together (like so
many fairies, or furies rather) and worse practices. As
if they had anew revived & celebrated the feasts of ye
Roman Goddess Flora, or ye beastly practices of ye mad
Bacchanalians."

It was all a long way from two-drinks-only per day at the
official tavern.

Morton was a man of the West Country, fascinated by his
native county's rural customs such as the rituals and celebrations
that took place on May Day and, being an intellectual of decidedly
libertine and romantic bent, combined the lot with alcohol, the
energy of his freed servants and, to be blunt, their need to find
sexual partners. So, the local tribes were invited to participate in
that infamous Maypole dancing episode. Drink flowed, having
been brewed on the spot. Morton himself described the events
in his three-volume history, polemic and propaganda book, *A
New English Canaan*, published in Amsterdam in 1637 and
promptly banned by the colonists in America – the first book to
be banned in the nascent United States.

The settlers "brewed a barrell of excellent beer, and provided
a case of bottles to be spent, with other good cheer, for all
comers of that day." There was a Maypole, guns, drums, pistols
"and other fitting instruments". The natives arrived to help and
participate. A very good time was duly had by … not quite all.
Some were less than happy. Those "separatists":

"The setting up of this Maypole was a lamentable
spectacle to the precise separatists: that lived at new
Plymouth. They termed it an Idoll; yea they called it
the Calf of Horeb: and stood at defiance with the place,
naming it Mount Dagon; threatening to make it a
woefull mount and not a merry mount …"

And there was singing. Lots of drinking and lots of singing:

> "There was likewise a merry song made, which (to make
> their Revells more fashionable) was sung with a chorus …
> which they performed in a dance, hand in hand about
> the Maypole, whiles one of the Company sung, and filled
> out the good liquor like Gammedes and Jupiter …"

This song I think reveals the sexual nature of what was going on
around the Maypole, which is a traditional symbol of fertility.
Hymen is the Greek god of marriage, feasting and fertility, and
there is no doubt that there was a great deal of inebriated sexual
congress if not around the Maypole of Merrymount, then in the
shadows and woods nearby. Incidentally, the location nowadays
in Quincy is a semi-industrial site near a Dunkin' Donuts.

> "Drinke and be merry, merry, merry boyes,
> Let all your delight be in Hymens joyes,
> Iô to Hymen now the day is come,
> About the merry Maypole take a Roome.
>
> Make greene garlands, bring bottles out;
> And fill sweet Nectar, freely about,
> Uncover thy head, and feare no harm,
> For hers good liquor to keepe it warme.
>
> Nectar is a thing assign'd,
> By the Deities owne minde,
> To cure the hart opprest with grief,
> And of good liquors is the chief,
>
> Give to the Mellancolly man,
> A cup or two of't now and than;
> This physick' will soone revive his bloud,
> And make him be of a merrier mood.

Give to the Nymphe thats free from scorne,
No Irish; stuff nor Scotch over worn,
Lasses in beaver coats come away,
Ye shall be welcome to us night and day."

This all happened in 1628. The Maypole was topped with deer antlers, just to make an explicitly pagan point, and it was all too much for the Puritans next door in Plymouth. A group of militiamen attacked the town, cut down the Maypole and arrested Morton for "supplying guns to the Indians". He was put in the stocks at Plymouth, brought to trial, and would undoubtedly have been executed for blasphemy had there not been much nervousness about his royal connections. So, he was marooned off the New Hampshire coast on a deserted island, presumably in the hope that he would die of starvation, but officially until an English ship arrived and could take him home. However, Morton's friendship with the local native tribes stood him in good stead and he was supplied with food by helpful and utterly bemused natives. He gained enough strength to organize his own escape back to England.

In retaliation for all the heathen goings-on at Merrymount, the Plymouth colonists renamed the place Mount Dagon, from 1 Samuel 5:2–7, which tells how the Ark of the Covenant was captured by the Philistines and taken to Dagon's temple in Ashdod. Next day the stone idol of Dagon was found lying prostrate before the Ark. It was rescued and re-erected, but the day after that it was again found prostrate before the Ark, this time with head and hands severed. The meaning was clear: Plymouth was the true home of the One God. Drinking and dancing and having sex around a Maypole, not to mention fraternizing with the locals, was always going to end in tears.

For the sake of balance and fairness (after all, I used to work for the BBC), I should probably give another account of the goings-on at Merrymount. Let the Puritans speak! William Bradford had come to America aboard the *Mayflower* and was the diametrical opposite of Morton: a hardline Puritan activist, unwilling to give native Americans an inch, let alone gunpowder, weapons and alcohol. And probably worse, he was from Yorkshire, almost the other end of England from Morton's southwestern outpost of Devon. He was also Governor of the Plymouth colony. Just as Morton wrote his epic justification in *A New English Canaan*, Bradford published what is still seen as the most authoritative account of the Pilgrim Fathers' journey from persecution in England through Holland to their early colonies in America. It is called *Of Plymouth Plantation* and was written between 1630 and 1651. His sheer loathing of Morton and everything he stood for simply reeks from his prose. Morton had arrived with Captain Wollaston, "but had little respect among them and was slighted by the meanest servants." Wollaston had headed off to Virginia, and while he was away, Morton had run riot, aided by alcohol, conspiring to get rid of Wollaston's man, Lieutenant Fitcher:

> "But this Morton … got some strong drink and other junkets, and made them a feast; and after they were merry, he began to tell them he would give them good counsel (which was) … easily received, so they took opportunity and thrust Lieutenant Fitcher out of doors and would suffer him to come no more among them …"

After this "they fell to great licentiousness and led a dissolute life, pouring out themselves into all profaneness. And Morton became lord of misrule and maintained (as it were) a school of atheism." They drank in vast quantities, they traded with the natives, began dancing around the famed Maypole, consorted with the native women and generally behaved in a cavalier, certainly less than Puritan fashion. Morton's misrule – as it was seen – had to end.

Lacking their leader, or host as he preferred to be called, Merrymount survived as a community for another year, despite its renaming after the broken idol of the Philistines. During a severe famine in winter 1629, as baldly described by Bradford, residents of New Salem led by John Endecott raided "Mount Dagon" for its corn supplies and destroyed what was left of the Maypole, denouncing it as a pagan idol and calling it the "Calf of Horeb". Morton returned to his former utopia soon afterwards, but most of his followers had scattered across the countryside. He was arrested, again put on trial and banished. The following year what had been the flourishing colony of Merrymount was burned to the ground and Morton sent home to England.

Back in England, Morton was briefly jailed but with the support of his mentor Gorges and, with the help of King Charles I, who was now seriously threatened by the mounting power of the Puritans at home and abroad, took legal action against the Massachusetts Bay Company, the power behind the Puritans' godly throne. He was heavily backed by the economic and political enemies of Puritanism and the company's charter was revoked in 1635. In 1637, Morton's magnum opus, *A New English Canaan*, was published, and in 1642 he prepared for a triumphant return to America, with his associate Gorges declared governor of the east coast colonies. There was a snag, however. The English Civil War had broken out, and the stage was set for the eventual dissolution of the English monarchy and the triumph of Puritan power at home and abroad. Gorges, always one to sense which way the wind was blowing, decided not to go to America to claim his governorship, which was already under threat from the colonists there. Fatefully, Morton crossed the Atlantic alone, to represent Gorges in Maine.

He was arrested in Plymouth and put on trial for sedition. The locals were having none of the King's appointment of Gorges; Morton was accused of being a Royalist agitator and imprisoned in Boston. His book was already banned. Ageing and unwell, he was given clemency and died aged 71 among what friends and supporters remained in Maine.

I am not alone in my fascination with Thomas Morton. Others who do not share his name have been part of a rehabilitation programme that has portrayed him as a pioneer of native American rights, and as an antidote to the solemn asceticism associated with the Pilgrim Fathers. Artists and writers are fascinated by him as the "anti-Puritan". He appears as a character in the Nathaniel Hawthorne story *The Maypole of Merrymount*, two novels by John Lothrop Motley, and a 1934 opera, *Merry Mount* by American composer Howard Hanson. There is an excellent biography by Peter C Mancall called *The Trials of Thomas Morton*, and its conclusion perhaps sums up his importance most soberly:

> "The Colonists who thrust Morton out of New Plymouth wanted to silence him. They had good reason to erase the influence of this potent antagonist whose actions defied their authority time and again."[9]

Morton liked a drink and used alcohol in the wild and licentious ceremonies he promoted. But there was a certain daft innocence in his Maypole-erecting sex orgies. He was a libertine High Anglican with a great deal of knowledge and understanding of rural Devonian new-paganism. He admired ordinary people in England and wanted to understand and collaborate with and protect the Native Americans he came in contact with. They in turn protected and helped him. And, of course, he wanted money and power.

Pitted against him were the hard-and-fast political and theological structures of Puritanism, which had history on its side. The Puritans were firmly against any integration with native American culture, to the extent of violence, the deliberate introduction of disease and eventually straightforward extermination. While alcohol was central, indeed essential to the building of colonial society, its use was carefully monitored and controlled. The beginnings of the temperance movement and prohibition could already be discerned.

---

[9]   Mancall, Peter C, *The Trials of Thomas Morton*, Yale University Press, New Haven CT, USA, 2019

And between Morton and Bradford, between Plymouth and Merrymount, we can see the start of America's central dichotomies: freedom and authority; enforced sobriety and wild drunkenness; devout Protestantism and the instinct to live outside religious law or within a much more liberal theological regime. Sin and redemption. Guns and flowers. Saturday night and Sunday morning. Today, if you go to Quincy, Massachusetts, you will be warmly welcomed by the Merrymount Residents' Association, whose website states, "Merrymount remains an integral yet unique part of Quincy, MA – minus the Maypole, but filled with warm and friendly neighbors, friends and families."[10]

Religious Whiskey

How do we get from the wild and sometimes violent religious fervour of Massachusetts in the 17th century to the production of whiskey in the often extremely religious Southern states of the USA today? It's all down to emigration, and those two countries where whiskey or whisky originated, Ireland and Scotland. Just as with the Pilgrim Fathers, religion was a powerful motivating factor, but this time Roman Catholics from Ireland were among those persecuted for their faith. And the peak periods of immigration in the 19th and early 20th centuries coincided with the rise of fundamentalist Protestantism and indeed the temperance movement in the USA.

The skills to distil whiskey may be most associated in the USA with Irish and Scottish immigrants, but it's interesting that the man most often termed the first legal commercial distiller in Kentucky, Evan Williams, was Welsh, though there is some doubt that he was in fact the first distiller of whiskey in Kentucky. And if you buy a bottle of Evan Williams Bourbon today, it will have been made in Louisville, where Heaven Hill, who own the name, make it.

---

[10] http://www.merrymountquincy.com/

Charles Cowdery, in his book *Bourbon, Strange: Surprising Stories of American Whiskey*, identifies as important not just the fleeing of Catholics from trouble in Europe, but their movement within the USA from persecution. Catholic families moved to Kentucky from Maryland after that state passed "anti-popery" laws in the 1700s.

One of that southern migration's leaders was a man called Basil Hayden. Hayden's grandson would later open a distillery and produce a whiskey called Old Grand-Dad, named for Basil and made nowadays by Jim Beam. Incidentally, this was one of the first American whiskeys I tasted, thanks to my friend Norrie Craig who was a graphic designer and printer responsible for making whiskey labels, and the UK distributor for Old Grand-Dad being one of his customers.

Elijah Craig was a Baptist minister, famously – and possibly wrongly – credited with making "Bourbon" whiskey for the first time by charring the inside of his oak barrels before filling them with spirit for ageing. In fact, this was customary among whisky distillers in the area of Kentucky he had moved to, following a whole host of run-ins with religious and political authorities including his fellow Baptists.

Craig was the man who established Georgetown, now a crucial centre for whiskey production, and he used the income from his distilling and other projects to fund his religious activities – something that went down well with some but not all of his Baptist colleagues. Indeed, Elijah Craig survives today as, appropriately, a brand of whiskey made by the Heaven Hill Distillery in Bardstown. You may be tempted to try the 18-year-old Single Barrel Elijah Craig Bourbon, from its description by Heaven Hill as "the oldest Single Barrel Bourbon in the world at 18 years … made in hand-selected oak barrels, you can rest assured that you and the angels have good taste. Each barrel of Elijah Craig 18 loses nearly two thirds of its contents to evaporation during the long years of ageing. This loss is known as the Angel's share."

Holy Flight – Tasting Notes

Monte Alban Mezcal

In the 1980s there was a rock'n'roll bar in the west end of Glasgow called Jimmy Chunga's, and it was the first place in the city to market mezcal seriously. We'd all gone down the tequila slammer route on occasion, but the idea of eating that white, alien-looking worm at the bottom of each mezcal bottle appealed to the daft, macho headcase element among Glasgow drinkers. If you were the lucky person who got the last drop out of the bottle, the worm in your glass and showed that you'd swallowed it, your name was engraved on a worm-eaters' plaque and displayed for all to see. I wonder what happened to it? Several of those whose names appeared there later had worldwide hit singles. Or, at least, became quite big in Albania.

Eating the worm, which is actually a moth larva found in the agave cactus used to make mezcal, is supposed to be a key to the soul of the person who eats it. We were always told you would have hallucinations, as the worm also feeds on the peyote plant, source of mescaline. Just like Carlos Castaneda's Don Juan. None of us ever did. It turns out the worm – which was traditionally eaten by local natives – was placed in the bottle as a tease for macho drinkers to eat it and impress possible partners.

I have never really liked mezcal. The "proper" way to drink it is from small glasses, accompanied by water from a separate glass. Monte Alban is 40 per cent alcohol by volume.

Colour: A pale, urinary yellow.

Nose: Unfinished wood panelling with a variety of spices and a kind of sweetened turpentine.

Palate: Smoother than you might have imagined but becoming rougher as it goes down. There's a kind of medical, as opposed to what we usually mean by medicinal, taste – you would have to imagine it was doing you good to drink it at all.

Finish: Peppery and spiky. Like you might expect from a cactus.

Of course, you can always rustle up a Mezcal Margarita by mixing it with lime juice, triple sec, Cointreau, agave syrup and some salt for the edge of the glass. Or have a proper drink instead.

Three American whiskeys, all made by Heaven Hill, though the final one is an independent bottling that may be quite difficult to source, even in the UK.

Evan Williams Kentucky Straight Bourbon Whiskey

Colour: Burned amber. Or caramel if you prefer.

Nose: Toffee apples, spearmint chewing gum, with a little chilli zing.

Palate: Milk chocolate. Hershey's with added creaminess. Wedding (fruit) cake, vanilla ice cream and some citrus zest.

Finish: Cinnamon and nutmeg spice.

Elijah Craig Kentucky Straight Bourbon Whiskey

Colour: Hold it to the light and it will look like one of Kentucky's lakes in the most golden of sunsets. Just watch out for the critters.

Nose: Honey and lemon. Perfect for a cold or flu treatment with a spoonful of bitter marmalade just to keep your energy levels up.

Palate: Apple crumble, with some rhubarb and cinnamon. A lot of brown sugar. Sweet and delicious.

Finish: The bitterness of the burned oak in the barrels used to age this starts to come through. But still a very attractive dram. Quite hefty at 47 per cent alcohol.

Heaven Hill Corn Whiskey 9-Year-Old (That Boutique-y Whisky Company)

That Boutique-y Whisky Company is one of several uber-trendy, friskily cool UK bottlers who pick up casks they rate and produce limited-edition bottlings with snazzy labels. In this case, they have a 9-year-old straight corn whiskey that I'm guessing was a bit of an experiment by Heaven Hill. Once 1,600-odd bottles have been produced in "Batch one", I'd assume that more will become available. There's always another batch if the first one sells.

Colour: Lighter yellowy corn-off-the-cob with overtones of oak furniture.

Nose: Corn on the cob with melted butter and a sprinkling of honey. Also chocolate. It ought not to work – it won't for everyone. Sweet. The ubiquity of banana flavours in this type of whiskey. A whiff of burned oak underneath it all.

Palate: Puddings with pepper. That's an apple pie with African lemon pepper, freshly ground, just to make your gums hurt.

Finish: Fruity, with Mexican concentrated cocoa powder and apple skins.

CHAPTER 10

OLD WAYS: MAGIC, WITCHCRAFT AND ADVENTURES IN CIDER

England, Scotland (Arran)
Cider, perry, whisky

Holy Flight
– *Smith Hayne Dry Still Cider*
– *Burrow Hill Sparkling Perry*
– *Arran 10-Year-Old Single Malt Whisky*

Shall we go a-wassailing? For many the word "wassail" conjures up images of carol singers roaming – sometimes not entirely soberly – from door to door, collecting cash for the local church. But delve into the custom's roots and you travel back in time, through Christianity to something much earthier and more pagan.

> "Here we come a-wassailing
> Among the leaves so green,
> Here we come a-wandering
> So fair to be seen …"

So begins one of the best known wassailing songs sung in England. But the custom is more associated with Twelfth Night rather than Christmas itself and it is really all about calling the future of spring and the renewal of the year, the coming of the light and the regeneration of crops, notably apples. And it is in the orchards of southern England that you will find wassailing still taking place today. It's a long way from neatly attired carollers strutting their choral stuff in the suburbs, and its relation to the pagan or Wiccan notion of making an offering to the Earth or local divinities is obvious. As the resource Witchpedia says: "A libation is a beverage poured out as an offering to a deity, spirit or beloved dead within a ritual context as a form of communion or to give honour and thanks. Libations vary by tradition. Alcoholic beverages, milk, honey, water and oil are all used as libations."[1]

Libations may be poured into a dedicated container such as a libation bowl or patera, onto a sacred object such as an altar or the statue of a deity or into the Earth.

At the National Trust's Dyrham Park Estate near Bath in England, wassailing in its original form has been revived, and a posting on the estate's Facebook page invited anyone who wished to come along on 6 January 2022:

"Create a hullabaloo this bright new year and help us scare away bad spirits for a bountiful orchard crop in the autumn! The festive season will culminate in a noisy celebration of wassailing on Sun 6 Jan, 11am–2pm, when visitors are invited to accompany the live music by bashing pots and pans in a traditional celebration to encourage the pear harvest …

We'll be singing and shouting the orchard into good health, join us for mulled perry and music. Feel free to bring your own percussion instruments, even if it's two wooden spoons!"[2]

---

[1] https://witchipedia.com/glossary/libation/

[2] https://www.facebook.com/events/dyrham-park-national-trust/dyrham-wassail/347053502520642/

This is wassailing as a pagan ritual designed to promote a good crop in the orchard by scaring away the evil, blighting spirits from the trees. There are many different forms of activity, but most are carried out in apple or pear orchards. People may bake cakes, then soak them in cider. This would be cider in the British sense of a sometimes very alcoholic drink, often referred to in the USA as "hard" cider. The non-alcoholic apple juice known as cider in the USA was familiar to me in my youth as Cidrax or Cirap, the source of much illicit excitement, as my friends and I would knock it back in the deluded belief that it would get us drunk. In proper wassailing people would drink cider and perry (pear cider) in large quantities. Guns are discharged, drums banged, there is dancing and shouting.

But there is a more sociable and less aggressively fertility-orientated aspect to it all. Wassailing in some parts of England might see groups of revellers going from house to house, visiting, drinking toasts and wishing the householders the best of health for the coming year. The word "wassail" may be rooted in Old English *was hál*, meaning "be hale" or "good health". However, wassailing is also the merest hop, skip and jump from the sometimes more sinister historical rural custom of charivari, shivaree or the skimmington ride.

Often carried out at the same traditional time as a wassail, this may be familiar to viewers of rural-set American TV shows such as *The Waltons* or *Dr Quinn, Medicine Woman*, and in its least malevolent form, as a pre-wedding bit of fun in the film *Oklahoma!*. But charivari or shivaree could involve hooded figures surrounding the house of someone who was perceived as infringing community custom or rules – perhaps through adultery – and scaring the living daylights out of the supposed culprit through making "rough music" by banging drums while consuming copious amounts of alcohol.

A proper wassail, however, is normally good-natured and in the depths of cider-making country is carried out with great attention to detail. There may be a torch-lit procession around the cider orchard, a Wassail King and Queen and a black-clad Master of

Ceremonies called the Butler. Some wassails will see a dozen small fires placed around the biggest tree, representing the 12 zodiac signs or 12 apostles. Apparently, in Herefordshire there can be a 13th fire, known as the Judas Fire, which people light then immediately stamp out to destroy the possibility of treachery.

The confusion or coalescence of religions continues in wassailing. The Butler may lead the crowd in appeal to Pomona, the apple goddess, for a healthy harvest. The smallest boy present, a child known (unfortunately, in my opinion) as the Tom Tit, is then lifted up to put cider-soaked bread into the branches of an apple tree to bring good luck. And then there's communal drinking, gunfire and a general hullaballoo.

If all this sounds like great fun, that's because it self-evidently is. And these Twelfth Night or Old New Year ceremonies are parallelled by other fiery events, notably in the north of Scotland in my own home, the Shetland Isles. Fire festivals to mark or hasten the advent of the light as spring beckons, albeit in the distance, take place in Up Helly Aa in Shetland (see Chapter 13 on Vikings and their mead-soaked lives), the burning of the Clavie in Burghead and the fireballs of Stonehaven.

All have roots in pre-Christian fertility and sun-welcoming paganism, though most have been modified by Christianity or, in Up Helly Aa's case – and this is not something much discussed – by post-World War I socialism and the temperance movement. This accounts for the fact that alcohol consumption in the post-burning social festivities is supposed to be discreet, if not invisible. Until folk, as they say locally, "fall by". Or just fall over.

Witches and Their Pointy Hats

The world of Wicca and witchcraft has spawned several books that offer spells and potions in liquid form, some promising aphrodisiac qualities or the potential to render a lover more amorous (or speechless, if enough vodka is applied). But it's interesting that most modern Wiccan practitioners are just as careful in their advice on alcohol use as adherents of the other world religions: it's fine in moderation.

Patti Wigington is a licensed Pagan celebrant and author of the *Daily Spellbook for the Good Witch*, *Wicca Practical Magic* and *The Daily Spell Journal*. In an article on the Learn Religions website, she writes, "In general, the Pagan population tends to have a very liberal attitude about the reasonable use of alcohol. It's not uncommon to have wine at a ceremony, although there are a number of covens dedicated to serving people in recovery, and those groups naturally have alcohol-free rituals. Most Wiccans and other Pagans will tell you that as long as you can maintain responsible behaviour, the use of alcohol or narcotics is a matter of personal choice."[3]

In the book *The Witch's Coven: Finding or Forming Your Own Circle*, Edain McCoy says that both tobacco and alcohol may be used in coven rituals, with tobacco as an offering or a "smudge" (a purifying incense) or smoked communally. Alcohol, often but not always wine, can be shared too, very much like a form of eucharist. But, he adds, "both can present problems if someone in the coven has asthma, heart problems or allergies is trying to quit smoking or is in recovery from alcoholism". While one or two covens may use drugs to "induce altered states of consciousness", for McCoy, they are merely an artificial support, and unnecessary "if you want to be a Witch of any power."[4]

The relationship between witches and brewing is a fascinating and controversial one. In March 2021, Laken Brooks, a doctoral student at the University of Florida, wrote an article for the online magazine The Conversation entitled: "Women used to dominate the beer industry – until the witch accusations started pouring in". Its general argument is that the production of beer was for millennia a household chore undertaken mostly by

[3]   https://www.learnreligions.com/drug-and-alcohol-use-2561717

[4]   McCoy, Edain, *The Witch's Coven: Finding or Forming Your Own Circle* (Llewellyn's Modern Witchcraft), Llewellyn Publications, Woodbury MIN, USA, 2003

women, until the 16th century when "a smear campaign accused women brewers of being witches. Much of the iconography we associate with witches today, from the pointy hat to the broom, may have emerged from their connection to female brewers."[5]

Brooks argues that anyone who travelled back in time to an English market in the Middle Ages would be struck by the sight of women wearing tall, pointed, Hogwarts-style hats. They would probably be standing in front of huge steaming cauldrons. But, she says, they weren't witches. They were brewers.

"They wore the tall, pointy hats so that their customers could see them in the crowded marketplace. They transported their brew in cauldrons. And those who sold their beer out of stores had cats not as demon familiars, but to keep mice away from the grain."

Cats, cauldrons and caps: it was all for the sake of the brew that was true, not the spell from hell.

It's a fantastically appealing idea, but one that provoked some controversy and opposition from other academics, especially when the article was republished in the *Smithsonian Magazine*, where the editors attached a number of qualifications and comments.[6] And yet Tara Nurin in the magazine *Craft Beer and Brewing* published a piece called, "How Women Brewers Saved the World", in which she states that beer and female brewers of beer go back much further in time and mythology. In Baltic myths, there is a goddess called Raugutiene who oversees beer production from heaven. Finland has a woman named Kalevatar bringing about beer by mixing honey with bear spit. And she points out that the beer anthropologist Alan Eames wrote in 1993 that real Norsemen – Vikings – would

---

[5] https://theconversation.com/women-used-to-dominate-the-beer-industry-until-the-witch-accusations-started-pouring-in-155940

[6] https://www.smithsonianmag.com/history/women-used-dominate-beer-industry-until-witch-accusations-started-pouring-180977171/

permit only women to brew ale for them. She quotes Eames as noting, "Viking women drank ale, flagon for flagon, along with the men."[7] And she adds: "Some historians see clear similarities between brewsters and illustrations selected for anti-witch propaganda. Images of frothing cauldrons, broomsticks (to hang outside the door to indicate the availability of ale), cats (to chase away mice), and pointy hats (to be seen above the crowd in the marketplace) endure today."[8]

My personal encounters with witches of any variety have been few and far between and did not involve alcohol. At least not at the time. All have been very pleasant individuals. I remember as a child been terrified by the born-again, reformed "queen of the witches" Doreen Irvine, after my mother attended a lecture by her. Irvine's book *From Witchcraft to Christ* is still in print. It should be said that Irvine's portrayal of so-called witchcraft bears little or no resemblance to the "Earth magic" of relatively wholesome modern Wicca and is instead a kind of strange, lurid Satanism. Still, it scared the living daylights out of me.

Not so the next set of witches I encountered on the sunny Isle of Arran in the early 1980s. This was a coven we were filming for BBC TV, and they met in an absolutely beautiful stream-side glen somewhere on the glorious island in the Firth of Clyde known as "Scotland in Miniature". I say "somewhere" as we – the entire film crew, producers and presenter – were blindfolded before being driven to this mysterious location.

There we experienced some lovey harp (*clarsach* – the small Gaelic harp) music and some rather restrained dancing. It was explained that everyone felt a bit hampered by the clothing the BBC insisted should be worn, as normally "sky dancing" would be the order of the day. Afterwards we went for a drink, but there was no ritual consumption of wine, beer or whisky. This was before the establishment of an official distillery on the island, though there has undoubtedly been a great deal of illegal

---

[7]   https://beerandbrewing.com/how-women-brewsters-saved-the-world/

[8]   Ibid.

distillation in years gone by. The small stills' whisky was known as "Arran Waters" and would be exported to the mainland where it was much prized.

Nowadays you can partake of some delightful drams courtesy of the Lochranza Distillery, which opened in 1995, and the much newer Lagg Distillery in Kilmore, which began distilling in 2019 and can therefore not legally sell its spirit as whisky until it is three years old at least. As this book is published, in fact.

Arran is a wonderful place; somewhere people have visions and dream dreams. Notably one Kay Morris, who in 1992 was owner of the nearby Holy Isle – famed for its miracle-working well, the cave once lived in by 6th-century monk St Molaire and the ruins of a 13th-century monastery. Its holy credentials are impeccable.

In 1992 Kay had a dream in which she was visited by the Virgin Mary and instructed to give the island to the Tibetan Buddhist community at Samye Ling in the Scottish Borders, which she duly did. The island is now the site of the Buddhist Centre for World Peace and Health and retreat houses where nuns and monks stay for three-year isolated stints with no outside contact.

Holy Isle itself, however, is very much open to visitors and there is a regular ferry from Lamlash on Arran. But there is one part of the island that fascinates me, though I have never travelled there – not, at least, without a blindfold.

I refer to the Fairy Glen, which back in my BBC days would have been a Forestry Commission site but has since been handed over to a local voluntary group known as Roots of Arran Community Woodland. Their 30-hectare site between Brodick, Arran's main village, and Lamlash has since 2002 been planted with beech, hazel, willow, oak, alder, blackthorn and fruit trees in a specially enclosed orchard area. The aim is to regenerate and increase the island's biodiversity.

Someday, hopefully on or around Twelfth Night, I will head there and see if I recognize the location from my last piece of cavorting with witches. And I will possibly do some wassailing.

A Bit of a Blur

On the evening before I began writing about wassailing, my friend and neighbour Margaret got in touch to say that she had been involved in some recent wassailing concerning her own apple trees (which, being in wind-scoured Shetland, are in a form of rigid polytunnel known as a Polycrub). And then suddenly wassailing was everywhere. I was sent a link to an obscure cover of *The Gloucestershire Wassailing Song* by, of all people, the globally successful rock group Blur.

Apparently, Damon Albarn and Graham Coxon from the band had sung the Wassailing Song when they were both pupils at Stanway Comprehensive in Colchester. During a break in the initial sessions for the album *Modern Life Is Rubbish* at Maison Rouge Studios in Fulham, London, the four members of the group alternate vocals on the verses, singing the refrain together. It's the only song in Blur's entire output that drummer Dave Rowntree sings on.

Only 500 copies of the Wassailing Song were pressed as a single and they were given away free at the band's 1992 Christmas gig at the Hibernian Club in Fulham by a man dressed as Santa Claus.

The record sale site Discogs has this note from someone who attended the gig, which would surely have been a classic case of extremely noisy wassailing, including the consumption of alcohol in large quantities and the secular worship of a band who were then not quite deities.

The gig took place at a point in Blur's career when the music press felt the band were finished. Tickets couldn't even be given away and the hall was less than half-full. However, Damon Albarn and the boys apparently played a blindingly good set and "at the end we all drunkenly queued up to get our free 7-inch from a Liverpudlian dressed as Santa." After about five minutes there was general mayhem when a barrier collapsed and, with records going everywhere, there was a mad grab for the rare vinyl. "A lot of them ended up littering the floor and being trampled on. Although 500 were pressed I'd say that a lot less than that were actually given away or survived the night," commented Iain in 2008.[9]

The Gloucestershire Wassailing Song

"Wassail, wassail all over the town
Our toast, it is white and our ale, it is brown
Our bowl, it is made of the white maple tree
With the wassailing bowl, we'll drink to thee."

(There are many, many verses to the song. Even Blur cannot make it all absolutely essential listening. So I have picked my favourites …)

"And here is to Dobbin and to his right eye
Pray God send our master a good Christmas pie
And a good Christmas pie that may we all see
With the wassailing bowl, we'll drink to thee

So here is to Broad Mary and to her broad horn
May God send our master a good crop of corn
And a good crop of corn that may we all see
With the wassailing bowl, we'll drink to thee

And here is to Colly and to her long tail
Pray God send our master he never may fail
A bowl of strong beer, I pray you draw near
And our jolly wassail, it's then you shall hear

Come, butler, come fill us a bowl of the best
Then we hope that your soul in heaven may rest
But if you do draw us a bowl of the small
Then down will take butler, bowl and all

---

[9]   https://www.discogs.com/release/541389-Gold-Frankincense-And-Blur-The-Wassailing-Song

Wassail, wassail all over the town
Our toast it is white and our ale it is brown
Our bowl it is made of the white maple tree
With the wassailing bowl, we'll drink to thee."

The association of cider, perry and other forms of alcohol produced from fruit trees with religion is ancient, and some would argue goes right back some 5,000 years to Mesopotamia and the *Epic of Gilgamesh*, thought to be the second oldest religious text. In it, the daughter of the sun god tries to convince Gilgamesh that his search for immortality is ridiculous, arguing that the pleasures of this world, here and now, are greater. Especially with fermented fruit juices. Her name? Siduri, or Sidre. And with Suduri or Sidre's blessing the wild *Malus sieversii* apple – ancestor of today's farmed *Malus domestica* – came from Asia's Tien Shan Mountains along the Silk Road and has ended up in fruit salads, juices and ciders the world over.

I have already discussed the links between agriculture, fruit and cereal production, fermentation, alcohol and religion (see pages 53–59). The apple, though, is a fruit both soaked in mythological and symbolic power and, in terms of its alcoholic potential, slightly usurped by both grape and grain.

The ancient Greeks believed that Dionysus, the god of wine and fertility, ecstasy (the condition) and general getting-out-of-it, created the apple, presenting it to Aphrodite, the goddess of love. It has always been associated with sex and fertility.

In classical mythology the Golden Apples of the Hesperides hang high. The Garden of the Hesperides was an orchard belonging to the goddess Hera. Golden apples from this orchard were part of Hera's trousseau when she married Zeus. The apples were looked after by those gardeners of the gloaming, the Hesperides, the nymphs of the evening. You can trace the Trojan War back to this particular orchard, as it was from there that Eris, goddess of discord, took the apple of discord. To cut a long story short, this led to Helen of Troy being abducted by Paris, and the Trojan War and all sorts of other calamitous events ensued. If only there had been some proper wassailing.

Then there was Heracles, who as one of his 12 Labours had to steal some of the legendary golden apples. He tricked Atlas into going and getting them while he took over the role of holding up the heavens on his shoulders. On Atlas' return, he managed to purloin the apples while swopping the burden back.

Would You Adam and Eve It?

Everyone associates apples, or an apple, with the Garden of Eden and the fall of humankind, thanks to that pesky snake, Eve and Adam. But the apple is never mentioned in the Bible as being the forbidden fruit. According to Genesis, "And the Lord God commanded the man, saying, Of every tree of the garden thou mayest freely eat: But of the tree of the knowledge of good and evil, thou shalt not eat of it: for in the day that thou eatest thereof thou shalt surely die."

So how did the apple get the blame? It could be simply a confusion between two very similar Latin words, the adjective *malum*, which means "evil", and *malus*, an apple tree. Or it could be a pun, the kind of pun someone comes up with while somewhat drunk on cider and determined to illustrate their command of a dead language.

Someone like John Milton, for example, who in 1667 had Satan in *Paradise Lost* seduce mankind from his creator with an apple, "the more to increase your wonder ... and, thereat offended, worth your laughter!"[10]

And so the apple became key to sinfulness, despite the Bible itself not explicitly making the fruit the source of All Bad Things. Solomon, though, is all for its sexual symbolism:

"As the apple tree among the trees of the wood, so is my

---

[10] https://www.poetryfoundation.org/poems/45718/paradise-lost-book-1-1674-version

beloved among the sons. I sat down under his shadow with great delight, and his fruit was sweet to my taste."

Unfortunately, and especially in the UK, cider (as in British hard cider, alcoholic cider) has gained a bad reputation as a cheap, sweet way of getting very drunk, very quickly. Fifty-six per cent of apples grown in Britain go to make cider and more cider is consumed here per head than anywhere else in the world. Most supermarkets still sell very strong, sugary "ciders" full of chemicals and made from imported apple juice. Legally, it can be called cider in the UK even if it's made with only 35 per cent apple juice. However, in both Britain and the USA, there is now a trend toward artisanal craft ciders and apple-based drinks that reflect a long tradition of high-quality beverages made with 100 per cent apple juice, often from a single type of apple.

Jane Peyton, an award-winning sommelier, writer and broadcaster, has written and talked extensively on the subject of cider. She comments, "I'm firmly in the 100% juice brigade thinking of cider as apple wine. That's what seventeenth-century English aristocrats did … King Charles I was said to have preferred cider over wine. If only Queen Elizabeth II was a cider drinker, then cider would regain its past glory and be borne the respect it deserves."[11]

I agree. Cider is a potentially wine-challenging substance. I have argued with one of the country's top wine connoisseurs that the best cider is as good as champagne (see page 103, where I relate how English cider producers were 17th-century pioneers of the "methode Champenoise" system – using secondary bottle fermentation to make sparkling cider). Today you can get still, sparkling, dry or sweet cider, barrel-aged, single estate or single variety, and it can cost anything up to £20 ($26) a bottle. Yet for many it's still something that provokes cries of "worst hangover in the world!"

All of which should encourage a bit more wassailing, even

---

[11] https://www.greatbritishchefs.com/features/cider-history-origins

among those famously religious cider makers, the monks of Ampleforth in Yorkshire, northern England, who, alas, have recently decided to move from fruit to grain and make beer. The malevolent spirits preventing apples becoming the new grapes and vintage, oak-aged cider usurping champagne as a celebratory drink must be sent packing.

In the words of yet another wassailing song, this one a 19th-century ditty from the southern English counties of Sussex and Surrey:

> "Stand fast root, bear well top
> Pray the god send us a howling good crop,
> every twig, apples big
> Every bough, apples now.
> Hail to thee, old apple tree!
> From every bough
> Give us apples now;
> Hatsful, capsful,
> Bushel, bushel, sacksful
> And our arms full, too."

Holy Flight – Tasting Notes

Smith Hayne Dry Still Cider

Amazing, really. I ordered a selection of craft ciders and perries for, uh, research, and this one was truly magnificent. Poised, sophisticated, austere, aristocratic. As befits what was once the drink of English kings and queens.

Colour: Slightly tawny.

Nose: Chalk and granite. Apple trees on a winter wind, maybe. Or frosty windfalls.

Palate: That cold stony feel. Bone dry, like a good Chablis. Unlike some ciders, it's not bitter or sharp, nor is it too sweet. Mouth-feel is fruity and citrusy and always fresh. Barley water mixed with mint leaves.

Finish: Then you're left with a touch of dankness as it goes down, and a burst of Granny Smith quenchiness.

Burrow Hill Sparkling Perry

Not like Babycham, which was so popular in the 1960s in the UK as "the genuine Champagne Perry". This is a much more refined beast.

Colour: Pale, like a good light English sparkling wine.

Nose: Sweet but fresh too, with notes of freshly cut grass, nettles and mint. Better than some cheap champagnes …

Palate: Fresh but with the pear drops sweetness you expect.

Finish: Fades quickly but demands further attention.

Arran 10-Year-Old Single Malt Whisky

This is not like a traditional peaty island whisky (you'll be able to get that from the other Arran distillery, Lagg, when it comes on stream). It's mild and on the lighter side of lowland and Speyside in style.

Colour: Light, like a cloudy sky just before dusk, caught by the fading sun.

Nose: Golfing on Arran's lovely Shiskine course on a hot summer's day. Grass, the scent of wooden-shafted golf clubs, the satisfying smack of steel against ball. A quick nip from a hip flask as the sun beats down and the hedgerow bushes send their aroma wafting over. Oops! Sliced!

Palate: Apples, appropriately enough. Quite sweet and Horlicksy (malted milk drink).

Finish: Edginess creeps in. You missed that putt, didn't you?

CHAPTER 11

DUNDERHEADS, ZOMBIES AND BARON SAMEDI

The Caribbean: Haiti, Cuba, Martinique
Rum

Holy Flight
– *Clairin Communal*
– *Clément VSOP Rhum Agricole*
– *Watson's Trawler Rum*

Not for the first time in research for this book, I find myself at risk of disappearing down a disorientating rabbit hole, or in this case, into a murky, bubbling pit of magical liquid containing all kinds of distillery waste products and very possibly the rotting bodies of goats. Letting my imagination run completely riot, these goats, possibly named Billy or Sally or Jim, were once used in voodoo (or vodou) rituals attended by Roger Moore, masquerading as a particularly languid 007 – Commander James Bond – in the movie *Live and Let Die*.

A receptacle used in the production of rum in its various forms is called a dunder pit, and it is traditionally where the stillage, or waste mash from the distillation process is dumped. In Scotland, this stuff is called draff and is valuable: it's collected and usually processed into animal feed. In America, the stillage is utilized in the production of the whiskey known as sour mash.

In some forms of rum production, this dunder is a source of aromatic, taste-making, downright funky compounds that are then added to the next mash (which contains the sugars that will eventually produce alcohol when it ferments and is distilled). It's fair to say that the addition of animal carcasses is rare in the commercial rum industry, but most rum distilleries will proudly point to their dunder pit and guides will gleefully shock tourists with tales of what may or may not once have been in there. And to tell the truth, would you mind the merest whiff, the ghost of rotting goat in that characterful Cuba Libre or rum punch?

I first heard the word "dunder" when I was seven years old, in the primary class of Mr McSmith, who would use the term "dunderhead" as a supreme insult. It was often applied to me, though I think I once received the strap. This was a peculiarly vicious and Scottish form of corporal punishment by which teachers would hit the offending pupil's hands with a hard leather belt called a tawse. Long illegal, in the 1960s it was commonplace and almost unconceivably painful when applied to the tiny, soft hands of children.

"YOU. ARE. A. DUNDERHEAD!" Mr McSmith would shout. Then you'd feel the crack of the divided leather landing on your skin and stifle the inevitable sobs. "Dunderhead" is an old insult, usually meaning a stupid, blockheaded person, and its origins are traced back to the Dutch word for a large, blunderbuss-like gun.[1] However, I think the modern urban slang usage, which refers to a man who has, ahem, a dirty or smelly penis,[2] probably reflects its true origin in Caribbean rum production. Because dunder pits do, undoubtedly, stink to high heaven. One can only hope that this was not a thought in the long-dead Mr McSmith's mind. There is, inevitably, a Dunderhead brand of rum.[3]

Rum and religion. Immediately, thoughts turn to Voodoo (or Voudo) and Santeria, the Caribbean religions of Haiti and Cuba.

---

[1] https://www.etymonline.com/word/dunderhead

[2] https://www.urbandictionary.com/define.php?term=Dunderhead

[3] https://www.drinkworthy.co.uk/products/dunderhead-rum

But we think that way because of popular culture and branding, whether that is movies such as *Live and Let Die*, the 1932 Bela Lugosi flick *White Zombies* or the 1988 film *The Serpent and the Rainbow* set in Haiti. The American flesh-eating, walking-dead zombie and the worldwide explosion of zombiedom as seen in countless horror films and TV shows since George Romero's *Night of the Living Dead* and *Dawn of the Dead* bears little relation to the traditional concept and is not rum-related. Unless, of course, you drink an awful lot of the stuff and turn yourself into a facsimile of one.

In an article in *The Atlantic* magazine, writer Mike Mariani explains the origin of the zombie myth with heartbreaking clarity. It was all to do with slavery. Between 1625 and 1804, the date of the Haitian revolution against French rule, zombiedom, he writes, "was a projection of the African slaves' relentless misery and subjugation. Haitian slaves believed that dying would release them back to *Lan Guinée*, literally Guinea or Africa in general, a kind of afterlife where they could be free. Though suicide was common among slaves, those who took their own lives wouldn't be allowed to return to *Lan Guinée*. Instead, they'd be condemned to skulk in the Hispaniola plantations for eternity, undead slaves at once denied their own bodies and yet trapped inside them – soulless zombies."[4] After the end of slavery, the story was incorporated into Vodou and some Haitians began to believe that shamans and priests could reanimate bodies as zombie servants. As slaves for all eternity.

Vodou or voodoo (Vaudou in French) is a result of the West African religion called Vodun, imported by slaves to what was then Saint-Domingue and is now Haiti, combining with the Roman Catholicism of their French owners. Vodun is a highly complex and widespread religion in West Africa based on the idea that everything is inhabited by a spirit. In Vodou and the associated Cuban variant called Santeria, the Christian God is understood to be the creator of those spirits and the entire universe.

---

[4]   https://www.theatlantic.com/entertainment/archive/2015/10/how-america-erased-the-tragic-history-of-the-zombie/412264/

At its simplest – and Vodou takes in the entire range of human behaviour and existence – Vodou is all about serving the spirits, praying to them and engaging in rituals to obtain health and advantage. The spirits – known as lwa – can enter the people engaged in rites, which may include song, dance, rhythmic music, eating and drinking. There can be priests and priestesses, and there are various branches of the faith scattered throughout Haiti in the form of both publicly accessible groups and secret societies.

Alcohol features in Vodou, particularly the local, micro-distilled form of Haitian rum called *clairin* in French or *kleren* in Haitian creole. There are thought to be between 500 and 600 clairin distilleries in Haiti, most of them unregistered and providing only for local residents. However, as an artisanal drink par excellence, some blended and single-producer clairins are now available to buy globally. Clairin is distilled in a small pot still from fermented sugar cane juice – not, as in the case of most rums, from molasses produced industrially from sugar cane. The sugar cane is cut by hand and its juice is usually left to ferment using the natural yeasts in open tanks. The Haitian climate means fermentation is normally swift, though the addition of citric fruits can delay things. And yes, waste from previous distillations, left to "mature" in a dunder pit, will be added to this mixture, too. Once distilled, the clairin is left unfiltered.

Each clairin is highly distinctive, depending on local terroir and tastes. It's a cruder drink, but clairin is similar to the French *rhum agricole* produced on the French overseas region, the island of Martinique. This is an industry in its own right, with AOC (*Appellation d'Origine Contrôlée* – Protected Designation of Origin) recognition by the French authorities.

I have never taken part in a Voudo ceremony, though I have drunk considerable quantities of rum. Once, notably, this included a form of clairin on the Caribbean island of Montserrat, on a journalistic trip many years ago before most of it was rendered uninhabitable by volcanic eruption. It was offered to me in a remote shack by a man who was introduced to me by the local police chief (then, as now, Montserrat was a

British colony) as "our local Rastafarian". In fact, Rastafarians do not drink alcohol, though the herbal additions to the murky rum cocktail I drank some of that day may well have contained another substance considered holy within Rastafarian practice. I don't remember clearly.

Rum is a very popular drink in Scottish coastal areas and especially in the Shetland Islands, where I live. Mostly, this is dark Navy rum, crudely made from molasses and very sweet, as issued to Royal Navy sailors in a daily ration until 1970. But there are spiced and lighter versions, albeit normally mixed with Coca-Cola or other fizzy and sweet sodas.

A few years ago I lent a bicycle to the son of a French couple who were staying at our local hotel. A month later, a bottle arrived in the post from the grateful family, who lived on the island of Martinique. It was my first experience of *rhum agricole*, a really lovely, very dry Martinique Trois Rivieres vintage, oak-aged rum.

Not that it would have borne many similarities to the raw cane distillate drunk by the ethnographer Jeffrey Vadala during his participation in various Haitian Vodou ceremonies. In an essay for the international anthropological database called Human Relations Area Files, he goes into detail about two religious practices. One is the Maya ritual in Yucatán, which involves the consumption of the local, mead-like honey drink called balché. The other is Vodou and the drink is clairin. In collaboration with a fellow ethnographer called Alissa Jordan, he attended divination events run by local leaders or *houngans*, and he was expected to bring clairin – which he calls kleren – bought from local household producers. He describes it as "clear, spicy and potent". Depending on the ritual, it could be mixed with things like "peppers, flowers, twigs, fruits, bones or spices".[5] It was also used as an embrocation, rubbed on sore backs, muscles and necks.

Not that there was much external-use-only application at the rituals attended by Vadala. "At rituals in Haiti I would first

---

5   https://hraf.yale.edu/a-divine-brew-alcohol-in-haitian-vodou-and-yucatec-maya-ritual/

present the kleren I purchased to the houngan (or the spirit possessing the houngan), who would take a swig and expect that I also take a few drinks with him and the other participants. When I came early to rituals, this frequently meant that the houngan, other critical participants and I had consumed a moderate amount of alcohol before the event began."[6]

There would then be prayers to God, the lwa and to Roman Catholic saints, with kleren consumed in between by the houngan and indeed everyone involved. "By the end of a given ritual event (which could last roughly 3–4 hours), everyone participating would have imbibed a fair amount, or at least feigned drinking it out of politeness."[7]

About halfway through the ceremony the houngan would enter a trance state of possession called *monte* or "being ridden" by the lwa or spirit. Typical aspects of this would be jerky bodily movements, glazed eyes and speaking in the voice of whichever spirit had possessed him. Vadala memorably quotes writer Harald Courlander, who witnessed a spectacular possession during such a ritual. When the spirit Pinga Maza entered the houngan, he became violent, made strange sounds and grabbed a machete, which was handily sitting on the altar. He then bashed himself on the head with the flat of it, continuously and fiercely, before beginning to quieten: "His assistants placed Pinga's red jacket on him. Now he spoke in the tired voice of an old man. He complained that he was hungry, that he had not eaten for a long while. His assistant handed him a razor blade. He placed it in his mouth, chewed it up, and swallowed it, washing it down with more of the white liquid in the bottle."[8]

---

[6] Ibid.

[7] Ibid.

[8] Courlander, Harold, *Drum and the Hoe: Life and Lore of the Haitian People*, University of California Press, Berkeley and Los Angeles, 1960, https://ehrafworldcultures.yale.edu/document?id=sv03-002

Eat the Glass

This instantly reminded me of an evening with my first editor, Mike Travers, who took me to what was then the less than salubrious area of Glasgow called Finnieston (now a mostly gentrified centre for upmarket dining and the quaffing of craft beers) for what was supposed to be a few drinks after work. It ended up in what's called a lock-in at a pub then owned by a former footballer and is probably now some kind of small-plates seafood joint. At around 2am the small, well-spoken man standing next to me at the bar (or supported by it) ordered a large whisky, downed it and then began eating the glass. Well, not the whole glass. This was a tumbler with a solid base and the bottom part was beyond him. He did, however, manage to consume and apparently swallow the edges, chewing them up with audible crunching and apparent enjoyment. "Och, don't mind him," said Mike. "He'll wash it down with the next pint."

Vadala saw houngans drinking more and more to enable the possessing spirit to see into the future or "remotely view" people in faraway places, as well as ancestors from the distant past. He makes the point that the non-commercial production of kleren, and the fact that it was limited to local people in a small area, contributed to its special significance for particular rituals. A bottle of Bacardi or Morgan's Spiced just wouldn't cut it.

Vadala concludes that "in both the Yucatán and Haiti, alcohol use shaped social relationships while also providing important ties to the past (in the case of Haiti, through the literal presence of the ancestors in the body of the houngan)."

It may seem an extreme and colourful expression of alcohol-in-worship, but I think we can see in these ceremonies the formalization in religious, ritual form of what used to happen in pubs: the introduction of the neophyte drinker to the practised masters of the art. The sharing of drinks, the common levels of inebriation that loosened tongues and, in some cases, drew out visions of the past, insights into the present, possible outcomes in the future. These were community events that brought people together, sealed relationships, created and affirmed identity. Like going to the pub. Or how going to the pub used to be.

And in common with perhaps less inebriated religious services, Haitian Vodou had and has music, movement, prayers, singing, prophecy and preaching. Transformation and ecstasy for some. Insight and instruction. A connection with the Divine, the ineffable. It's no surprise, then, that attempts to sell booze using readily recognizable images from Vodou have become commonplace.

The Branding

The iconography of Vodou has proved just too attractive for the producers of even very loosely associated alcoholic drinks to ignore. The promise of spiritual transformation through drink may be portrayed in a cartoon, jocular fashion, but it is there, along with the lurid association with horror films and the offer of zombification, should you choose to accept it. Which seems, given what we have seen as the roots of the "zombie" concept, unsettling to say the least.

The writer, ethnographer and folklorist Tony Kail has written and illustrated an entertaining blogpost about the use of Vodou images in alcohol marketing, starting with the drawing of Baron Samedi, in top hat, tailcoat, with staff and panda makeup, on the label of Louisiana brewery Abita's raspberry lager Purple Haze (note the connection to Jimi Hendrix's song *Voodoo Chile*, protected by heavy-duty copyright and presumably unusable).[9] The Baron also features, to an almost ludicrous extent, in Campari's Baron Samedi Spiced Rum, which is sold in a black, coffin-shaped box adorned with traditional Vodou symbols. Oddest perhaps of all is the portrayal by Colorado's Trinity Brewing of the Vodou (and Vodun) spirit Legba on their Pappy Legba Kriek or Belgian cherry beer. Kain says: "The

---

9   https://memphishoodoo.medium.com/invoking-spirits-hoodoo-voodoo-african-religions-in-the-alcohol-industry-389e3b6dfd2d

art used to depict the spirit is true to the lore surrounding his manifestation as an old man walking with a cane and standing at the crossroads."[10]

This ties in to a piece of mythology central to American music and forever associated with the blues musician Robert Johnson: the idea that, if you stood at a crossroads at midnight, you would meet a mysterious man who would offer you your heart's desire in exchange for your soul. By the early to mid-20th century, this was not the West African spirit known as Legba, but Satan himself. And it's a story that has emerged in different cultures, notably in Europe in the German legend of Faust, and with the Italian violinist Paganini doing devilish deals, for both their short-term benefit and long-term damnation.

Bluesman Son House, who knew Robert Johnson and insisted Johnson had been a poor guitarist until he disappeared for a few weeks and returned a brilliant player. "He sold his soul to the devil to play like that," Son House is supposed to have said. Johnson allegedly took his guitar to the crossroads of Highways 49 and 61 in Clarksdale, Mississippi, where the devil retuned his instrument in exchange for his soul. And the rest is mystery. And confusion – the story was first told of the older blues player Tommy Johnson, who died in 1956 aged 60. Robert Johnson died in 1938, aged only 27, after a troubled life during which he made friends and enemies, notably among the women and men he betrayed. Somebody took it personally and poisoned his whiskey during a performance in a juke joint. As far as I know nobody has produced a Robert Johnson whiskey, or if they have, it has not gone down too well.

Tony Kail poses this question: "Is this use of African religious culture simply an homage to the liquid's use in rituals? It appears that many of the companies that feature Voodoo-inspired aesthetics want to use the symbols and names associated with the religion but do not necessarily want to be associated with the actual religious culture."

---

[10] Ibid.

As in the selling of mezcal and tequila, sacred images are being appropriated for the commercial purposes of selling alcohol, Kail argues, and his conclusion is extremely thought-provoking: "The images that are used in alcohol marketing are provocative and shocking, providing quite a contrast to the rich culture of spirituality that thousands of adherents to the religion enjoy throughout the world. Advertising designers would certainly opt to use those images that stir us as opposed to images that bring peace and communicate spirituality."[11]

Pirates

"Fifteen men on the dead man's chest –
…Yo-ho-ho, and a bottle of rum!
Drink and the devil had done for the rest –
…Yo-ho-ho, and a bottle of rum!"

Of course, if we're to talk about the branding of rum, piracy and pirates would have to figure. If you mention the Caribbean, then there must be pirates. And what better location for pirates to obtain and imbibe some rum?

The relationship between the sea, sailors and rum has already been highlighted (see page 199), but in the 17th and 18th centuries there were practical reasons for the presence of rum in large quantities aboard ships of all kinds. It was a cheap form of alcohol, readily available, and could be used to disinfect drinking water. In fact, Caribbean rum was usually very strong, and diluting it with water meant there was less chance of instant inebriation aboard ship. The resultant mixture, grog, became a Royal Navy staple.

Were pirates religious? That's an odd question, really, given the vast range of piracy over the centuries, from the Islamic Barbary pirates to modern-day Somalis and the officially sanctioned privateering of the late 18th and early 19th century,

---

[11] Ibid.

where chaplains aboard ship would not have been unusual. Christianity at its most elemental tends to survive at sea for those brought up in the faith, in the face of almost any descent into wickedness. There's a small but significant sign that even pirates were concerned for their eternal souls in the list of goods sent by New York merchant Frederick Philipse to his agent Adam Baldridge on the island of St Marie, off Madagascar, in 1689.

Baldridge arrived on St Marie to trade with the pirate companies then infesting the Indian Ocean. Philipse sent "Western" commodities that were otherwise unavailable in the region, which Baldridge then exchanged with the pirates for their pillaged loot. Philipse supplied clothes and tools, but also "some books, Catechisms, primers and horne books, [and] two Bibles ..."[12]

What of the 15 men dancing on that dead man's chest? The verse quoted above is to be found in Robert Louis Stevenson's *Treasure Island* and is thought to be the main reason pirates are now so commonly associated with rum. From Long John Silver to Johnny Depp in one quick swallow. There is an argument that the "15 men on the dead man's chest" are actually the producers of rum, stamping down the body of a dead man into a dunder pit in order to add a particular tang to the rum consequently produced. But Stevenson himself first came across the three words "Dead Man's Chest" in a Charles Kingsley book about the West Indies, and it took just those words to inspire the entire story of *Treasure Island*.

Apparently, in the early 1700s the pirate Edward Teach – better known as Blackbeard – punished a crew who had mutinied against him by marooning them on a tiny islet called Dead Man's Chest, surrounded by high cliffs and without water. Each man was given a cutlass and a bottle of rum, Blackbeard hoping that they would kill each other. But when he returned a month later, 15 had survived.

---

[12] Deposition of Adam Baldridge, 5 May, 1699, CO 5/1042, no. 30ii, quoted at https://www.reddit.com/r/AskHistorians/comments/47m6kq/during_the_golden_age_of_piracy_how_important_was/

In fact, Stevenson himself was interested in the effects of alcohol and other mind-altering substances, and someone profoundly affected by his own alcohol consumption and its effects on others he was close to. Some have argued that his seminal novella *Dr Jekyll and Mr Hyde* is a meditation on the way alcohol can alter someone's personality. There is a book by Thomas L Reed Jr arguing this at length called, *The Transforming Draught: Jekyll and Hyde, Robert Louis Stevenson and the Victorian Alcohol Debate.*[13]

Religion, on the other hand, was definitely not to Stevenson's taste. He utterly rejected Christianity, which caused his father and mother considerable distress. He was living a bohemian and fairly dissolute life in Edinburgh in 1873, when his father stumbled on a document spelling out the constitution of the LJR (Liberty, Justice, Reverence) Club, of which Stevenson and his cousin Bob were members.

"Disregard everything our parents have taught us" it began. He asked his son about the club and his beliefs, to which RLS replied that he no longer believed in God, "Am I to live my whole life as one falsehood?" His father was distraught: "You have rendered my whole life a failure", and his mother said the news was "the heaviest affliction" that she had ever experienced.

"O Lord, what a pleasant thing it is", Stevenson wrote to his friend Charles Baxter, "to have just damned the happiness of (probably) the only two people who care a damn about you in the world."[14]

But Stevenson did understand rum, and the comfort it can bring. Ten years after that final crushing parting from his parents, he wrote one of the greatest books in world literature. A children's book, but not a children's book, *Treasure Island* was

---

[13] Reed Jr, Thomas L, *The Transforming Draught. Jekyll and Hyde, Robert Louis Stevenson and the Victorian Alcohol Debate*, McFarland & Company, Jefferson NC, USA, 2006

[14] Stevenson, Robert Louis, *Selected Letters of Robert Louis Stevenson*, Yale University Press, New Haven CT, 2001, p. 29

read to me by my mother. I have read it to my children. She terrified me with it, and I terrified my offspring, too. All my life I have searched for my Admiral Benbow, a seafront pub offering shelter and respite. All my life I have feared the coming of the Black Spot … Who can forget that wonderful opening to Chapter 3:

"About noon I stopped at the captain's door with some cooling drinks and medicines. He was lying very much as we had left him, only a little higher, and he seemed both weak and excited.

'Jim,' he said, 'you're the only one here that's worth anything, and you know I've been always good to you. Never a month but I've given you a silver fourpenny for yourself. And now you see, mate, I'm pretty low, and deserted by all; and Jim, you'll bring me one noggin of rum, now, won't you, matey?'

'The doctor—' I began.

But he broke in cursing the doctor, in a feeble voice but heartily. 'Doctors is all swabs,' he said; 'and that doctor there, why, what do he know about seafaring men? I been in places hot as pitch, and mates dropping round with Yellow Jack, and the blessed land a-heaving like the sea with earthquakes – what do the doctor know of lands like that? – and I lived on rum, I tell you. It's been meat and drink, and man and wife, to me; and if I'm not to have my rum now I'm a poor old hulk on a lee shore, my blood'll be on you, Jim, and that doctor swab'; and he ran on again for a while with curses. 'Look, Jim, how my fingers fidgets,' he continued in the pleading tone. 'I can't keep 'em still, not I. I haven't had a drop this blessed day. That doctor's a fool, I tell you. If I don't have a drain o' rum, Jim, I'll have the horrors; I seen some on 'em already. I seen old Flint in the corner there, behind you; as plain as print, I seen him; and if I get the horrors, I'm a man that has lived rough, and I'll raise Cain. Your doctor hisself said one glass wouldn't hurt me. I'll give you a golden guinea for a noggin, Jim.'"[15]

Holy Flight – Tasting Notes

Clairin Communal

I love the note from the online drinks dealer Master of Malt – who do one-shot samples of many products they sell, including Clairin Communal – that this drink "is produced naturally with no herbicides or pesticides." It's a blend of four clairins from the communes of Cavaillon, Barraderes, Pignon and St Michel de l'Attalaye, made by hand and about as organic as a drink can get. This is "white" rum in that it's clear, unaffected by oak ageing, and made from sugar cane juice as described above. Be careful! A lot of people don't like the taste neat and mix it with ... well, Coca-Cola, fruit juice ... indeed, almost anything to take the taste away. But if you go for it straight ...

Colour: Clear.

Nose: All fruit and flowers with an acidic, fizzy edge. If someone told you this had been made in a recently cleaned bathtub full of rose hip syrup, you wouldn't be very surprised.

Palate: You know that mango juice that's been left out on the breakfast buffet a little too long? Mix it with tonic water and you're on the right track.

Finish: Fruit, touch of bitterness and sea salt. Possibly best mixed with something else unless you really are after that full-on Haitian ritual experience. As I was once told by an Islay resident when I mentioned one of the local whiskies, "You can clean windows with it."

---

[15] Stevenson, Robert Louis, *Treasure Island*, Cassell & Company Limited, London, 1883, Chapter 3

Clément VSOP Rhum Agricole

Well, this is very good. Martinique Rhum Agricole is not like Bacardi (Cuban or expatriate) or any of the molasses-based drinks that creep into alcopops or provide, I must admit, such an ideal cold-weather addition to ginger beer or ginger wine (see below). These Martinique rums can be delicate, restrained, sophisticated or rough as turpentine if you choose badly. This, though, is a delight. Matured for a year in virgin French oak barrels, it then spends three years in charred bourbon barrels. It was awarded a Gold rating by the Beverage Tasting Institute and also received 96 points out of a possible 100 from *Wine Enthusiast.*

Colour: Deep, burnished gold.

Nose: There is oak and sweetness coupled with vanilla ice cream in a Baked Alaska kind of way, plus a tart fruitiness lurking in there, too. You can almost hear the sugar cane rustling in the breeze.

Palate: Typically light for this type of rum, but with the depth of all that oak ageing, too. But the fruitiness that makes this so different from dark, cheap molasses-based drinks is also evident. There's a real delicacy to it.

Finish: Toffee from the oak, but with spiced apple pie, cinnamon – and brown sugar, funnily enough.

Watson's Trawler Rum

Down and dirty, a mixture of rums from Barbados and Guyana. Cheap too, as drunk by, well, trawlermen. And women. Mostly mixed with Coke but in my neck of the bog, from small glasses, not drowned in mixer and used as a chaser for heavy beer. A double shot of this added to Stone's or Crabbie's Green Ginger Wine has a wondrous effect on the common cold in my experience, and mixed with ginger beer, it (or Shetland's own dark rum, Stewart's) has been offered to me as a cure for seasickness. Ginger root is often used as a herbal salve for nausea, and I know at least one Royal National Lifeboat Institution member who insists on ginger snap biscuits as a *mal-de-mer* curative. Possibly dipped in rum.

Colour: Dark, furniture-stain brown.

Nose: Raisins, dried fruit generally, road tar and rope ends. Yo ho ho! Also black molasses. Smells sticky.

Palate: The spirit comes through warmingly. Treacle tart and the blackest of black coffee – an espresso with ten teaspoonfuls of sugar.

Finish: Well, there might be oak in there but it's hard to tell among all that syrup of figs stickiness. Actually, it's great! You're all at sea in a hurricane, heading home with a full catch of illegal mackerel and all is well with the world. Probably.

CHAPTER 12

SAKE, WHISKY AND JESSIE ROBERTA'S JOURNEY

Japan
Sake and whisky

Holy Flight
– *Ben Nevis 10-year-old Single Malt Whisky*
– *Isake Classic Sake*
– *Yoichi Single Malt Whisky*

Jesse Roberta's story has fascinated me since I first encountered her in 1991, in the manager's office at the then rather bedraggled Fort William's Ben Nevis Distillery.

The distillery, which had fallen on hard times, had the previous year been taken over by the Japanese spirits company Nikka, owned since 1954 by the conglomerate Asahi. There were some leaflets from Nikka telling the story of why Takeshi Taketsuru, Nikka's then boss, had moved heaven and earth to buy this little piece of Scotland's spirits industry. His adoptive mother, Rita Taketsuru, born Jesse Roberta Cowan, had eloped in 1920 with her family's lodger, Masataka or Massan Taketsuru, travelling to Japan with him. There, after many trials and tribulations, Massan started Japan's first malt whisky distillery in the far northern snowfields of Hokkaido. It was the beginning of Nikka and what is now the world-beating and award-winning Japanese whisky industry. And their tale remains one of the great transglobal love stories. Rita would embrace Japanese culture, adopt two Japanese children, and endure harassment and accusations of spying during World War II, before dying young in 1953. She would become a kind of saint in Japan, her and Massan's story the subject of books, a thriving visitor centre and even a wildly popular daytime soap opera.

She was to become, as some of the local people who grew to adore her said, "more Japanese than the Japanese", dressing exclusively in Japanese clothes and becoming such an expert in Japanese cuisine that you can now go on a dedicated Rita Taketsuru culinary tour, drink and eat at Rita's Bar and buy a recipe book containing all her signature dishes. And all that time, she remained a dedicated churchgoer and Christian. We will return to her story later in this chapter.

Rita's life illustrates how the Japanese national religion, Shintō, affected her despite her Christianity. Because Shintō is not just a matter of faith-in-a-bubble or something exclusively conducted within temples by monks. It is inherent in the Japanese approach to work, family life, politics, the land and ethics. To become as adapted and absorbed into Japanese life as Rita did meant her Scottish Presbyterianism had to be conjoined with Shintō, that whisky and rice wine had to be mutually consumed. Add some shōchū (a distilled spirit typically made from mixed grains and/or sweet potatoes) into the mix, and you may be heading for a hangover of truly international proportions.

A Way, Not a Religion

So what is Shintō? As with so much else in what is a short book covering an enormous amount of ground, this is a subject that has produced entire libraries, and of all the great world religions, Shintō seems one of the most enigmatic and elusive. Some practitioners define it not as a religion but as "a way", and see it as integrated with custom, tradition and State. There is also an argument that Shintō is a fairly modern system of belief and action, only coming into proper focus in the 19th century as a way of defining "Japaneseness" and linked to the imperial court and a Japanese way of life.

You may associate the sublime beauty, order and calm of a Japanese garden with Shintō, and that would to an extent be correct. Buddhism is also crucial to the appearance of what is thought of in the West as a "Japanese" garden and, while the two faiths, or aspects of faith, walk hand in hand horticulturally, there are differences in style.

Shintō's creation myth involves eight perfect islands and the lakes of the gods, or *shinchi*. Ancient Shintō shrines to the *kami*, the gods and spirits, were widely scattered in Japan and often included rocks or trees marked with cords of rice fibre – *shimenawa* – set in a context of white stones or pebbles, symbolizing purity. And so you get the pale gravel courtyard in Shintō shrines, imperial palaces, Buddhist temples and gardens.

These gardens were also strongly influenced by the Chinese philosophy of Daoism and Amida Buddhism, which arrived from China around AD 552. These stories tell of five mountainous islands inhabited by eight immortals living in harmony with nature, who had the ability to fly on the back of a bird – the crane. A giant sea turtle supported the islands, a scenario that will immediately resonate with any readers of Terry Pratchett's *Discworld* books. In that universe, the great A'Tuin is a Giant Star Turtle – species *Chelys galactica* – who carries four giant elephants called Berilia, Tubul, Great T'Phon and Jerakeen. They in turn support the Discworld on their ample backs. In Shintō, there is an absence of elephants and the five Chinese islands became one called Horai-zen or Mount Horai, symbol of a perfect world. This philosophy is much featured symbolically in the classic Japanese garden, along with rocks representing turtles and cranes.

My understanding is that the word Shintō refers to a way of life aligned with the worship of various traditional gods, many of them integrated with natural phenomena, and became popular in distinguishing particularly Japanese beliefs from those that were intrinsically Buddhist. It's linked to the seasons and is about traditional practices as well as the gods, beliefs and rituals associated with these practices. Sin is not big in Shintō but growth, fertility and purity are important. Buddhism is traditionally concerned with transcendence, going beyond the worldly to a place of nirvana, whereas Shintō focuses on the ordinary aspects of living and getting by in the best way possible. According to the *Encyclopedia Britannica*, "Shintō is more readily observed in the social life of the Japanese people and in their personal motivations than in a pattern of formal belief or philosophy. It remains closely connected with the Japanese value system and the Japanese people's ways of thinking and acting."[1] Its promotion in the 19th century was linked to the imperial family's desire to assert the primacy of the gods and practices of the emperor over local gods and practices.

There are Shintō shrines and temples, and there is more to them than monks and gardens. And there is sake.

Chewing the Rice

Making an alcoholic beverage from whatever source of sugar was most readily available is part of human culture, as we've seen, so making beer and wine from rice was an obvious developmental step in a country where that was the staple crop. Sake had fairly brutal beginnings: the earliest form, *kuchikami-zake*, was made simply by chewing grains of rice. This would then be spat into a pot and the enzymes in the saliva, along with natural airborne yeasts, would be left to produce an alcoholic beverage perhaps even less appetizing than neat Buckfast Tonic.

However, the pleasures and power of sake soon became evident to Japan's rulers, and the making of sake was gradually appropriated by the imperial court for festivals, rituals and of course for more frivolous partying. But from about AD 878 onwards, as power passed into the hands of the

---

[1] https://www.britannica.com/topic/Shinto

military, private brewing was encouraged, along with paying taxes on everything sold. But sake made in Shinto temples and at shrines remained tax-free, so understandably this became widely available. It is much less common now. Sake was and is used in ceremonies, too. The little white porcelain flasks called *miki-dokkuri* and their associated cups can be seen on altars of shrines throughout Japan, and in the ceremony of *O-miki* a priest will drink a small amount of sake in an act of prayerful unification with the gods. There are also many legends and stories associated with divinities and the drink, which is placed as an offering on Shinto shrines as a matter of course.

In one of the tales about legendary dragon Yamata-no-Orochi, the shintō storm god Susano-o has the goddess Kushinada-hime's parents brew a particularly strong type of sake. He then uses it to get the dragon so drunk that it falls asleep, after which he kills it. It is the first mention of sake in the collection of Japanese myths and tales called the *Kojiki*.

There are stories of the gods getting together to drink sake, and it's natural that sake has its very own god, Kusu-no-kami, offspring of Susano-o, born when that deity made a pledge with Amaterasu, the goddess of the sun, while on his way to the Land of Ne-no-kuni (origin of all things). He is also the god of fire and is sometimes identified as Senju-Kannon (the thousand-armed Avalokiteshvara) found in both Shintō and Buddhism.

Sake is drunk for pleasure, but its consumption can also be an act of purification, bringing humans and gods together. The rice wine is important in Shintō wedding ceremonies, with the bride and groom serving each other with it in much the same way that in some traditional Scottish weddings the couple drink whisky from a silver quaich (a traditional cup with two handles) to symbolize their unity. Sake is often given out at shrine festivals to worshippers. There may even be preliminary consumption before that, strictly necessary for the rituals.

Party of the Gods

The Saka Shrine at Izumo City in Shimane Prefecture is one of many in the area, but it is highly regarded because of its connection to Kuso-no-Kami and a legend about a massive party that apparently took place there, involving all of the gods and a very great deal of sake. On 13 October, head brewers from all the sake breweries in the area gather there, and in preparation for this, the head priest of the shrine brews *doburoku*, an unrefined sake. The brewers drink this and pray that the coming season of brewing will bring a tasty product and lots of sales. Oh, and members of the public can, if they're lucky, have a taste of the doburoku, too. I found this post on TripAdvisor by Odoridu-Aki, here translated from Japanese:

"When you go up the stone steps on the approach to the shrine, you will find the main shrine, and next to it, you will have a mini-sized cup that is often used for tasting, and you will have doburoku drawn from the jar. It feels good to have two glasses. A banquet! At Yokote Shrine, I was able to appreciate the Kagura dance. A place where you can go once. With a driver who does not drink, it is perfect."

Speaking of the need to avoid inebriation, it is important not to confuse sake with *shōchū*, which is much stronger than sake, as it is distilled to between 25 and 35 per cent alcohol by volume. And not just from rice, but also from barley, sweet potatoes, buckwheat or sugar. Anything, really. It's been made since at least the 16th century. After the missionary Francis Xavier visited Kagoshima Prefecture in 1549, he wrote: "The Japanese drink arak made from rice ... but I have not seen a single drunkard. That is because once inebriated they immediately lie down and go to sleep."[2]

And there is a tenuous Shintō connection to shōchū in the graffiti found on a roof plank at the Kōriyama Hachiman shrine in Ōkuchi, Kagoshima. The carpenters working there in 1559

---

[2] https://web.archive.org/web/20050307194210/http://www.denen-shuzo.co.jp/chisiki/tisiki07.htm

inscribed this complaint, "The high priest was so stingy he never once gave us shōchū to drink. What a nuisance!"[3]

When Rice Wine Met Whisky

Masataka Taketsuru came from a rice wine dynasty, but in the years after World War I, his family thought there might be a future in making whisky and sent their son to study in Scotland. Even today, you will find folk in the whisky industry who shake their heads ruefully at what they see as a piece of enormously successful industrial espionage. "He came here to steal our secrets," one now-deceased veteran distiller once told me. The status of the Japanese whisky industry and its ownership of several distilleries in Scotland tells its own story. Suntory and Nikka are now names as familiar to connoisseurs as Laphroaig and Macallan, though it must be said that until recent changes in Japanese law, some of the drams sold as Japanese contained a great deal of imported Scottish liquid.[4]

The reputation of Japanese whisky is extremely high, but it was not always thus. In Ian Fleming's 1964, Japan-set James Bond novel *You Only Live Twice*, Bond's source Dikko Henderson gets drunk on Suntory whisky and sake. Next day, when he complains about having a hangover, he's told by Bond: "You shouldn't have poured all that sake on top of the Suntory. I can't believe Japanese whisky makes a good foundation for anything." To which Henderson replies, "You're wrong about Suntory. It's a good enough brew. Stick to the cheapest, the White Label, at around fifteen bob a bottle. There are two smarter brands, but the cheap one's the best."[5]

---

[3]   History of Suntory: https://www.suntory.co.jp/customer/faq/001805.html

[4]   "Whisky makes in Japan accused of relabelling Scotch", https://foodanddrink. scotsman.com/drink/whisky-makers-in-japan-accused-of-relabelling-scotch-whisky-as-japanese/

[5]   Fleming, Ian, *You Only Live Twice*, Jonathan Cape, London, 1964, Chapter 5

Fleming was of course a pioneer of product placement in literature and the film versions of his books were and remain no exceptions. The movie version of *You Only Live Twice* features Sean Connery as Bond quaffing Suntory White Label in his friend Tiger Tanaka's garden. But there's no sign of any sake.

Taketsuru studied organic chemistry at Glasgow University before travelling to various Scottish distilleries, taking copious notes and learning on the job as an unpaid apprentice. In the little town of Kirkintilloch, north of Glasgow, the Cowan family were in a state of financial embarrassment. Dr Samuel Cowan had died in 1918 of a heart attack, leaving Jesse Roberta (later known as Rita in Japan), her sisters Ella and Lucy and brother Ramsay in the care of their mother Robina. The family were struggling with the upkeep of a rather grand nine-room house called Middlecroft, and Samuel, in the days before the National Health Service, had died with unpaid and uncollectable fees of almost £600 ($787) outstanding – the equivalent of almost £24,000 ($31,500) today. To add to the tragedy, Jesse Roberta's fiancé had been killed in Damascus during the war. Nevertheless, she was a highly educated career woman, with a degree in English and Music from Glasgow University and, unusually for the day, a driving licence. She had driven her father to appointments and was also a successful piano teacher.

So, in 1919 Robina was looking for a lodger and the handsome 25-year-old Masataku took up the offer, having heard about the room through fellow student Ella. He was immediately popular with the family, teaching young Ramsay the martial art ju-jitsu. He also took part in social occasions, including, family lore has it, a New Year duet of *Auld Lang Syne* between Massan and Jesse Roberta, during which they fell in love. There's also a great visual image, remembered by grand-nephew Harry Hogan, of them pulling a silver sixpence and a ring respectively as tokens from a Christmas pudding or clootie (cloth-boiled) dumpling. And realizing they were meant to be together.[6]

---

6   "Astonishing tale of Scots woman who took whisky to Japan", *Daily Record*, 13

In January 1920, the couple married at the Calton registry office in Glasgow's Great Hamilton Street. Jesse Roberta's mother did not attend and probably did not know what was afoot. The witnesses were her younger sister Lucy and her friend Jessie Henderson, sister of Dr Samuel Henderson, who now ran Dr Cowan's surgery at Middlecroft. Robina tried to have the marriage annulled and Massan faced parental disapproval, too.

After a period living in Campbeltown in Kintyre, where Massan worked for the Hazelburn Distillery, the pair began the long journey to Japan by sea. It took them 10 months, and Jesse Roberta, who was never in particularly good health, was not a robust passenger. Becoming known as Rita in Japan, she would visit Scotland just once, in 1931. Her sister Lucy came to Japan in 1959 on a visit, but those were her only subsequent contacts with her home country and family apart from copious letters.

Massan went to work on his return, hoping to put into practice the lesson he'd learned in Scotland, but when his employer seemed keen only to make cheap spirit, he resigned. The couple lived hand to mouth with Rita supporting them through English and music lessons. Then, in 1923, Massan was taken on by Shinjiro Torii – founder of the Suntory group – to help build a whisky distillery in Yamazaki. There were personality problems, and again Massan went his own way. Yamazaki would later become the site of one of Japan's best distilleries, with the Yamazaki 2013 single malt sherry-cask bottling being named Best Whisky in the World in 2015 in the prestigious Jim Murray's *Whisky Bible*.

Snowbound

In 1934, Massan and Rita moved to the northern island of Hokkaido, near Russia, which in winter is often snowbound. They picked it for its similarities to the Highlands of Scotland,

May 2012, https://www.dailyrecord.co.uk/news/uk-world-news/astonishing-life-of-scots-woman-who-877833 though it was also famous for its orchards, and at first Massan raised cash by producing apple juice in large quantities. Finally, having set up the Nippon Kaju KK firm – now called Nikka Whisky – Massan built a distillery at Yoichi with the help of two investors, installing a copper pot-still directly fired by powdered coal on the Scottish model. They even planted heather around the doors. It was 1935 before that first pot-still arrived and spirit production started. Taketsuru could not afford a second still at the time, so the traditional wash-and-spirit, twin-still process couldn't be used. In 1939 the first whisky was vatted, along with Nikka's other distillate, brandy, and a year later the first consignments left the distillery for sale, exactly twenty years after Taketsuru and Rita had left Scotland. The story of Japanese single malt whisky had begun.

And then there was war. At first, this proved a major advantage for the Taketsurus. The Imperial Japanese Navy had been a major consumer of imported Scotch whisky before the war, and as supplies dwindled, turned to the Yoichi distillery instead. It was declared a war industry.

For Rita, the war was a source of great heartbreak and trouble. You can only imagine what it was like, despite her strenuous efforts to become "more Japanese than the Japanese". After Pearl Harbor, in December 1941, the *tokubetsu keiji bu* (Imperial Special Detective Division or secret police) searched the Taketsuru home because they saw a radio aerial antenna on their roof and suspected that Rita was a spy, communicating with the British or Russians. It's worth remembering that Japan was subject to major and successful spying missions by the Russians during World War II. Agents would follow Rita and she was prevented from travelling on the Hokkaido-Honshu ferry. Children would call her names like "ketō! ketō!" ("hairy foreigner! hairy foreigner!") and threw stones at her. To this she would sternly reply (in Japanese), "I'm Japanese, just like you children."

Many locals shunned her, apparently causing her to lament, "If only my nose was just a little less prominent, if my eyes and hair were black like the Japanese."[7] Nevertheless, she remained staunchly loyal to her husband and to the town. She was proud to continue teaching those children whose parents remained supporters and friends. She was still struggling with health problems that had afflicted her since the Kirkintilloch days.

Rita and Massan had adopted a daughter, Rima, in 1930, who grew up troubled and disturbed by the way her mother was treated during the war. But after the war, they adopted Massan's 20-year-old nephew Takeshi, who was groomed to take over from Massan.

Rita died in 1961, aged 64, of cirrhosis. There's no record of her having had a serious drinking habit, although the Japanese soap opera Massan portrays her as taking a dram or two. She did not thrive in the cold Hokkaido winters and it was in her winter home, Kanagawa's Kamakura City, that she died. Massan was so upset that he spent two days alone in his room, neither eating nor drinking, and he did not attend the cremation. He apparently begged for her ashes to be brought to him so he could sleep with them by his side. After Rita's cremation, they held a formal funeral in Yoichi. Those terrible wartime days had been forgotten, as the townspeople lined part of the cortege route with garlands of flowers in her honour.

Massan would live for another 19 years, establishing Nikka as the powerhouse in whisky production it remains, and passing on control to his and Rita's adopted son, Takeshi. He and Rita were reunited in a grave overlooking the distillery in Yoichi. In a highly unusual move, the gravestone is in English.

Pastor for Free

There was an odd aspect to the funeral, too. It was undertaken by the new pastor of Yoshioka, the local church, who had met Rita before her death. Establishing that she was both baptized and

---

[7] "Becoming Legally Japanese", https://www.turning-japanese.info/2015/06/rita.html

devout, he waived his fees after he witnessed a huge outpouring of grief and affection for Rita. It was, he thought, a great witness to the power of Christianity, then as now very much a minority religion in Japan. Through a trust set up in Rita's name, Takeshi and Massan then funded the establishment of a kindergarten associated with the church.

Go to the distillery today and you will find a museum commemorating Rita's life. In Japanese culture, she is celebrated as the queen of Japanese whisky. There are, as well as the TV series and numerous books, the cookery tour and the merchandise, manga comics and much more. It's interesting that the establishment of whisky production in Japan brought to the forefront of Japanese culture a Scottish woman who was utterly determined to absorb Japanese culture, withstood all the hazards of being an enemy alien during World War II, stood completely with her husband no matter what, and remained a convinced Christian. Yet none of this was anathema in terms of Shinto practice and belief, which has no set dogma and is all about family social convention, tradition and discipline – things Rita was committed to.

The distillery itself produces great whisky. The warehouses sit silently under snow for much of the year, and inside the pot stills are old-school Scottish in design. Each is adorned with a Shinto garland.

The words that follow come from a song performed by Scottish folk ensemble Mavis Grind and the Fitful Heads. You can find it online at thebeatcroft.co.uk

Jessie Roberta in the Empire of the Sun

"She gazed from Kirkintilloch to the Campsies high above
She gave Scotland up for whisky, she gave it all up for love
In 1920 Masataka Taketsuru came
Impressed with his Ju-Jitsu skills, asked her to change
* her name*

Jessie Roberta, in the Empire of the Sun
Jessie Roberta, you were his only one

You sailed on the White Anchor Line
You left the River Clyde
Your mother and your sisters
Stayed at Middlecroft and cried
And Massan said he'd build a Campbeltown for you
In the Hokkaido snows he made that dream come true

Chorus

And when the war broke out you couldn't help but be afraid
You hid your peelie wallie[8] west of Scotland face away
they ransacked your house, said you were a spy
Somehow you and Taketsuru's Campbeltown survived

Massan truly loved you, loved you till his dying breath
And now you lie together in the mystery of death
But your garlands bloom in that Hokkaido chill
The water of your life forever flowing from those stills."[9]

Holy Flight – Tasting Notes

Ben Nevis 10-Year-Old Single Malt Whisky
Around 2017 there was a fuss about Ben Nevis 10, as the food writer and broadcaster Rachel McCormack revealed in her book *Chasing the Dram* that the bottling of Ben Nevis then available contained whiskies a lot older than 10.

The rule is that when a whisky claims to be 10 (or 12 or 25)

---

8   "Peelie wallie" – Scots term for being pale and wan

9   Jessie Roberta in the *Empire of the Sun*, written by Scar Quilse/Mavis Grind. Copyright Control, used by permission.

years old, then the youngest whisky used to make it must be that age when bottled. So, Ben Nevis 10 is a minimum of 10 years old. Despite being a single malt, it contains a blend of different, older Ben Nevis expressions, and as Nikka, Japanese owners of Ben Nevis, had been exporting all the young spirit to age it in Japan (then selling it as Japanese whisky), the only thing the local management could do was use older whiskies. As there is a tendency for older whiskies – that's whiskies that have been in the cask for longer – to be better and a lot more expensive, Ben Nevis 10, which never sold at a premium price, was a bargain. Needless to say, there was a bit of a run on supplies. The warehousing has been regulated further since then, and the Ben Nevis 10 you get these days is not as tasty as the 2017 version. But it's still a good dram. Masataku Taketsuru and Rita would be proud.

Colour: Mid-golden brown, but varies depending on the bottling.

Nose: This is a West Highland malt, and typical of the style – a touch of peat but not overwhelming, Nescafé, toasted porridge and wedding (fruit) cake with some lighter leafiness. There's marmalade in there, too. Think Paddington Bear post-lunch on a wet Fort William Day (and it's always wet in Fort William).

Palate: Dry with the peat coming through more strongly now, then toffee apples made with cooking varieties. Definitely some oats.

Finish: Quite smooth. Just the very thing to take up to the top of Ben Nevis, Britain's highest mountain, and take the merest nip of in celebration at having conquered it. Not too much, though, as it's also an extremely dangerous mountain and people die there all too frequently, despite the well-worn path to the top.

Isake Classic Sake

I'm not a huge fan of sake and have never really spent the time doing that heat-it-up, chill-it-down, swill-it-all-around thing. So I'm including this as a good representation of a premium-priced sake, readily available worldwide. It's 14.7 per cent alcohol, which is pretty much the same as Buckfast Tonic, but this is a lot nicer. Well, a bit.

Colour: Clear with faint greeny-yellow overtones.

Nose: All depends on whether or not you heat it; flowery.

Palate: Soft and slightly sticky. Nuts and floral spice.

Finish: Melon cocktail.

Apparently if you chill it there are chalky, lemongrass elements detectable, but this is something I have been unable to check myself.

Yoichi Single Malt Whisky

The whisky produced by Nikka at Taketsuru's Yoichi distillery, site of the Rita Museum and made to the original exacting standards, using traditional, direct-fired stills and peaty in the classic Scottish West Highland style – just like Ben Nevis. This no-age-statement whisky is a blend of various Yoichi ages and is a classic representation of the distillery's style. It's not cheap but neither is it ludicrously expensive. Even if you can just about get two bottles of Ben Nevis for the same price, depending where you shop.

Colour: Tawny.

Nose: Hefty, but the undoubted phenolic content from peat never overwhelms. It's quite smooth. Citrus fruits and spices head into flowery territory, but the aroma of peat smoke in the malted barley is always present.

Palate: No ignoring the peat now, but there's chocolate and nuts in there, too. Like eating a Swiss milk chocolate bar face down in a bog, only more alcoholic. With a touch of non-citrus fruit, but there's also the tang of a sweet lime marmalade.

Finish: It just goes on and on, the peat turning all oaty and fruity before a little hint of salt and ozone creeps in. Sort of like a Campbelltown malt, which is nice as that's where Rita and Massan lived for a while after they eloped.

CHAPTER 13

HERE COME THE VIKINGS AGAIN

Scandinavia, Shetland, England (Lindisfarne)
Beer, whisky and mead

Holy Flight
— *Lerwick Brewery Blindside Stout*
— *Scapa Skiren Single Malt*
— *Lindisfarne Mead*

Largs is a small holiday town on the Firth of Clyde, about 30 miles from Glasgow, and it has been one of my favourite places since I first tasted home-made Italian ice cream and smelled the tang of salt, vinegar and fishy chip fat on the evening air.

I have never publicly consumed an alcoholic drink in Largs, but I have worshipped in the local Gospel Hall, sung choruses at open-air meetings and eaten large quantities of Nardini's ice cream and fish and chips, washed down with Barr's Irn Bru (see page 119). I have gazed at The Pencil, the monument to Scottish King Alexander III's defeat of King Haakon of Norway's forces in 1263, the battle that brought to an end Viking harassment of Scotland's mainland, though not Norse influence over the islands.

Vikings are still part of Largs's lore and street geography, pub names and touristic mythology. But long gone is the item that planted the romance of the Vikings in my head and heart as a youngster – the gigantic facsimile of a Norse war galley that used to jut from an Art Deco building that was once the 1,300-seat Viking cinema. We kids would shriek with excitement each time we passed that fake boat's ferocious-looking dragon's head prow, but before long the building was the headquarters and bottling plant of J H Wham and Son, who produced a truly horrible blend of sweet South African wine and Scotch whisky called Scotsmac. It was a favourite of schoolboys and girls on an illicit bender as it was cheap and effective; alcoholics liked it too. In fact, it was not unlike the much mentioned Buckfast Tonic Wine or other electric soups of Scottish industrial culture. It was affectionately known as Wham's Dram or sometimes Bam's Dram.[1]

Scotsmac is no longer available for sale. It had gone through several owners by the time it vanished from the cheaper British supermarkets' shelves in 2018, and its 15 per cent alcohol, viciously hangover-inducing axe-blow to head and heart, thankfully, became a thing of the past. I once conducted a tongue-very-much-in-cheek "guided tasting" that involved Scotsmac, Buckfast Tonic Wine, Irn Bru and English St George's Whisky. It's fair to say that the audience left discombobulated and desperately seeking a proper drink.

And that was it for me and Vikings really, once childhood has departed. Or so I thought. Then, for reasons spelled out in two other books, I ended up living in the Shetland Islands, that northernmost of British archipelagos halfway to Scandinavia, and Vikings came rampaging back into my life.[2]

Shetland was not abandoned by Haakon of Norway after the Battle of Largs. He retreated to Orkney and plotted a foul and violent vengeance on Alexander and his Scots, but Orkney's damp and dodgy vapours claimed his life. Most of Scotland was

---

[1]   Bam: Scots vernacular for a foolish and potentially violent person

[2]   Morton, Tom, *The Further North You Go*, Shetland Times Ltd, Lerwick, 2013; Morton, Tom, *In Shetland, Tales from the Last Bookshop*, Looderhorn Books, Shetland, 2017

left alone by the berserkers, but it would be almost another 200 years before Shetland and Orkney passed from Scandinavian (by then, Danish) hands into the clutches of the Scots. In 1472, the deed was done. Three years earlier Margaret, daughter of the King of Denmark, had married James III of Scotland. A dowry of 60,000 florins had been agreed the previous year, with Orkney and Shetland as security against non-payment. None of that sum was ever paid and on 20 February 1472, the Scottish crown annexed Orkney and Shetland, groups of islands that to a large extent (and genetic research has proved this) had been populated by Norse settlers and their descendants.

And that heritage is still very much in evidence today, in the remnants of Udal law that relate to the seabed and coastline, in the local dialect, placenames, the design of inshore fishing boats and, not least, in the annual fire festivals called Up Helly Aa.

The biggest of the Up Helly Aa events is in Shetland's capital, Lerwick, but there are a dozen or so smaller ones in communities throughout the isles. They are among several Scottish winter fire festivals, mostly in northern coastal towns, founded to herald the coming of the lighter nights and to provide an excuse for, well, partying very hard indeed.

Up Helly Aa in Shetland was originally a town festival and basically an excuse for sustained youthful mayhem. From the early 1800s onward, groups of inebriated young men would set tar barrels alight and drag them through the streets at Christmas, New Year and "Auld Yule" by the abandoned Julian calendar, more commonly Twelfth Night. It's been argued that soldiers returning from the Napoleonic Wars had acquired a post-traumatic taste for fire, explosions and general drunken violence. Gangs would cheerfully attack the premises of anyone who'd upset them during the previous year, and it all became a tad too riotous and dangerous. Police and troops were called in, and the whole thing was banned around 1874. A few years later, amid an upsurge of romantic sentiment about the islands' Viking heritage, the first torchlight procession was held with Viking dress apparent and, in a flurry of Victorian do-goodery, the Up Helly Aa Society was formed to promote total abstinence and keep young men from the demon drink by encouraging dressing up and well-behaved dancing, dramatic performance and singing songs about Grand Old Rapists and Pillagers On the Ocean Wave.

The whole thing grew to its current status in Lerwick as a mass event involving up to 1,000 "guizers", the leading band of whom are the Jarl or leader's squad, dressed in Viking finery. A massive war galley is towed through the streets and set on fire in a local playpark. Much partying, dancing and drinking ensues until breakfast the next day and beyond. The idea of total abstinence or even moderation has long been forgotten.

The festival spread to rural areas where women have been allowed to participate as more than tea makers and dance partners, and at last the Lerwick event - hitherto resolutely macho - is planning to allow females to march, drink and disport themselves should they so desire.

I have been to many Up Helly Aa processions and post-match parties, and there is something thrilling and energizing about the sheer joyful exuberance of it all: the smell of paraffin from the burning torches; the eruption of flame from a burning longship (some in the rural areas, sent flaming out to sea). The men dressed as Vikings mostly recognize the essential absurdity of what they're doing, though there have been cases of the Lerwick festival's motto – "We axe (demand) for whit we want" – being taken too seriously.

It's a bit of community theatre with partying and dressing up thrown in, and while some local folk cast glances of political and economic jealousy towards Norway, it doesn't really reflect a desire to be un-Scottish or un-British and suddenly parade around wearing raven's feathers, carrying a hatchet. It's a bit of fun. And curiously, its resemblance to real Viking activity really comes down to the drinking.

This is because alcohol was absolutely critical to Viking culture, as reflected in the Norse mythology that underpinned it. Vikings liked to do things drunk, and the legendary berserker, the "bear men" or "wolf warriors", portrayed in tombs and carvings as biting their shields ferociously, were off their heads on mead or beer and doses of the plant *Hyoscyamus niger* (henbane), not fly agaric mushrooms as is often asserted.

In a way that anticipated the later creation of small or mild ales during the Industrial Revolution in the UK (1760–1840) as a means of making drinking water safe through sterilization, the Vikings drank a great deal of beer. Fermentation was key to making liquid ingestion non-toxic, so you had wine made from berries and other fruits, fermented milk (known as syrah) and mead, brewed from honey. It's lately become apparent from the excavation of Viking tombs that women not only fought on equal terms in Viking war parties alongside their male counterparts – even leading them – but also that they were in charge of the drink, making, serving and meting out the mead.

Wine made from berries was common and fairly downmarket; wine made from grapes had to be imported from more southern climes and was expensive. It was the chosen drink of Odin, chief of the gods, and, as such, god of alcohol in all its forms. Lesser gods had to be content with mead and partaking of it was necessary for anyone who fancied becoming a poet or a bard. Alcohol was an integral part not just of social functions, but also the signing of political treaties, sorting out of wills after a death and sealing of land deals. You can see aspects of this still in the trotting out of the drinks trolley or the cracking open of a bottle of champagne after a business agreement or the signing of a treaty.

But alcohol was also something to be shared, with religion at the core of this. The gods had gifted alcohol to humanity, now humanity had to pass that gift on: buy your round. British, indeed northern European drinking culture remains based on this idea. The pub is a place to meet, to share alcohol and stories and create or reflect community. And in Viking culture, you had the *sumbl*.

A sumbl, or *symbel*, was a drinks party thrown by a chieftain and held in his mead hall. Women again were key here in serving the drink, controlling who got it and when, classifying guests according to their status. They stopped fights, made sure enmities were not (necessarily) carried to their fatal conclusions. They were seen as peace bringers, and absolutely crucial to proceedings. Again, the social ebb and flow of a modern party can be discerned here. The most famous examples of sumbls occur in the poem *Beowulf*, which concerns events that allegedly took place in the 6th century, though the manuscript dates from sometime between the 8th and 11th centuries.

Hrothgar hosts a sumbl for his warriors at Heorat, presided over by Queen Wealhtheow.

> "Adorned in her gold, she graciously saluted the men
> in the hall, then handed the cup first to Hrothgar, their
> homeland's guardian, urging him to drink deep and enjoy
> it because he was dear to them. And he drank it down
> like the warlord he was, with festive cheer."[3]

After serving Hrothgar, Queen Wealhtheow serves the warriors according to rank, with Beowulf coming last, as at this point he is an unproven warrior.

> "So the Helming woman went on her rounds, queenly
> and dignified, decked out in rings, offering the goblet to
> all ranks, treating the household and the assembled troop,
> until it was Beowulf's turn to take it from her hand."[4]

As Mark Forsyth writes in his book *A Short History of Drunkenness*, "you needed a queen because women were a

---

[3] *Beowulf*, trans. Seamus Heaney, *The Norton Anthology of English Literature*, gen. ed. Stephen Greenblatt, 9th ed., Vol A, Norton, New York, 2012, pp.36–108, lines 614–619

[4] *Beowulf*, lines 620–624, as above

rather important part of the mead hall feast. Women – or peace-weavers as the Vikings called them – were the ones who kept the formal footing of the feast going, who lubricated the rowdy atmosphere and provided a healthy dose of womanly calm. They were in charge of the logistics of the sumbl."[5]

On a typical evening, you would drink first to Odin, then to two other gods or goddesses, including Thor (Odin's son), Freyr (the god of fertility) and his sister Freya (goddess of same), and possibly Njord (god of the sea). Drinking escalated and what was said was given great credence, as due to alcohol's source being Valhalla, home of the gods, everything you said when drunk was seen as potentially divinely inspired. Things could and did get tricky. The drinking inspired loyalty and bonding. It reminds me of a story about the band The Strokes, who apparently always rehearsed blind drunk, as it was necessary to perform blind drunk – they required band unity and they needed to be drunk to remember the words and the chords.

Marriages and funerals were also events hallmarked by alcohol consumption. Again, one thinks of more modern celebrations, notably during my stint as a reporter for *The Scotsman* newspaper, when I heard someone in Inverness discussing what she said had been "the perfect Ferry[6] funeral – the police, fire brigade and ambulance were called."

And there was always mead, as befitted an event held in a mead hall. Mead is a big part of Norse mythology. There is an eternal sumbl in Valhalla involving the souls of warriors killed in battle. Who get no respite, as they are fated to fight each other (while drinking) to see who qualifies for the Last Battle, Ragnarök, at the end of the world. Mead flows from the udders of holy goats. This is not something I suggest you investigate if you happen to see a passing goat, be it (or you) drunk or sober.

---

[5]   Forsyth, Mark, *A Short History of Drunkenness*, Penguin, London, 2018

[6]   The Ferry – an area of the Scottish Highland capital, Inverness, with a reputation in the past for certain social issues

And then there's the Mead of Poetry. This is an incredibly complicated story for which I have some affection, in that it purports to explain the origins of poetry and literature, though some may see it more as a tale of how tabloid journalism started.

War between two sets of gods – the Aesir of Asgard and the Vanir of Vanaheim – was drawing to a close. To solemnize the peace, both sides spat into a pot, making out of this a man called Kvasir, who turned out to be so clever he could answer any question anyone cared to ask of him (note the "spitting in a pot" similarity to the origins of primitive fruit beers in Japan as described in Chapter 12).

Off Kvasir went, answering questions left, right and centre. Then, alas, he met Fjalar and Galar, two dwarves (in the Lord of the Rings sense of the word) who claimed they had a question for him. They lied! They killed Kvasir and drained his blood into two pots and a kettle. They then made mead out of the blood by blending honey with it – special mead that provided anyone who partook of it the gist of wisdom and poetry (alcohol made from spittle and blood – a basic brewing skill).

The mischievous – that's one word for them – dwarves explained to anyone enquiring after the whereabouts of Kvasir that he had choked to death on his own brilliance as he couldn't find anyone to ask him a question. Then, they took a giant called Gilling out boating and drowned him, killing his grieving wife by dropping a millstone on her head. Their son, Suttung, was understandably upset, and threatened the dwarves with a nasty death, also by drowning. In exchange for their lives, they gave the magical mead to Suttung. He hid it in his daughter Gunnlod's room.

News of magical mead travels fast, and word eventually reached Odin of the substance's potential and what had been going on. Off he went in search of it, on his way accidentally killing nine slaves belonging to Suttung's brother Baugi, whose house Odin ended up staying in. Baugi was upset about the loss of his slaves and Odin saw his chance. He offered to carry out the work of all nine slaves if, and only if, Baugi could get him a taste of the magical mead belonging to his brother.

Time passes.

A whole summer, in fact (passing of the season, gathering of the harvest, making and maturing of the brew). Odin finishes the nine slain slaves' tasks and demands the mead as payment. He and Baugi visit Suttung but no mead is forthcoming. Magically, Odin gets Baugi to drill a hole into Suttung's house, turns himself into a snake and slithers inside (sexual symbolism, clearly reminiscent of Al Wilson's great Northern Soul record "The Snake"). There Odin seduces Gunnlod, sleeping with her for three nights and persuading her to give him three drinks of mead, one for each sexual act.

Odin (as if there aren't enough names in this story, he is now operating under the name Bolverk, or Evil Deed) takes ruthless advantage. Presented with the two pots and the kettle, he consumes the contents of all three, turns himself into an eagle and flies off toward Asgard, home of the gods. Suttung, not best pleased, turns himself into an eagle too and flaps off in pursuit. As you would. Reaching Asgard, Odin spits the mead into a variety of handy receptacles prepared by the inhabitants, but Suttung is close behind. What can Odin do? Not even the cartoon *Wacky Races* could prepare for you this. Odin expels undigested mead in the form of liquid excrement from his eagle-anus, splattering Suttung but preventing the pursuit. This is traditionally the mead of the bad poet, boring conversationalist or lousy academic. The mead gathered in the pots and vats of Asgard is the mead of good poetry, and it is subsequently shared out so that poetry and good, if rather inebriated, chat can continue for all eternity.[7]

The myth has various versions but the key points seem to be the links between literature and alcohol, the divine origins of fermentation, its transformative effects and links with sexual conquest.

---

[7]   Sturlson, Snorri, 1179–1241, *The Prose Edda*, Penguin Classics, London, 2005 (illustrated edition)

The coming of Christianity to Scandinavia saw the production of beer, fruit wine and mead move (as it had elsewhere) into the hands of the Church. Monks recognized the value of these commodities and gradually, supported by Christianized kings, wrested authority from Odin and his pesky spittle. In 1295 a charter was issued by the Swedish prince Eric Magnusson prohibiting the brewing or sale of alcoholic beverages, as well as drinking parties, outside of established and recognized taverns except of course for monks, who claimed they had to brew beer and ale "for religious and health purposes". Permission was duly granted. And, in the Viking tradition, "holy" mead and ale continued to be consumed at weddings, funerals, feasts and christenings.

I would say it still is, but punitive taxes and duties mean that alcohol in the Scandinavian countries tends to be expensive. Which is why yachts tend to appear off my home, the Shetland Islands, each spring and summer, anxious to avail themselves of cheap or duty-free booze they can ship back to the Faroes, Iceland, Norway, Denmark or Sweden in large quantities. What they do with it is anyone's guess. Drink it probably. Maybe they turn themselves into eagles and spit or defecate it over customs officers.

Someday I will try to find out.

Holy Flight – Tasting Notes

Lerwick Brewery Blindside Stout
Founded in 2012, the Lerwick Brewery is fairly new, and has been the most northerly brewery in the UK since the closure of Valhalla in Unst, Shetland's northernmost island. This is my favourite of all their beers; it's a highly successful dark IPA that conjures up for me memories of the night in Cork when I encountered Murphy's Stout for the first time (see page 123).
Colour: Dark ruby brown.
Nose: Malty and dark with lots of wedding-cake fruitiness.

Palate: Lighter than you'd expect from that blackness, roasted nuts and burned toast. It has a great deal of character.

Finish: Small bubbles, so doesn't ransack your tastebuds; leaves a fairly smoothe aftertaste.

Scapa Skiren Single Malt

Skiren is Old Norse for the sparkling summer light you get in Orkney, where this whisky comes from. The Scapa distillery is right next to the sea, not too far from its competitor Highland Park in Kirkwall, and its products have often been dismissed as less characterful than its better-known local cousin. Notably by myself. Recently, I bought a bottle in the community shop that sits right in front of the St Rognvald Hotel, and I have to say I was very impressed.

This has been aged only in "first fill" American oak (that would be barrels bought in kit form from the USA, where it is illegal to re-use barrels that have had whiskey in them previously) and it has a delightful, supple smoothness, lacking the sweet sherry oak notes of Highland Park but with a gloriously assured fruitiness and a charcoal tang from the treatment the American oak casks would have had across the Atlantic – all are charred internally to add character to the whiskey made there.

Colour: Sandy, light gold.

Nose: Salt and sweetness, a walk along a storm-tossed beach on a cloudy day. Firm leathery notes with a hint of seaweed.

Palate: This is a really assured whisky, with the merest hint of heathery island influence. There is a salt shoreline aspect, but you could be forgiven for thinking this was a Speyside malt. The American oak makes it creamy and smooth.

Finish: Burn-free and long-lasting, vanilla pods and gorse bushes in the snow. Very nice indeed.

Lindisfarne Original Mead

Lindisfarne, or Holy Island, is reached by tidal causeway from the Northumberland coast in the north of England. The island is steeped in the Celtic, Roman and Viking traditions, and it's thought it was first settled by monks who arrived with St Aidan, via Iona. The monks brought their expertise in both beekeeping and the uses of honey to make mead, and this mead was seen by the locals, understandably, as holy – an elixir that could be used to heal the sick, promote long life and provide a little bit of comfort from the ferocious North Sea weather.

Lindisfarne Mead as sold today from the winery on the island comes in three varieties – original, dark, pink and spiced – and includes more than just fermented honey. It uses what's thought to be a Roman, rather than Viking or Celtic recipe. So in addition to honey, ingredients include water, wine and raw alcohol, as well as various herbs and spices. The taste is described by the makers as "light, smooth, with a sharp aftertaste – reminiscent of a sweet-wine." The label is based on the artwork of the Lindisfarne Gospels, which were created at Lindisfarne Priory on the island in the 7th century.

Put it this way: it's better than Buckfast Tonic.

Colour: Yellow-oaky gold.

Nose: A smell of honeysuckle in the sunshine.

Palate: Slightly tart with honey coming in.

Finish: Cinnamon and ginger with a substantial, sweet punch.

CHAPTER 14

GIVE A DOG A BONE

Shetland, Switzerland
Rum and beer

Holy Flight

– *Stewart's Dark Rum*
– *St Bernardus Abt 12*

Lulu was a smooth-coated St Bernard, 170lbs (77kg) of somnambulance for 98 per cent of the time. However, when she roused herself, normally because her gigantic nose was telling her that bacon was frying or that somewhere within an area of 20 square miles (52 square kilometres) a barbecue was planned, she could become frisky. And when 170lbs (77kg) of canine was in play mode, you had to beware. One swoosh of that massive tail could decimate a table of glassware. She once broke two of my ribs. By accident. She was, without a doubt, the best-natured and gentlest dog I have ever come across.

The problem with Lulu was her tendency to lean. This is a St Bernard trait and relates to their usefulness as rescue dogs in the snow-bound fastnesses of the Alps. It seems that when they nose out a lost climber or skier, they burrow in beside them and use their ample bodies to warm up their companion. In Lulu, this resulted in her silently approaching unsuspecting strangers, sitting down beside them, and then allowing her entire weight to fall on their legs. Toppling can and did result.

Immensely territorial, craving human companionship, loyal – and just … big. That's St Bernards. We've had three. We adopted the runt of the same litter Lulu came from after her show potential was destroyed by a faulty eye. Lucy, she was called. She did not live long. The sheer physical size and personality of these dogs means they fill large spaces in your life. Taking Lucy to the vet for her final journey, emaciated and yet still enormous, was a dreadful experience. And then there was Rug, another rescue St Bernard, gloriously grumpy and, as you may guess from her name, prone to lying decorously on the floor for hour after hour. Now Lulu has gone, too. Her loss was devastating, but she was 12, a good age for a mastiff-type dog, and she had lived a happy life, raiding the local hotel for kitchen scraps until her dying day. In the end, her ample heart just gave out.

Once you've had a St Bernard, really no other dog will do. It's like having a horse in the house, one with human characteristics. Faithful. Loving. True. Very large.

These dogs were associated for centuries with the Great St Bernard Hospice in Switzerland, which was named after St Bernard of Menthon and remains a hostel or refuge for travellers through the Great St Bernard pass in the Alps, near the border with Italy.

St Bernard of Menthon, the 11th-century archdeacon of Aosta, regularly saw travellers arriving terrorized and distressed by the nefarious attentions of locals, so he decided to put an end to banditry in the area. An order of Augustinian monks was established to staff the refuge he founded, and they built a church, but it wasn't until the 17th century that the famous and extremely big dogs of St Bernard made their appearance – originally as guard animals. There were always bad people about, even up in the mountains.

The St Bernard breed was created at the hospice from cross-breeding local dogs, and by 1709, something approximating the breed we know and love existed. St Bernards' usefulness in rescuing folk who were lost in the snow meant they were intensively bred for size, strength and their ability to smell out those buried in avalanches. And, of course, they carry barrels of brandy.

Except they don't, other than for the benefit of tourists and in our house – we bought one from eBay and occasionally annoyed Lulu by attaching it to her collar.

It's thought that only one dog actually had a brandy container attached. According to *The Percy Anecdotes* by Thomas Byerley, first published in 1823:

"The breed of dogs kept by the monks to assist them … has been long celebrated for its sagacity and fidelity. All the oldest and most tried of them were lately buried, along with some unfortunate travellers, under a valanche [*sic*]; but three or four hopeful puppies were left at home in the convent, and still survive. The most celebrated of those who are no more, was a dog called Barry. This animal served the hospital for the space of twelve years, during which time he saved the lives of forty individuals. His zeal was indefatigable. Whenever the mountain was enveloped in fogs and snow, he set out in search of lost travellers. He was accustomed to run barking until he lost breath and would frequently venture on the most perilous places. When he found his strength was insufficient to draw from the snow a traveller benumbed with cold, he would run back to the hospital in search of the monks. When old age deprived him of strength, the Prior of the Convent pensioned him at Berney, by way of reward. After his death, his hide was stuffed and deposited in the museum of that town. The little phial, in which he carried a reviving liquor for the distressed travellers whom he found among the mountains, is still suspended from his neck."[1]

---

[1] Byerley, Thomas, *The Percy Anecdotes,* T. Boys, London, 1826, pp.25–6

Monks. St Bernards. Alcohol. Now, where have I heard that before? Ah yes, the Cistercians of Mount St Bernard Abbey in Britain, where they make that wonderful, spiritually elevating, incredibly strong and sweet Tynt Meadow Trappist ale (see page 132).

Thank God there's still a bottle or two of that in the larder. And just to set it in some kind of saintly context, there's also a full-on Belgian abbey beer, actually called St Bernardus, which is a ferocious liquid, guaranteed to warm hearts and the most avalanche-chilled body. It was once a classic Trappist brew, but as it is no longer brewed within the walls of an abbey, it can't be called that anymore. Be very, very careful with it.

Not usually to be found in the restorative miniature casks attached to rescue St Bernards is dark rum. Yet Stewart's Rum has a long and very particular association with the Shetland Islands.

The brand was originally produced in Edinburgh in the 18th century by two Shetland brothers and was owned for many years by local wholesaler Hughson Brothers, who bought the J & G Stewart company after it was discovered that 90 per cent of the rum it produced was sold in the islands. A blend of Demerara rums from Guyana, this is a traditional drink of local fishermen and much loved by "deep sea" merchant seamen, too. It has become enfolded in Shetland culture and is mostly drunk mixed with Coca-Cola. Cuba Libre? Well, sort of.

The popularity of rum in Shetland is partly rooted in the islands' maritime tradition, and partly in changes in customs duty that came in during the 18th century and made spirits like rum, gin and whisky cheaper to buy and drink than beer. Particularly if consumed in illegal shebeens or "tippling houses". These were common in Shetland at that time, and indeed throughout Scotland. I was interested to find that a minister with a similar name to my own – Rev Thomas Marton – was concerned for his local parish of Langholm, in the Scottish borders, in the 1790s. Beer, he said, was "the natural and wholesome beverage of the country" whereas the "unlicensed dram and tippling houses", where spirits such as rum were sold, were "haunts of vice where the young of both sexes are tempted from the straight and narrow."[2]

So rum, while associated with the various forms of Caribbean native religion (see pp.195–200), and of course piracy (see pp.200–209), does not sit well with the stern Protestantism of the north. Or, for that matter, with the Catholicism of Ireland. Ruibin's Bar in Galway ran into a spot of local trouble after it began serving a cocktail called "Ruibin's Holy Water", a mixture of spiced rum, brandy, grapefruit, bitters and milk, with "communion on the side". One social media commentator said, "This is a disgrace. For Catholics, the Eucharist is sacred. Your mockery is deeply upsetting."[3] A sentiment with which the Rev Thomas Marton would undoubtedly have agreed.

Holy Flight – Tasting Notes

Stewart's Dark Rum

Stewart's is a Shetland institution.

Colour: A dark, viscous reddy-brown.

Nose: Treacle, figs and burned sugar.

Palate: Surprisingly thin. Lots of liquorice and caramel, with those golden syrup and treacle notes. The alcohol kicks in with a strikingly delicate, slow warmth.

Finish: A bitterness left behind dissipates into a kind of numbing, dark, cheap glow.

St Bernardus Abt 12

One of the best beers in the world, some say. Certainly, one of the strongest at a whopping 10.5 per cent alcohol. An absolute classic of Belgian abbey beers, with a complicated history involving sets of monks who came, went, brewed, made cheese,

---

[2]   Cooke, Anthony *A History of Drinking: The Scottish Pub since 1700*, Edinburgh University Press, Edinburgh, 2015

[3]   https://www.irishcentral.com/news/galway-bar-holy-water-cocktail-communion

gave the head cheesemaker a licence to brew, then finally pulled out of brewing. Blessed, as they say, are the cheesemakers. Now St Bernardus is a thriving brewery without spiritual portfolio.

Colour: Dark, with a substantial, ivory head.

Nose: Fruit, notably those darned cherries again, roasted malt and a distinct yeastiness.

Palate: The alcohol doesn't really become noticeable until you've dived into the fruity, malt-bready, raisin-and-biscuit-chocolate-bar mixture that tastes of dark chocolate.

Finish: Smoothly wanders off without necessarily revealing at first that it has brought you to the verge of unconsciousness.

CHAPTER 15
THE MOON
UNDER WATER

England
Beer

Holy Flight
– *Theakston's Old Peculiar*
– *Newcastle Brown Ale*

George Orwell's 1946 essay "The Moon Under Water" is about the pub as church, the perfect hostelry where you can find solace, refuge and redemption through mostly the beer, with some company and conversation thrown in. I have searched for it all my life.

"In the Moon Under Water", writes Orwell, "it is always quiet enough to talk …" There is no radio, piano, or the modern equivalent, the Bluetoothed Spotify playlist, and if there is any singing "it is of a decorous kind". In the way of the TV show *Cheers*, "the barmaids know most of their customers by name, and take a personal interest in everyone." All are middle-aged women, two of them with dyed hair "in quite surprising shades," and all customers are called "'… dear'. Definitely not 'ducky'. Pubs where the barmaid calls you 'ducky' always have a disagreeable raffish atmosphere."[1]

---

[1]   https://www.orwellfoundation.com/the-orwell-foundation/orwell/essays-and-other-works/the-moon-under-water/

Despite having been in several pubs actually called The Moon Under Water – there are 13 J D Wetherspoon outlets in the UK with that name – I never found this elusive perfect pub. Until I realized I lived just five minutes' walk away.

From my fourth year in high school to my final year at university, Orwell was my constant English literature companion, primarily his novels *1984* and *Animal Farm*. They were easy books to memorize chunks of, they were accessible, readable, interesting and credible from an examiner's point of view. His non-fiction and essays, with special reference to *Down and Out in Paris and London* (the image of the roast chicken that was retrieved from a filthy lift shaft, then plated and served by an insanitary chef at the Georges V Hotel in Paris has stalked my entire culinary life), shed light on the allegorical fiction. But one short magazine article, "The Moon Under Water", written for the BBC magazine *The Listener*, has reverberated throughout pub design and intellectual drinking far beyond my own fascination for both these things.

"The Moon Under Water" is a description of the ideal pub, at least from Orwell's point of view in the 1940s. It begins with a description of the eponymous pub, which appears to really exist. Then Orwell explains that it doesn't, other than in his mind, though some city bars come close. Here are the crucial elements he demands in a hostelry:

— The architecture and fittings basically have to be Victorian in feel and design.
— Games like darts can only be played in the Public bar. The Lounge bar should be arrow-free for safety reasons. Presumably the modern trend for axe-throwing is anathema. It certainly should be.
— The pub should be quiet enough to talk in without shouting, with no radio (these days, that would include background music like the aforementioned Spotify or Tidal playlist or a jukebox) and no piano, other than at Christmas. Where you actually get and how you move that festive piano is not mentioned.

- The bar staff, women of "a certain age", should know their customers by name and take an interest in everyone.
- It should sell tobacco and cigarettes, aspirins (or other non-prescription painkillers) and stamps, and be "obliging about letting you use the telephone".
- There should be "a snack counter where you can get liver-sausage sandwiches, mussels (a speciality of the house), cheese, pickles and … large biscuits with caraway seeds." Let's include crisps. Or as they say in the USA, chips. And nuts.
- In an upper lounge or restaurant, for six days a week, customers should be able to obtain "a good, solid lunch – for example, a cut off the joint, two vegetables and boiled jam roll – for about three shillings."
- "The perfect pub should serve "a creamy sort of draught stout."
- The Moon Under Water should never serve a pint of beer in a straight glass without handles. This is where I would disagree with George. Straight pint glasses, slightly flaring, are to my mind the greatest receptacle for decent ale.
- There should be a garden with a play area for children. Hmm … I'm not so sure …

I think what Orwell was arguing for was not so much the perfect pub as one that includes all the elements that the drinker may wish to avail themselves of, depending on the circumstances. Surely there are pubs where a garden is irrelevant and where you decidedly don't wish to have children present? Companionship should be there for those who seek it, but it should be avoidable if you don't. A proper pub should be a place where you're welcomed, but it's acknowledged that sometimes you just want to drink alone. There will be bars where you expect to find live music and places where silence rules. I still remember my first exposure to the Jolly Judge, hidden down a narrow alley off the Royal Mile in Edinburgh, and finding it had no background music, was comfortingly regular in shape – a feature I find incredibly soothing in a pub – and that it somehow deadened sound so that private conversations could not be easily overheard. My favourite in Aberdeen is now alas closed – called Under the Hammer and set in a basement beneath an auctioneer's, it was almost perfectly square, but had one or two small alcoves that offered a sense of sanctuary. The famous Crown in Belfast, with its dark wooden booths, is like a church equipped with a host of confessionals. Most British cities have a range of pubs that would suit me, and some that would suit Orwell in most aspects. But it strikes me that what Orwell is describing, and what the person who seeks a regular haunt wants, is a form of church.

In the UK, there are many redundant church buildings that have been converted into licensed premises. Some have dreadful punning names, like Soul, in Aberdeen. My friend Iain Shaw, musician and artist, mounted a photography exhibition of churches that had found other uses. It was called "Jesus Has Left the Building". But a church usually feels uneasy when it assumes an alcoholically lubricating role. Oran Mor in Glasgow, a massive former kirk in the busy and bohemian West End of the city, whose name in Gaelic means "The Great Melody of Life", is a warren of bars, function suites, venues and restaurants, and always feels to me like a living creature. One that is only just about tolerating a kind of teeming blasphemy.

There is one form of blasphemy that the Bible condemns as "the unforgivable sin", and that is blasphemy against the Holy Spirit. Any church that has been consecrated would usually, though not always, be deconsecrated before devilish drinking (or, for that matter, completely innocent imbibing) can take place within. Church architecture aimed at drawing the collective into awe and worship of the Divine sits uneasily with the more earthly concerns of many drinkers. There can be an awkward collision of nomenclature, such as in the enormous bar complex called the Church on the Hill in Glasgow. Altars sometimes contained reliquaries, with bones or bits of clothing associated with martyrs and saints. Using one as counter top or cocktail-mixing surface does seem a little strange. One company that was marketing a "Holy Spirits" Advent calendar containing miniatures of whisky changed the name after objections from people concerned for the copywriters' eternal souls. If they had any, which some within the advertising industry would doubt.

But what does a drinker seek? Drink, obviously. However, the kind of pub that serves a particular place and a set of customers who come because it is "their" local provides much more than that. It offers sanctuary; anonymity and silence should you seek it; company and conversation, if that's what you need; physical and intellectual stimulation and sustenance. And redemption and forgiveness even if you misbehave and are barred, unless you have blasphemed against the Holy Spirit or done something truly terrible like insisting soap operas must be watched on the television. That's if there is a television, which there shouldn't be. And sometimes you do want a bit of trouble, disagreement and action.

Like in church.

The relationship between church and drink is seen at its most ... peculiar, in the one that exists and has done for 800 years between the church of St Mary the Virgin in Masham, North Yorkshire and the local brewery, Theakston's. I always thought the "peculier" referred to was a witch's cat, but I was very wrong. Its actual definition is an ecclesiastical district, parish, church or chapel that falls outside the jurisdiction of the local bishop's diocese. From the 12th century onward, the church has been able to govern itself and the surrounding area, with the aid of the Peculier Court of Masham, consisting of 24 men and the local vicar. To this day, apparently, the Peculier (or Peculiar in modern spelling), which in this context means "Particular", retains the right to rule on such matters as "drunkenness, brawling, swearing, scolding, not bringing your children to be baptized, bidding church wardens to do their worst when they order you to church and carrying a skull out of a churchyard to lay under a person's head to charm him or her to sleep."[2]

---

[2] "Michael Theakston Obituary", *The Times*, 30 October 2004

When the Theakston Brewery began operations in Masham in 1827, the first beer made was called Old Peculier, and there has been a strong relationship between brewery and church court ever since. Theakston's used the official seal of the Peculier Court of Masham on the beer's label and, in 1999, paid for a new stained-glass window in the church in that design.

There is a contract between the vicar and Theakston's permitting the use of this seal and it was last signed in 1989, when a new portrait of the Virgin Mary and the Baby Jesus was commissioned and paid for by the brewery. The contract lasts until 2040.

Holy Flight – Tasting Notes

Theakston's Old Peculier

Old Peculier is one of my favourite beers, and one of the first non-generic pints I ever tasted. On draught this beer can be extraordinary – a dark ruby red verging on black, and strong without being in any way aggressive. The beer is only 5.6 per cent alcohol, which in my younger days was a lot, but is now almost run of the mill for craft beers. Still, it pays to treat this stuff carefully. You could end up in front of a court … feeling a bit … strange.

Colour: A glorious deep dark red, almost black. Disturbing.

Nose: Fresh fruit-and-nut chocolate bar, just snapped open, with a hoppy, liquorice overtone.

Body: Dark cherry, Vimto (a British soft drink made from cherries, blackcurrant and chemicals) and with a pleasant bitterness that somehow smooths out as you drink more and more.

Finish: Damp leaf mould. Earth, pepper and a wee bit of spice. A very good beer indeed, better on draught but fine from the bottle.

Newcastle Brown Ale

I should say immediately that these notes refer to the British version of this old-school beer, not the USA one, which has a different recipe and is made by Lagunitas in California and Illinois. I'm including it because it is the kind of beer Orwell would have liked. Ever since I first tasted it in my teens, I've found it a bit bland and rather too sweet for my liking.

Colour: Light, muddy water brown.

Nose: Well-used leather schoolbag that has been carrying sherbet fountains and jam sandwiches, with some mild nuttiness.

Palate: Bitter and sweet, sweet and bitter, not quite satisfying somehow. It was called "Big Newkie" by the quarrymen I worked with when I left school, and its bland, undemanding sweetness was the very thing to wash away all the granite dust. It's a bit watery.

Finish: Quickly, then move on to something more interesting. But it's a session beer you can drink a lot of. Probably ill-advisedly.

CHAPTER 16

ONE LAST DRINK …
OR TWO

Scotland (Edinburgh)
Whisky and beer

The Final Holy Flight

– *Deuchar's India Pale Ale*
– *Glenkinchie 12-Year-Old Single Malt Whisky*

And here we are then, coming to the end of this strange, informative and I hope entertaining journey into the wild world of spirited, sometimes spiritual drinking. Have I found the sacred, in a glass? Many, many times. And I hope that as you've read, and sampled some at least of the suggested aperitifs, quenchers, uplifters, brain-shrinkers and digestifs, some semblance of insight into the Divine has crept in. Or at the very least, you've not been arrested for being drunk and disorderly. No one likes to be disorderly.

Where to end this planet-spanning trip? I'm returning to the subject of buildings where alcohol can be consumed, and churches that have been converted to aid the pursuit of this spiritual quest. I have recently been reading Francis Spufford's eye-wateringly forceful defence of Christianity, *Unapologetic*. In the chapter entitled Big Daddy, Spufford describes, at length, the effect of entering a church building. Here's a brief snatch from his musings: "The calm in here is not denial. It's an ancient, imperturbable lack of surprise. To any conceivable act you might have committed, the building is set up to say, ah, so you have, so you did. Yes. Would you like to sit down?"[1]

A church is designed to awe, to impress, but also to welcome. Where can I find one that welcomes me with intimacy and offers a drink as well? I know. Edinburgh.

Perhaps the soaring scale of traditional church architecture is ill-suited to the intimacy necessary for proper pub culture, but there are smaller religious buildings that have been turned into drinking houses, and do not necessarily carry the sense of God gazing balefully down upon the consumers of mood-altering liquids. Or maybe I'm just more at home in them.

The Grassmarket Mission was founded in 1886 to provide social and spiritual care for families in what was one of the poorest parts of Edinburgh. The Mission particularly targeted those affected by alcohol abuse, and so it must be with mixed feelings that the current trustees of the Mission, which still exists and continues its work among the desperate and homeless of Edinburgh, look at its former premises.

This is because the former Grassmarket Mission Hall, kitchens and offices at 94–96 Grassmarket are now partly a hotel and mostly Biddy Mulligan's, a sprawl of Irish-themed bars and restaurants. One, on the ground floor, is called the Wee Pub, and proudly proclaims that it is the Smallest Pub in Scotland, holding just 20 people. Above the entrance, the building's original use is remembered in carved sandstone. The words "Grassmarket Mission Hall" remain and will always be there.

The Wee Pub, in truth, is a cosy space. And you can hire it for private use – it then stops being a public bar, of course, and so lacks the randomness, the risk of encounter that makes a pub a pub. But still, as a place to sit, converse and drink with friends, in one of the oldest parts of Scotland's capital, it has its attractions. You can contemplate your place in the world, meditate on history and religion. Life and death.

---

[1]   Spufford, Francis, *Unapologetic: Why, Despite Everything, Christianity Can Still Make Surprising Emotional Sense*, Faber and Faber, London, 2012

From the 14th century onward the Grassmarket was a centre for cattle and horse trading, and then in the 17th century it became a major market for all kinds of goods. But it was also Edinburgh's traditional place of public execution. Among the many hanged on the scaffold just outside what is now the Wee Pub was one Margaret (Maggie) Dickson, a fishwife who was executed in 1724 for murdering her illegitimate child just after birth. After the hanging, her body was taken to Musselburgh on a cart. However, on the way there she awoke from what was clearly not doom, but a swoon. Under Scots Law, her punishment had been fully carried out, and she could not be sentenced to death for a second time for the same crime. It would be several years before the words "until dead" were added to the sentence of hanging, opening up the possibilities of lengthy or continuous neck-stretching until permanent oblivion was accomplished. How Maggie lived the rest of her life, what guilt she felt, can only be imagined.

There were many religious executions, too, and in 1937 a memorial was created to commemorate the Protestant Covenanters (those who had signed the National Covenant in 1638 opposing changes to religious practice in Scotland by King Charles I) who died on the gallows between 1661 and 1688 in what was known in Scotland as "the killing time". So the Wee Pub, in the former mission hall, is no Moon Under Water, really. It is a place of melancholy memory.

However, there is another pub in Edinburgh (and Edinburgh has many) where the building's former status as a mission hall not only gives the place its name, but offers fewer reminders of death, poverty and violence. The Auld Hundred in Rose Street is named after the tune associated with the 100th Psalm, which would often have been sung there during the 18th century when this building, too, was a mission hall.

The Auld Hundred has a carefully restored traditional public bar on the ground floor, with welcoming old sofas and no sense of divine disapproval. Upstairs is an excellent restaurant. And sometimes, as you sip whisky, wine or beer, gin, Green

Chartreuse, cognac or just some tap water, the management will allow you to sing that slow and stately song, best known in the translation of the 100th Psalm by Thomas Kethe, a Scotsman who was forced out of his country to Geneva in the late 16th century.

And if you start singing, even just humming one of the most famous hymn tunes in history (as sung at Queen Elizabeth II's Coronation) people will, I guarantee, join in, sipping from and swinging their glasses in irresistible time. No matter their religion, no matter what they're drinking. They won't be able to help themselves, because in that once-holy place, these are sacred words that are also inclusive, that celebrate life, and faith and, dare I say, all the things in creation. I will drink to that.

"All people that on earth do dwell,
sing to the Lord with cheerful voice.
Serve him with joy, his praises tell,
come now before him and rejoice!

Know that the Lord is God indeed;
he formed us all without our aid.
We are the flock he comes to feed,
the sheep who by his hand were made.

O enter then his gates with joy,
within his courts his praise proclaim.
Let thankful songs your tongues employ.
O bless and magnify his name.

Trust that the Lord our God is good,
his mercy is forever sure.
His faithfulness at all times stood
and shall from age to age endure."[2]

---

[2]   William Kethe, d.1594.

And seeing that this book ends as it began, in Scotland, perhaps this song, sung to the ancient folk melody known in Gaelic as *Ag òl Airson Saoradh* (Drinking for Salvation), could be a useful encore.

The Water of Life

As I'm about to show, all the places so poetically mentioned below are locations of whisky distilleries.

From the place of peaks and mountains	*Arran*
To the hollow of the mill	*Lagavulin*
From a rock on stony ground	*Craigellachie*
To the speckled hill	*Benriach*
From the plain of the new Ireland	*Blair Atholl*
To where the river ends	*Bunnahabhainn*
Between two waters	*Edradour*
Blackberries in the glen	*Glendronach*

> *Oh the water, oh the water of life*
> *It runs so clear*
> *Oh the water, oh the water of life*
> *The source is here*

From Mary's Well	*Tobermory*
Past Juniper Hill	*Tomatin*
To the Warning Peak	*Tullibardine*
We'll take a boat	*Scapa*
To Kenneth's Glade	*Rosebank*
Let the Sons of Allan speak	*Macallan*
Monks will guide us	*Mannochmore*
To the Little Bay	*Oban*
By the Glen of Peace	*Glenmorangie*
Black Waterfalls	*Dallas Dhu*
Rough Ground	*Glengarioch*
And smooth	*Glenlivet*
Where laughter will not cease	*Royal Lochnagar*

That is a holy flight to take you beyond these words into a world of the spirits. Where who knows what your ultimate destination will be?

The Final Holy Flight – Tasting Notes

Deuchar's India Pale Ale

Deuchar's is an Edinburgh institution. Made at the Caledonian Brewery in Slateford Road, before anti-pollution laws were introduced the hoppy smell of Caley's activities would hang over the city like a blessing or a curse. Tragically, as this book went to press, it was announced that the ancient Caledonian brewery would close and production of Deuchars would move outside the city.

On draught, it's less than 4 per cent alcohol and the ideal place to drink it is in one of the great Edinburgh pubs. The draught ale reacts with the east coast air to produce a unique consumer reaction ... or maybe it's just better looked after. On the other hand, it tastes very good in certain Glaswegian howffs (haunts) too, so perhaps it's all nonsense.

In a bottle or can it's not quite the same beast, but if you're reading this at home, it is widely available. And by the way, India Pale, or IPA, is so called as it was discovered that a more heavily hopped beer could survive the long sea trip to England's 18th-century colonies in the Indian subcontinent.

Colour: Bright, orangey kipper brown.

Nose: Lots of hops and and herbal earthiness. Too bubbly in bottle, but that's the price you pay for not being in Scotland.

Palate: Malt, flowery with some muted citrus.

Finish: Quite bitter and mouth-drying. Fly to Edinburgh immediately and try the cask version.

Glenkinchie 12-Year-Old Single Malt Whisky

There is a whisky distillery in Scotland itself, at Holyrood, near the parliament and the palace. However, it's not bottling and selling its own whisky yet, so instead, chase your Deuchar's with a wee dram of Glenkinchie 12, made in the East Lothian village of Pencaitland outside the city.

A lowland malt, it is smooth and unabrasive, like its west coast equivalent, Auchentoshan. Sitting there with this book, a pint of Deuchar's and a dram of this relatively cheap and rather lovely whisky, you may dream dreams and see visions. Try not to fall off your seat.

Colour: Amber nectar, thin honey.

Nose: Fresh hazelnuts with honey and almonds.

Palate: Sweet, with apples and a touch of stewed prunes creeping in along with the barrels it was aged in.

Finish: Hand-mown lawn cuttings collected while eating an apple cereal bar in the sunshine.

EPILOGUE: THE MORNING AFTER

Something which may arise in some minds, before or after reading this book: are you an alcoholic, Tom? In pursuing fermented liquids and distilled spirits, have you become enslaved by their demonic power and exchanged holiness for dissolution?

Such a binary question!

The danger, as should be evident from the stories in this book, is always present that the drinker will become captivated by what is a psychoactive substance. As the old saying goes: first you take a drink, then the drink takes a drink, then the drink takes you.

It will be clear from the preceding pages that alcohol in a religious context has been used sometimes to induce states of perception more conducive to manipulation; as a way of making money; as a comforting balm in times of difficulty and pain; and especially, as a signifier of unity, a ritual symbol of togetherness, of communion. We drink, in many different faiths, or none, as a sign of our oneness.

Those who seek enlightenment through drinking, who use alcohol as a solution to their mental or spiritual problems, are doomed to be disappointed. Thoughtful, enlightened, moderate drinking, however, taking joy in the beauty of where and how a particular liquid is crafted, meeting its makers, going to the source, can be illuminating and enlivening.

Alcohol is a dangerous thing. A little can be healthy, perhaps. In its making we see the craft of humankind, the splendour of nature, the exactitude and brilliance of science. And at its core is the transformation, through fermentation and distillations, of agriculture into ... liquid light. Poetry in solution. The sacred in a glass. It is a living symbol, a metaphor, a story in a bottle.

There are two Bible sayings I keep in my heart. Well, more than two, but these will suffice for now. One is Paul's admonition to his friend and follower Timothy, already quoted herein, to "take a little wine [for] thy stomach's sake",[1] and the other is from in Psalms and King David, who enjoyed the occasional bucket. Or two. "Wine, that maketh glad the heart ..."[2]

---

[1] 1 Timothy 5:23, KJV

[2] Psalm 104, verse 15

ACKNOWLEDGMENTS

This book owes its existence to Ella Chappell, who suggested the idea and allowed me to pursue it. The fact that it is in your hands, either digitally or in paper and ink form, is due to Ella and all her colleagues at Watkins Publishing. Grateful thanks to Ingrid Court-Jones for salvation from gratuitous howlers.

For some sections of the book, I am indebted to Paul Kelbie at *Discover Scotland* magazine, and the indulgence of Bill Campbell and Peter Davidson at Edinburgh's late lamented Mainstream Publishing, who allowed the ship *Spirit of Adventure* to set sail all those decades ago. Rob Allanson and Kenneth Hamilton, my companions on the Journey's Blend motorcycle adventure, and Rob solo as editor of *Whisky Magazine* and facilitator of the Five Nations whisky journey, deserve credit for forbearance and expertise. Jim Lister and Stephen Wright of Fairpley put up with a lot at the Belladrum Festival's Verb Garden and pioneered the Malt and Barley Revue. And John Lamond incited me to try serious port.

Angus MacRaild shared his knowledge, the Glug-Glug Club some of its secrets and Jon Beach the wondrous hospitality of Fiddlers in Drumnadrochit. Andrea and Paul at the St Magnus Bay Hotel know all about the St Rognvald Hotel, which almost had a chapter on its own; Mike Travers and Craig Samet started all this, if they had but known, at Project Scotland. The *Shetland Times* newspaper and *Shetland Life* magazine gave me far more chances than I really deserved.

Finally, I owe all of this to the late George Thomas and Euphemia Jones Adam MacCalman Morton. Never to be forgotten, always honoured. Slainte.